Robert Musil

SELECTED WRITINGS

The German Library: Volume 72

Volkmar Sander, General Editor

Robert Musil

SELECTED WRITINGS

Edited by Burton Pike

Foreword by Joel Agee

CONTINUUM · NEW YORK

1986

The Continuum Publishing Company
370 Lexington Avenue, New York, NY 10017

The German Library
is published in cooperation with Deutsches Haus,
New York University
This volume has been supported by a grant
from The Marie Baier Foundation, Inc.

Library of Congress Cataloging in Publication Data

Musil, Robert, 1880–1942.
Selected writings.

(The German library; v. 72),
1. Musil, Robert, 1880–1942—Translations, English.
I. Pike, Burton. II. Title. III. Series.
PT2625.U8A2   1985   833'.912   86-8849
ISBN 0-8264-0305-0
ISBN 0-8264-0304-2 (pbk.)

Acknowledgments will be found on pages 346
which constitute an extension of this page.

Contents

Foreword

I am looking at a photograph of a sixty-year-old man in a gray suit with broad lapels. He is wearing a bow tie. There are dark leaves behind him, and the lines of a sunlit house. His right hand dangles across the armrest of the wicker chair in which he is sitting with one leg draped over the other. The left hand, wearing a signet ring, rests on a round table and is loosely holding a cigarette. The face could be that of a European diplomat or businessman of a now extinct type: refined, austere, intellectual. The dark, dense eyebrows add an expression of calm virility. The only incongruous detail is the eyes: they are closed. One assumes at first the snapshot was taken at the moment of blinking. But it is impossible to imagine this face with the eyes open, because all its features and in fact the whole gesture of the body, which at first glance appeared so urbanely relaxed in its well-tailored suit, are drained of motility, as if drugged. At any minute, the cigarette may drop from between those slackly curved fingers. Is this a picture of mortal exhaustion or of extremely attenuated contemplation? Probably it is both. The man depicted is Robert Musil, at whose funeral in 1942—less than two years after the photograph was taken—the eulogist applied to Musil a statement Musil had made about Rilke: "He was not a summit of this age—he was one of those elevations upon which the destiny of the human spirit strides across ages."

Today, no one would dream of describing a human being in such grandiose terms—a political program perhaps, or a space mission, but not a person, and certainly not a writer. It may have something to do with the expectations writers have of themselves, and with a rather diminished sense, generally, of the human spirit's having any

sort of destiny. Perhaps it's better that way. A more modest perspective may open up a vision of what is staring us in the face: that
unless we supply the essential necessities to the collective body of
man, the spirit may have to find another planet for the fulfillment
of its destiny. Musil himself was coming to a similar conclusion
near the end of his life (chastened, perhaps, by the enormity of the
war and by his personal experience of severe poverty): "The most
important thing is not to produce spiritual values, but food, clothing, security, order. . . . And it is just as important to produce the
principles necessary for the supply of food, clothing, etc. Let us call
it—the spirit of indigence." Elsewhere he described himself as
"building a house of cards as the earth begins to crack."

The house of cards (but I prefer a different image Musil coined
for his work: "A bridge out into space") was a huge, phenomenally
ambitious construction, thirty years in the making and never finished, titled *The Man Without Qualities*—a satire on the collapse
of the Austrian empire, a utopian novel about untried possibilities
of being, a visionary expedition "to the edge of the possible," an
essay in the philosophy of history, a critique of the major ideologies
of the twentieth century, an attempt to combine the different ex-
actitudes of reason and mysticism. The book that was virtually
unknown in its author's lifetime is now being celebrated by some
prominent critics as "the greatest novel in the German language,"
"greater than *Ulysses* and *A la recherche du temps perdu*" (as if
works of this order of imagination could be ranked), and even "the
greatest novel ever written," which is surely a very silly thing to
say, but it does give some indication of the book's moral and im-
aginative energy.

Only a portion of *The Man Without Qualities* has been published
in this country, and the translation rarely rises above a workmanlike
level. Most of Musil's earlier fiction, however, is available in English; some of the best of these works are collected in this volume.
American readers who want to acquaint themselves with Musil are
thus in a position not unlike that of Soviet readers (though the
reasons are different) who can read Joyce's *Portrait of the Artist
as a Young Man* in Russian but are denied access to the complete
Ulysses: One is disappointed, because so much interest attaches to
the unknown masterpiece, yet one has cause to be grateful, for here

in one's hands is the master's work, his lesser work perhaps, but, as one discovers in the reading, not in any way minor.

About a year before he began to write *Young Törless*, the twenty-one-year-old Musil "gave away" the essential plot of the book to some young novelists of the naturalistic school which was in vogue at the time. The story, drawn from memory, of the sadistic punishment of a boy caught stealing from his fellow students at an elite boarding school, did not interest him especially, and, by his own account, he eventually wrote the book mainly as a remedy for boredom. This astonishing first novel, published in 1906, proved to be one of the most politically prescient books of its time. Three decades later, Musil wrote in his journal: "Reiting, Beineberg [central characters in *Young Törless*]: Today's dictators in nucleo. Also the concept of 'the mass' as an entity to be subjugated." Curiously, he does not mention Törless, whose startlingly uncompassionate experimentation with the suffering Basini is just as symptomatic a presage of a certain species of intellectual who in the early Thirties took a mystical and esthetic and sexual interest in the latest revival of organized barbarity at the heart of European civilization.

If *Törless* was written out of boredom, it does not show any sign of it. Musil must have very quickly developed an intense interest in several dark puzzles concealed within his simple plot—problems which a naturalistic treatment would have left unexamined, and which fortunately proved unfathomable, so that four decades later he was still exploring them in *The Man Without Qualities*. There is, for instance, young Törless's discovery of the *interchangeability* of human destinies and the uncanny proximity, in each human soul, of good and evil, the sublime and the depraved: that there is no essential difference between his genteel mother and the crudely alluring prostitute he visits; that if Basini, in every way an undistinguished boy, could find himself covered, as a result of a moment's lapse in "the heavy, pale, poisonous leaves of infamy," it could happen to Törless as well; that, hypersensitive though he is, Törless becomes an accomplice in torture; "that between those people whose lives moved in an orderly way between the office and the family as though in a transparent and solid building of glass and iron, and the others—outcast, blood-stained, debauched and filthy, wandering through labyrinthine halls full of roaring voices—there was not only a passageway but a secret place where their limits touched and the border could be crossed at any moment."*

One is reminded of Jean-Paul Sartre's treatment, half a century later, of the same problem in his plays, novels, and stories, whose characters also feel the vertiginous pull of terrifying possibilities. Like Musil, Sartre saw himself faced with an enigma that eluded the grasp of reason, indeed of language. But where Sartre shored up the anguished consciousness with a thoroughly rational framework against the encroachments of the "absurd," Musil never employed his considerable powers of analysis in a systematic way—and in this philosophical debility (or was it an abstinence?) lay the strength of the poet Robert Musil. He did not freeze, as Sartre did, in nauseated horror on the edge of the abyss, but recognized its soundless depths as an intimate part of his nature, and one as likely to be a source of delight as of terror. Nor did he ever indulge in the hysterical emotionalism of the literary expressionists (some of whom later claimed *Young Törless* as a forerunner of their movement) or offer himself as a medium for dictations from the unconscious, like the surrealists. Instead, he expended himself, throughout his adult life, in an effort to link the incommensurable worlds of the rational and the essentially unnameable; and though others before him had struggled with the same impossible task (I'm thinking especially of the holy stammerings of the Christian, Jewish, and oriental mystics, to whom Musil was to some extent indebted), he was probably the first to set about building one pylon of the mystical bridge, the one on the hither shore, out of the kind of intellectual steel one associates with science (further tempered, in his case, with the unsentimental habits of mind he had developed in his training as an engineer), and to insist on subjecting his materials to rigorous testing by a highly corrosive irony. He did this precisely because the other shore, the destination and magnetic source of all his fiction, was a realm of intangible, transient, imaginary, and sometimes scarcely imaginable feeling-states that are ordinarily the province of dreamers, ecstatics, and madmen.

Among the texts collected in this volume, "The Perfecting of a

---

*I have slightly amended the wording of the English translation of this and other passages cited herein.

Love" represents the most extended foray into that nebulous zone. Conceived as an elegantly erotic magazine story, Musil expected to dash it off in two weeks but took two and a half years to finish it. One need only peruse it anywhere after the first two pages to gain a sense of the nature of his difficulty, for it is to no small extent a difficulty the reader has to contend with as well. What there is of a story line can be summed up in a single sentence: A woman experiences in the act of adultery the fulfillment of her love for her husband. But this summary is misleading, for very little happens in the way of physical action or even physical description. Of the seducer's appearance, for instance, we know only that he is big and has a beard; of the woman's (and this only by inference), that she is attractive; the nameless husband is almost invisible to the reader. The settings, too—a living room, a train, the streets of a small town, a seedy hotel room—are like places in a dream. The story's single, sustained focus of attention is the heroine's virtually disembodied psyche, for her seduction takes place in depths of the soul to which the seducer can have no access (so that it is he, not her husband, who is betrayed); and this gradual, inexorable divesting and shedding of moral security and merely habitual identity down to the last shreds of self-possession culminates, with beautiful and exact paradoxy, in Claudine's recovery of her inviolate, solitary self along with the certainty of her love. But what is the nature of this self that unfolds its mysterious core, petal by petal, yet remains unrevealed to the end? The name "Claudine" signifies not a character so much as a shifting force field of tensions and relations, a vaporous, oscillating flux of impulses and memories, impressions and feelings, without causal linkage between past and present; not an identity but a spectrum: the light of a consciousness refracted into a multitude of self-perceptions ranging from sublime devotion to masochistic subjection, from confident presence in the world to an eerily vacuous absence from its own gestures and acts.

"The Perfecting of a Love," published together with another, even more tenuously structured novella (not included here) in a volume called *Unions*, was almost unanimously panned by the press—a particularly bitter disappointment after the very respectful response to *Young Törless*. A note of doubt and tough self-interrogation creeps into Musil's journals. He prods himself with Goethe's admonition to "just reach into the fullness of human life."

It's telling, too, how this extremely acrimonious and jealous critic of other writers expresses enthusiastic admiration, repeatedly, for naive realists like Gorky, Sigrid Undset, and Selma Lagerlof. He never followed their example. Not that he was incapable of it: there are stunningly vivid observations and descriptions throughout his fiction; but it seems that he was, overall, not really interested in "the fullness of human life" as such, and it was probably in keeping with his own constitutional makeup that he had his Man Without Qualities propose the wholesale abolition of reality—the word itself hardly ever appears in his work without implied ironic quotes. (What sort of engineer would he have been? One wonders.)

In the novellas collected under the title *Three Women* ("Grigia," "The Lady from Portugal," and "Tonka"), Musil reverted to traditional narrative forms. But the theme—the secret theme, I'm tempted to say, because it is partly disguised by social and psychological issues (especially in "Tonka") and by deftly sketched, sometimes wonderfully accurate details of character and setting—is still that of transcendent love and mystical union, and its treatment is not traditional at all. Where the mystics' *via unitiva* prescribed a symbolic death for the aspirant, one of Musil's heroes achieves gnosis through literal, physical death, another by the death of the woman he loves, and the third by a propitiatory ritual in which suicide or murder seem the only probable outcomes. All three novellas are, appropriately, set in border regions, and in each one a woman figures as the unparticipating catalyst for a man's solitary illumination. (In this, Musil departs radically from the conventions of the classical romance, on which these tales are in part predicated: imagine Tristan exulting in the ecstasy of union with the *image* of his beloved while Iseult stands by, dies, or sips the waters of a distant spa.)

The all-consuming irony which, in *The Man Without Qualities*, is developed into an instrument of enormous subtlety and range, is completely absent in *Three Women*, as it is in *Törless*. An intimation of it is given in the self-portrayal of the seducer in "The Perfecting of a Love" (incidentally, I can think of no other writer, male or female, with such a merciless eye for the various ridiculous styles of masculine self-importance) and in the short stories, sketches, and miscellaneous articles collected in 1935 in a slim volume called *Nachlass zu Lebzeiten* (Posthumous Writings of a Living Man; in the present volume translated as "Pre-Posthumous Papers"). Most of these pieces were written as entertainments for Sunday newspaper supplements and magazines—hence their seemingly throwaway lightness and insouciance. This casualness of manner is deceptive. For instance, when, at the beginning of his delightful speculation on the question of whether a horse can laugh, Musil concedes that perhaps "since the war" (he means World War I) horses may have stopped laughing, any reader conscious of the use of horses in battle will feel the stab of truth jabbing the complacency of the amusement aroused by the opening sentences. Similarly, the two and a half pages on "the fly-paper Tanglefoot" push ironic detachment way past the point where the reader can continue to smile in comfortable superiority. Are these still insects being described, or a certain human subspecies, Homo Europaeus—or ourselves, at this point—sinking in the slime and poison of modern history? There is a kind of visionary optics at work here, a way of seeing that combines exact observation and a summoning up of a separate, mythical and imaginary reality.

This faculty of simultaneously rational and mythical perception is perhaps Musil's most characteristic, idiosyncratic quality, for one finds it expressed in all his fiction, and most often in the way he formulates his images. The sad, inarticulate Tonka in the story titled with her name, for instance, is startlingly and beautifully likened—literally out of nowhere—to "a snowflake in summer," which is really quite perfect, combining as it does the ideas of miraculous singularity, impossible yet undeniable purity, evanescent beauty, and a kind of innocence that cannot survive the harsh daylight of the doubting, dissecting intellect. In "Grigia," to give another example, a gramophone "wheels its way" through the boredom and stifled lust in an engineers' mess hall "like a gilded tin cart trundling over a soft meadow strewn with marvelous stars," a simile that just barely adheres to its rickety, commonplace object, while almost all its elements—gold, meadow, starlike flowers—yearn away in the direction of an enchantment (and it is not clear whether it is a curse or a blessing) that is luring the hero toward death.

"The Blackbird" is the last of the miscellaneous prose pieces collected in *Nachlass zu Lebzeiten*. It is the most enigmatic and cunningly encoded of all of Musil's stories. The first sentence tells us that "it is important to know who is reporting" the tale. It is, of course, always important to know that, so the instruction seems unnecessary. But Musil was never careless with words: he wouldn't let a phrase drop like loose change from the pocket of a sentence: he must have said it for some purpose.

Two old friends meet after a long separation. They are called Aone and Atwo—a nomenclature that suggests an identity underlying their difference—and we are told that their relationship is very much like the kind "every single person entertains with the various gentlemen he successively addresses as I." Atwo tells the story—actually three stories in one—about himself. But someone else is "reporting" Atwo's account, as well as Aone's uncomprehending response (in which Atwo professes to be completely uninterested). Is it far-fetched to assume that the rational, rather unimaginative Aone and the precariously haunted, poetic Atwo are aspects of the same personality, and that the unnamed narrator *is* that divided psyche? Or is the narrating voice that of a psychic function transcending those of Aone and Atwo by combining them— a synthesizing intelligence that knows how to strike sparks of ineffable magic from the cold stone of reason while keeping the lure of the devouring unconscious at bay?

But exegesis itself is risky, at best, with a writer like Musil; and we might do well to read him with an ear for the substratum of mystery in his stories and in ourselves rather than attempt to decipher a code that dissolves on inspection. Atwo puts it plainly enough at the end of "The Blackbird": "It's as if you hear a whispering, or just a rushing sound, without being able to tell the difference!"

JOEL AGEE

Introduction

This volume contains Musil's first novel, *Young Törless*, four of his five major novellas, and selections from the collection of sketches and prose poems Musil published under the untranslatable title *Nachlass zu Lebzeiten*, here rendered as "Pre-Posthumous Papers." These works complement the excellent new translation to be published by Alfred A. Knopf of the monumental novel *The Man Without Qualities*, which was left unfinished at Musil's death in 1942. Aside from *The Man Without Qualities*, this volume presents most of Musil's prose ficton. His other important writings include the play *Die Schwärmer* (The Visionaries), the farce *Vinzenz und die Freundin bedeutender Männer* (Vincent and the Girl Friend of Important Men), incisive essays on German and European culture and politics, a great many sketches and feuilleton pieces, an extensive body of book and theater reviews, diaries, letters, and a considerable quantity of fragmentary material belonging to *The Man Without Qualities*.

Musil was born in 1880 to a family of the upper-middle-class Austrian technocracy. He was trained as a mathematician, behavioral psychologist, and engineer, and also studied philosophy. He wrote his doctoral dissertation on Ernst Mach and could have had a distinguished scientific career: the zealous young scientist in "Tonka" and Ulrich, the central character in *The Man Without Qualities*, are partial self-portraits. The disintegration of the ramshackle Austrian Empire was for him a paradigm of how political and social institutions, as well as personal relations, had fallen apart. Literature seemed to Musil to offer the only real hope of uniting intellect and feeling, social action and moral action, of putting together again the smashed Humpty-Dumpty of twentieth-century European culture.

From 1908 to 1914, and again after the First World War, Musil was active as a journalist, reviewer, and contributor to serious cultural magazines. From 1911 to 1914 he was a librarian at the Technical University in Vienna; in 1914 he became an editor of the influential periodical *Die neue Rundschau* in Berlin. After the war, in which he saw service as an officer in the Austrian army on the Italian front (Hemingway was somewhere on the other side), Musil worked for several years as a bureaucrat in the Austrian Foreign Ministry and the War Department. Thereafter he devoted himself entirely to writing, although impoverished by the post-war inflation. When the Nazis occupied Austria in 1938, Musil, who had from the beginning been an astute dissector of the phenomenon of Nazism, fled with his wife to Switzerland, where they lived precariously. Attempts to help the Musils emigrate to Philadelphia, where Martha Musil's daughter and her family lived, proved unsuccessful, although supported by Einstein and Thomas Mann, among others. Musil died of a stroke in Switzerland in 1942 at the age of sixty-one.

Musil's outer life was undramatic. In 1911 he married Martha Marcovaldi, née Heimann, who had had two children by a previous marriage. A native of Berlin, Martha was a painter, independent-minded, and cosmopolitan. The couple had a close relationship; aside from his wife Musil had few intimate friends. Always well-dressed, he invariably displayed in public a reserved, correct demeanor. He was not unsociable, but discouraged personal intimacy; a very private person, he was very much an interested observer of the world. Paradoxes abound in Musil's life and thought.

His inner life was intense. Nietzsche had marked a break between the European present of the late nineteenth century and the German past, "German" being understood in its broader cultural rather than its narrow political sense. Musil, like his contemporaries Rilke, Kafka, Thomas Mann, and Wittgenstein—the list could well be longer—belonged to the first generation for whom Nietzsche's challenge to revalue values became, in an almost programmatic way, the order of the day. The moral framework of the Europe they had inherited in no way corresponded to a culture reforging itself on its own through industrialism, mushrooming capitalism, and rapid development in all fields of science and technology.

> In Goethe's world the clatter of the weaver's loom was considered a disturbing noise. In Ulrich's time they were just discovering the music of machine shops, steam hammers, and factory sirens. Not that people were quick to notice how a skyscraper towers over a man on a horse. On the contrary, even to this day those who want to make an impression will not mount a skyscraper but a high horse; they will move like the wind and see like an eagle, not a giant refractor. Their feelings have not kept up with their intellect; the difference in development between these two faculties is about that between the vermiform appendix and the cerebral cortex. (*The Man Without Qualities*, tr. Sophie Wilkins, © Alfred A. Knopf, Inc.)

In the line of Emerson and William James, as well as of Nietzsche, Musil came to literature as an experimental moralist. He wrote in his diary on November 14 or 15, 1910, that "literature is a bolder, more logical recombination of life. A calling into life or analyzing out of possibilities. . . . It is a zeal which starves the skin off one's bones for the sake of an intellectually emotional goal." His major characters move out from the illusory security of fixed positions in life along an experimental path, the path of possibility, hesitantly tapping toward some unseen utopian place where life's contradictions might be reconciled. Being on this path requires that everything in life, particularly questions of individual, social, and moral value, be rethought and redefined.

Musil was an acute dissector of culture and society, and he was also technically familiar with the newest scientific insights into the cognitive workings of the mind. (Trained as a behaviorist, he was also later well-read in the literature of psychoanalysis.) Musil insisted that life is not a sequential narrative of actions or ideas, but a web in which these are inextricably bound up with sensations and emotions. He presents his major characters with moral dilemmas, placing his figures in a realistic historical and natural setting which is sketched rather than described. With one exception, "The Lady from Portugal," all his fiction takes place in a European setting from, roughly, 1900 to 1920.

Musil's characters, the minor as well as the major ones, are all extremely human. Not one of them but is caught in the tangle of his character, place, and time. None of them are abstractions. Living is for them a process of groping toward ideal constant relationships with other people and toward a utopian society that must somehow be possible. (There are no pure existentialists in Musil's world.) The impossibility of attaining constant relationships is, however, also a given; these characters are forced by their creator to work within a fluid field of ever-shifting perceptions, sensations, emotions, and ideas. Because they are caught in this web of being human, they cannot possibly reach a fixed ideal goal. The result is an ethical dilemma. How, except in a mystic continuum, can one attain a state of ideal equilibrium and at the same time remain faithful to the quicksilver fluidity of thought and sensation which constitutes living? (The mystic note is liminally present throughout Musil's work, and comes to the fore in the later, unfinished part of *The Man Without Qualities*. Musil never solved the problem, however.) Some of Musil's characters succeed a bit and for a short time, others fail. There is even a hint of sadness in their searching: "We have won reality and lost dream," Musil says of the modern temper. His created people are seekers the way Rilke's poet-figures and Kafka's and Thomas Mann's characters are seekers, which reminds us again of Musil's ties to his generation.

While concerned with these themes, Musil's fiction is extremely varied in form and subject matter. As a writer he was a perfectionist and a polisher. Part of this was psychological—for long periods he suffered from writer's block—but more important, it seems to me, was the difficulty of what he was trying to do, which involved forging an entirely new kind of literary language. An artistic as opposed to a naturalistic language, it is powerful, compressed, highly wrought, and difficult to capture in translation. Within a metaphoric envelope thought is fused with the penumbra of perceptions, sensations, and emotions which surround it in life. As a writer Musil was interested not in the unconscious, but in the boundary where subconscious thoughts become conscious ones. The metaphorical tropes attempt to capture a situation the way people live it, as an ebbing and flowing which cannot be dissected rationally, either in cross section or sequentially. This of course has implications for the narrative process, the telling of a story; it de-emphasizes action and linear progression. This process is overseen by a narrator who is himself partly within and partly outside the characters. For Musil this complex style is truest to life.

Like Kafka and Rilke, Musil regarded language itself as an integral part of his subject, not merely a vehicle of expression. The goal of his style and of his art was to unite intellect with feeling, precision with soul, and this union, which may not be attainable for his characters, succeeds brilliantly on the level of language. Musil's aim was not to be poetic but realistic. His entire work is an untiring series of experiments in new forms of narrative prose in order to express a truer understanding, based on modern scientific knowledge, of cognition and states of feeling, of how the mind works and relates to the world it is part of.

Young Törless was published in 1906; "The Perfecting of a Love" in 1911 in *Unions*; *Three Women* in 1924; *Pre-Posthumous Papers* in 1936; and "Art and Morality of the Crawl" in 1932.

The best book in English on Musil, which places his life and thought within the broader European context it demands, is *Robert Musil and the Crisis of European Culture, 1880–1942* by David Luft (University of California Press). Also informative are *Wittgenstein's Vienna* by Allan Janik and Stephen Toulmin (Simon and Schuster), *Robert Musil: Master of the Hovering Life* by Frederick G. Peters (Columbia University Press), and my own *Robert Musil: An Introduction to His Work* (Cornell University Press).

B. P.

YOUNG
TÖRLESS

"*In some strange way we devalue things as soon as we give utterance to them. We believe we have dived to the uttermost depths of the abyss, and yet when we return to the surface the drop of water on our pallid finger-tips no longer resembles the sea from which it came. We think we have discovered a hoard of wonderful treasure-trove, yet when we emerge again into the light of day we see that all we have brought back with us is false stones and chips of glass. But for all this, the treasure goes on glimmering in the darkness, unchanged.*"

MAETERLINCK

It was a small station on the long railroad to Russia.

Four parallel lines of iron rails extended endlessly in each direction, on the yellow gravel of the broad track—each fringed, as with a dirty shadow, with the dark strip burnt into the ground by steam and fumes.

Behind the station, a low oil-painted building, there was a broad, worn dirt-road leading up to the railway embankment. It merged into the trampled ground, its edges indicated only by the two rows of acacia trees that flanked it drearily, their thirsty leaves suffocated by dust and soot.

Perhaps it was these sad colours, or perhaps it was the wan, exhausted light of the afternoon sun, drained of its strength by the haze: there was something indifferent, lifeless, and mechanical about objects and human beings here, as though they were all part of a scene in a puppet-theatre. From time to time, at regular intervals, the station-master stepped out of his office and, always with the same turn of his head, glanced up the long line towards the signal-box, where the signals still failed to indicate the approach of the express each time, which had been delayed for a long time at the frontier; then, always with the very same movement of his arm, he would pull out his pocket-watch and, then, shaking his head, he would disappear again: just so do the figures on ancient tower-clocks appear and disappear again with the striking of the hour.

On the broad, well-trodden strip of ground between the railway-line and the station building a gay company of young men was strolling up and down, walking to right and to left of a middle-aged couple who were the centre of the somewhat noisy conversation. But even the blitheness of this group did not ring quite true; it was as if their merry laughter fell into silence only a few paces away, almost as if it had run into some invisible but solid obstacle and there sunk to the ground.

Frau Hofrat Törless—this was the lady, perhaps forty years of age—wore a thick veil concealing her sad eyes, which were a little reddened from weeping. This was a leave-taking. And she found it hard, yet once again, having to leave her only child among strangers for so long a period, without any chance to watch protectively over her darling.

For the little town lay far away from the capital, in the eastern territories of the empire, in thinly populated, dry arable country.

The reason why Frau Törless had to leave her boy in this remote and inhospitable outlandish district was that in this town there was a celebrated boarding-school, which in the previous century had developed out of a religious foundation and had since remained where it was, doubtless in order to safeguard the young generation, in its years of awakening, from the corrupting influences of a large city.

It was here that the sons of the best families in the country received their education, going on then to the university, or into the army or the service of the State; in all such careers, as well as for general social reasons, it was a particular advantage to have been educated at W.

Four years previously this consideration had caused Hofrat and Frau Törless to yield to their son's ambitious plea and arrange for him to enter this school.

This decision afterwards cost many tears. For almost from the first moment when the doors of the school closed behind him with irrevocable finality, little Törless suffered from frightful, agonising homesickness. Neither lessons, nor games on the wide luxuriant grasslands of the park, nor the other distractions that the school offered its inmates, could hold his attention; he took almost no interest in these things. He saw everything only as through a veil and even during the day often had trouble in gulping down an obstinately rising sob; at night he always cried himself to sleep.

He wrote letters home almost daily, and he lived only in these letters; everything else he did seemed to him only a shadowy, un-meaning string of events, indifferent stations on his way, like the marking of the hours on a clock-face. But when he wrote he felt within himself something that made him distinct, that set him apart; something in him rose, like an island of miraculous suns and flashing colours, out of the ocean of grey sensations that lapped around him, cold and indifferent, day after day. And when by day, at games or in class, he remembered that he would write his letter in the evening, it was as though he were wearing, hidden on his person, fastened to an invisible chain, a golden key with which, as soon as no one was looking, he would open the gate leading into marvellous gardens.

The remarkable thing about it was that this sudden consuming fondness for his parents was for himself something new and disconcerting. He had never imagined such a thing before, he had gone to boarding-school gladly and of his own free will, indeed he had laughed when at their first leave-taking his mother had been unable to check her tears; and only later, when he had been on his own for some days and been getting on comparatively well, did it gush up in him suddenly and with elemental force.

He took it for homesickness and believed he was missing his parents. But it was in reality something much more indefinable and complex. For the object of this longing, the image of his parents, actually ceased to have any place in it at all: I mean that certain plastic, physical memory of a loved person which is not merely remembrance but something speaking to all the senses and preserved in all the senses, so that one cannot do anything without feeling the other person silent and invisible at one's side. This soon faded out, like a resonance that vibrates only for a while. In other words, by that time Törless could no longer conjure up before his eyes the image of his 'dear, dear parents'—as he usually called them in his thoughts. If he tried to do so, what rose up in its place was the boundless grief and longing from which he suffered so much and which yet held him in its spell, its hot flames causing him both agony and rapture. And so the thought of his parents more and more became a mere pretext, an external means to set going this egoistic suffering in him, which enclosed him in his voluptuous pride as in the seclusion of a chapel where, surrounded by hundreds of flickering candles and hundreds of eyes gazing down from sacred images, incense was wafted among the writhing flagellants. . . .

Later, as his 'homesickness' became less violent and gradually passed off, this, its real character, began to show rather more clearly. For in its place there did not come the contentment that might have been expected; on the contrary, what it left in young Törless's soul was a void. And this nothingness, this emptiness in himself, made him realise that it was no mere yearning he had lost, but something positive, a spiritual force, something that had flowered in him under the guise of grief.

But now it was all over, and this well-spring of a first sublime bliss had made itself known to him only by its drying up.

At this time the passionate evidence of the soul's awakening vanished out of his letters, and in its place came detailed descriptions of life at school and the new friends he had made.

He himself felt impoverished by this change, and bare, like a little tree experiencing its first winter after its first still fruitless blossoming.

But his parents were glad. They loved him with strong, unthinking, animal affection. Every time after he had been home on holiday from boarding-school, and gone away again, to the Frau Hofrat the house once more seemed empty and deserted, and for some days after each of these visits it was with tears in her eyes that she went through the rooms, here and there caressing some object on which the boy's gaze had rested or which his fingers had held. And both parents would have let themselves be torn to pieces for his sake.

The clumsy pathos and passionate, mutinous sorrow of his letters had given them grievous concern and kept them in a state of high-pitched sensitiveness; the blithe, contented light-heartedness that followed upon it gladdened them again and, feeling that now a crisis had been surmounted, they did all they could to encourage this new mood.

Neither in the one phase nor in the other did they recognise the symptoms of a definite psychological development; on the contrary, they accepted both the anguish and its appeasement as merely a natural consequence of the situation. It escaped them that a young human being, all on his own, had made his first, unsuccessful attempt to develop the forces of his inner life.

*   *   *

Törless, however, now felt very dissatisfied and groped this way and that, in vain, for something new that might serve as a support to him.

*   *   *

At this period there was an episode symptomatic of something still germinating in Törless, which was to develop significantly in him later.

What happened was this: one day the youthful Prince H. entered the school, a scion of one of the oldest, most influential, and most conservative noble families in the empire.

All the others thought him boring, and found his gentle gaze affected; the manner in which he stood with one hip jutting forward and, while talking, languidly interlocked and unlocked his fingers, they mocked as effeminate. But what chiefly aroused their scorn was that he had been brought to the school not by his parents but by his former tutor, a doctor of divinity who was a member of a religious order.

On Törless, however, he made a strong impression from the very first moment. Perhaps the fact that he was a prince and by birth entitled to move in Court circles had something to do with it; but however that might be, he was a different kind of person for Törless to get to know.

The silence and tranquillity of an ancient and noble country seat, and of devotional exercises, seemed somehow to cling about him still. When he walked, it was with smooth, lithe movements and with that faintly diffident attitude of withdrawal, that contraction of the body, which comes from being accustomed to walking very erect through a succession of vast, empty rooms, where any other sort of person seems to bump heavily against invisible corners of the empty space around him.

And so for Törless acquaintance with the prince became a source of exquisite psychological enjoyment. It laid the foundations in him of that kind of knowledge of human nature which teaches one to recognise and appreciate another person by the cadence of his voice, by the way he picks up and handles a thing, even, indeed, by the timbre of his silences and the expressiveness of his bodily attitude in adjusting himself to a space, a setting—in other words, by that mobile, scarcely tangible, and yet essential, integral way of being a human entity, a spirit, that way of being it which encloses the core, the palpable and debatable aspect of him, as flesh encloses the mere bones—and in so appreciating to prefigure for oneself the mental aspect of his personality.

During this brief period Törless lived as in an idyll. He was not put out by his new friend's devoutness, which was really something quite alien to him, coming as he did from a free-thinking middle-class family. He accepted it without a qualm, going so far as to see it, indeed, as something especially admirable in the prince, since it intensified the essential quality of this other boy's personality, which he felt was so unlike his own as to be in no way comparable.

In the prince's company he felt rather as though he were in some little chapel far off the main road. The thought of actually not belonging there quite vanished in the enjoyment of, for once, seeing the daylight through stained glass; and he let his gaze glide over the profusion of futile gilded agalma in this other person's soul until he had absorbed at least some sort of indistinct picture of that soul, just as though with his finger-tips he were tracing the lines of an arabesque, not thinking about it, merely sensing the beautiful pattern of it, which twined according to some weird laws beyond his ken.

And then suddenly there came the break between them.

Törless blundered badly, as he had to admit to himself afterwards.

The fact was: on one occasion they did suddenly find themselves arguing about religion. And as soon as that happened, it was really all over and done with. For as though independently of himself, Törless's intellect lashed out, inexorably, at the sensitive young prince; he poured out torrents of a rationalist's scorn upon him, barbarously desecrating the filigree habitation in which the other boy's soul dwelt. And they parted in anger.

After that they never spoke to each other again. Törless was indeed obscurely aware that what he had done was senseless, and a glimmer of intuitive insight told him that his wooden yardstick of rationality had untimely shattered a relationship that was subtle and full of rare fascination. But this was something he simply had not been able to help. It left him, probably for ever, with a sort of yearning for what had been; yet he seemed to have been caught up in another current, which was carrying him further and further away in a different direction.

And then some time later the prince, who had not been happy there, left the school.

* * *

Now everything around Törless was empty and boring. But meanwhile he had been growing older, and with the onset of adolescence something began to rise up in him, darkly and steadily. At this stage of his development he made some new friends, of a kind corresponding to the needs of his age, which were to be of very great importance to him. He became friends with Beineberg and Reiting, and with Moté and Hofmeier, the boys in whose company he was today seeing his parents off at the railway station.

Remarkably enough, these were the boys who counted as the worst of his year; they were gifted and, it went without saying, of good family, but at times they were wild and reckless to the point of brutality. And that it should be precisely their company to which Törless now felt so strongly drawn was doubtless connected with his own lack of self-certainty, which had become very marked indeed since he had lost touch with the prince. It was indeed the logical continuation of that break, for, like the break itself, it indicated some fear of all over-subtle toyings with emotions; and by contrast with that sort of thing the nature of these other friends stood out as sound and sturdy, giving life its due.

Törless entirely abandoned himself to their influence, for the situation in which his mind now found itself was approximately this: At schools of the kind known as the *Gymnasium*, at his age, one has read Goethe, Schiller, Shakespeare, and perhaps even some modern writers too, and this, having been half digested, is then written out of the system again, excreted, as it were, through the finger-tips. Roman tragedies are written, or poems, of the most sensitive lyrical kind, that go through their paces garbed in punctuation that is looped over whole pages at a time, as in delicate lace: things that are in themselves ludicrous, but which are of inestimable value in contributing to a sound development. For these associations originating outside, and these borrowed emotions, carry young people over the dangerously soft spiritual ground of the years in which they need to be of some significance to themselves and nevertheless are still too incomplete to have any real significance. Whether any residue of it is ultimately left in the one, or nothing in the other, does not matter; later each will somehow come to terms with himself, and the danger exists only in the stage of tran-

sition. If at that period one could bring a boy to see the ridicu-
lousness of himself, the ground would give way under him, or he
would plunge headlong like a somnambulist who, suddenly awak-
ing, sees nothing but emptiness around him.

That illusion, that conjuring trick for the benefit of the personality's development, was missing in this school. For though the
classics were there in the library, they were considered 'boring', and
for the rest there were only volumes of sentimental romances and
drearily humorous tales of army life.

Young Törless had read just about all of them in his sheer
greed for books, and this or that conventionally tender image
from one story or another did sometimes linger for a while in his
mind; but none had any influence—any real influence—on his character.

At this period it seemed that he had no character at all.

Under the influence of this reading, he himself now and then
would write a little story or begin an epic romance, and in his
excitement over the sufferings of his heroes, crossed in love, his
cheeks would flush, his pulse quicken, and his eyes shine.

But when he laid down his pen, it was all over; his spirit lived
only, as it were, while in motion. And so too he found it possible
to dash off a poem or a story at any time, whenever it might be
required of him. The doing of it excited him, yet he never took it
quite seriously, and this occupation in itself did not strike him as
important. Nothing of it was assimilated into his personality, nor
did it originate within his personality. All that happened was that
under some external pressure he underwent emotions that tran-
scended the indifference of ordinary life, just as an actor needs the
compulsion that a role imposes on him.

These were cerebral reactions. But what is felt to be character
or soul, a person's inner contour or aura, that is to say, the thing
in contrast with which the thoughts, decisions, and actions appear
random, lacking in characteristic quality, and easily exchangeable
for others—the thing that had, for instance, bound Törless to the
prince in a manner beyond the reach of any intellectual judgment—
this ultimate, immovable background seemed to be utterly lost to
Törless at this period.

In his friends it was enjoyment of sport, the animal delight in being alive, that prevented them from feeling the need for anything of this kind, just as at the *Gymnasium* the want is supplied by the sport with literature.

But Törless's constitution was too intellectual for the one, and, as for the other, life at this school, where one had to be in a perpetual state of readiness to settle arguments with one's fists, made him keenly sensitive to the absurdity of such borrowed sentiment. So his being took on a vagueness, a sort of inner helplessness, that made it impossible for him to be sure where he stood.

He attached himself to these new friends because he was impressed by their wildness. Since he was ambitious, he now and then even tried to outvie them in this. But each time he would leave off half-way, and on this account had to put up with no small amount of gibes, which would scare him back into himself again. At this critical period the whole of his life really consisted in nothing but these efforts, renewed again and again, to emulate his rough, more masculine friends and, counterbalancing that, a deep inner indifference to all such strivings.

Now, when his parents came to see him, so long as they were alone he was quiet and shy. Each time he dodged his mother's affectionate caresses under one pretext or another. He would really have liked to yield to them, but he was ashamed, as though he were being watched by his friends.

His parents let it pass as the awkwardness of adolescence.

Then in the afternoon the whole noisy crowd would come along. They played cards, ate, drank, told anecdotes about the masters, and smoked the cigarettes that the Hofrat had brought from the capital.

This jollity pleased and reassured the parents.

That there were, in between times, hours of a different kind for Törless was something they did not know. And recently there had been more and more of such hours. There were moments when life at school became a matter of utter indifference to him. Then the putty of his everyday concerns dropped out and, with nothing more to bind them together, the hours of his life fell apart.

He often sat for a long time—gloomily brooding—as it were hunched over himself.

* * *

This time too his parents had stayed for two days. There had been a lunching and dining together, smoking, a drive in the country; and now the express was to carry Törless's parents back to the capital.

A faint vibration of the rails heralded the train's approach, and the bell clanging on the station roof sounded inexorably in the Frau Hofrat's ears.

"Well, my dear Beineberg, so you'll keep an eye on this lad of mine for me, won't you?" Hofrat Törless said, turning to young Baron Beineberg, a lanky, bony boy with big ears that stuck out, and eyes that were expressive and intelligent.

Törless, who was younger and smaller than the others, pulled a face at this repugnant suggestion of being given into his friend's charge; and Beineberg grinned, obviously flattered and with a shade of triumphant malice.

"Really," the Hofrat added, turning to the rest of them, "I should like to ask you all, if there should be anything at all the matter with my son, to let me know at once."

This was going too far, and it drew from young Törless an infinitely wearied protest: "But, Father, what on earth do you think could happen to me?" although he was well used by now to having to put up with this excess of solicitude at every leave-taking.

Meanwhile the others drew themselves up, clicking their heels, each straightening the elegant sword at his side. And the Hofrat went on: "One never knows what may happen. It is a great weight off my mind to know I would be instantly informed. After all, something might prevent you from writing."

At that moment the train drew in. Hofrat Törless embraced his son, Frau von Törless drew the veil tighter over her face to hide her tears, and one after the other the friends once more expressed their thanks for having been entertained. Then the guard slammed the door of the carriage.

Once again Hofrat and Frau von Törless saw the high, bare back of the school building and the immense, long wall surrounding the park; and then there was nothing to left and to right but grey-brown fields and an occasional fruit-tree.

*   *   *

Meanwhile the boys had left the railway station and were walking, in two single files, along the two edges of the road—so avoiding at least the densest and most suffocating dust—towards the town, without talking to each other much.

It was after five o'clock, and over the fields came a breath of something solemn and cold, a harbinger of evening.

Törless began to feel very mournful.

Perhaps it was because of his parents' departure, or perhaps it was caused only by the forbidding stolid melancholy that now lay like a dead weight on all the landscape, blurring the outlines of things, even a few paces away, with lack-lustre heaviness.

The same dreadful indifference that had been blanketed over the surrounding countryside all that afternoon now came creeping across the plain, and after it, like a slimy trail, came the mist, stickily clinging to the fresh-ploughed fields and the leaden-grey acres of turnips. Törless did not glance to right or to left, but he felt it. Steadily as he walked he set his feet in the tracks gaping in the dust, the prints left by the footsteps of the boy in front—and he felt it as though it must be so, as a stony compulsion catching his whole life up and compressing it into this movement—steadily plodding on along this one line, along this one small streak being drawn out through the dust.

When they came to a halt at a crossroads, where a second road and their own debouched into a round, worn patch of ground, and where a rotten timber sign-post pointed crookedly into the air, the tilted line of it, in such contrast with the surroundings, struck Törless as being like a cry of desperation.

Again they walked on. Törless thought of his parents, of people he knew, of life. At this time of day people were changing for a party or deciding they would go to the theatre. And afterwards one might go to a restaurant, hear a band playing, sit at a café table. . . . One met interesting people. A flirtation, an adventure, kept one in suspense till the morning. Life went on revolving, churning out ever new and unexpected happenings, like a strange and wonderful wheel. . . .

Törless sighed over these thoughts, and at each step that bore him closer to the cramped narrowness of school something in him constricted, a noose was pulled tighter and tighter.

Even now the bell was ringing in his ears. And there was nothing he dreaded so much as this ringing of the bell, which cut the day short, once and for all, like the savage slash of a knife.

To be sure, there was nothing for him to experience, and his life passed along in a blur of perpetual indifference; but this ringing of the bell was an added mockery, which left him quivering with helpless rage against himself, his fate, and the day that was buried.

Now you can't experience anything more at all, for twelve hours you can't experience anything, for twelve hours you're dead. . . . That was what this bell meant.

*   *   *

When the little band of friends reached the first low-built wretched cottages, this mood of gloom and introspection lifted from Törless. As though seized by some sudden interest, he raised his head and glanced intently into the smoky interior of the dirty little hovels they were passing.

Outside the doors of most of them the women-folk were standing, in their wide skirts and coarse shifts, their broad feet caked with dust, their arms bare and brown.

If they were young and buxom, some crude Slav jest would be flung at them. They would nudge each other and titter at 'the young gentlemen'; sometimes, too, one would utter a shriek when her breasts were too vigorously brushed against in passing, or would answer a slap on the buttocks with an insulting epithet and a burst of laughter. There were others who merely watched the swift passers-by with a grave and angry look; and the peasant himself, if he happened to come on the scene, would smile awkwardly, half unsure what to make of it, half in good humour.

Törless took no part in this display of overweening and precocious manliness.

The reason for this lay doubtless to some extent in a certain timidity about sexual matters such as is characteristic of almost all only children, but chiefly in his own peculiar kind of sensuality, which was more deeply hidden, more forceful, and of a darker hue than that of his friends and more slow and difficult in its manifestations.

While the others were making a show of shameless behaviour with the women, rather more for the sake of being 'smart' than from any lascivious urge, the taciturn little Törless's soul was in a state of upheaval, surging with real shamelessness.

He looked through the little windows and the crooked, narrow doorways into the interior of the cottages with a gaze burning so hotly that there was all the time something like a delicate mesh dancing before his eyes.

Almost naked children tumbled about in the mud of the yards; here and there as some woman bent over her work her skirt swung high, revealing the hollows at the back of her knees, or the bulge of a heavy breast showed as the linen tightened over it. It was as though all this were going on in some quite different, animal, oppressive atmosphere, and the cottages exuded a heavy, sluggish air, which Törless eagerly breathed in.

He thought of old paintings that he had seen in museums without really understanding them. He was waiting for something, just as, when he stood in front of those paintings, he had always been waiting for something that never happened. What was it . . . ? It must be something surprising, something never beheld before, some monstrous sight of which he could not form the lightest notion; something of a terrifying, beast-like sensuality; something that would seize him in its claws and rend him, starting with his eyes; an experience that in some still utterly obscure way seemed to be associated with these women's soiled petticoats, with their roughened hands, with the low ceilings of their little rooms, with . . . with a besmirching of himself with the filth of these yards . . . No, no . . . Now he no longer felt anything but the fiery net before his eyes; the words did not say it; for it is not nearly so bad as the words make it seem; it is something mute—a choking in the throat, a scarcely perceptible thought, and only if one insisted on getting it to the point of words would it come out like that. And then it has ceased to be anything but faintly reminiscent of whatever it was, as under huge magnification, when one not only sees everything more distinctly but also sees things that are not there at all. . . . And yet, for all that, it was something to be ashamed of.

*   *   *

"Is Baby feeling homesick?" he was suddenly asked, in mocking tones, by von Reiting, that tall boy two years older than himself, who had been struck by Törless's silence and the darkness over his eyes. Törless forced an artificial and rather embarrassed smile to his lips; and he felt as though the malicious Reiting had been eavesdropping on what had been going on within him.

He did not answer. But meanwhile they had reached the little town's church square, with its cobbles, and here they parted company.

Törless and Beineberg did not want to go back yet, but the others had no leave to stay out any longer and returned to the school.

The two boys had gone along to the cake shop.

Here they sat at a little round table, beside a window overlooking the garden, under a gas candelabrum with its flames buzzing softly in the milky glass globes.

They had made themselves thoroughly comfortable, having little glasses filled up now with this liqueur, now with another, smoking cigarettes, and eating pastries between whiles, enjoying the luxury of being the only customers. Although in one of the back rooms there might still be some solitary visitor sitting over his glass of wine, at least here in front all was quiet, and even the portly, ageing proprietress seemed to have dozed off behind the counter.

Törless gazed—but vaguely—through the window, out into the empty garden, where darkness was slowly gathering.

Beineberg was talking—about India, as usual. For his father, the general, had as a young officer been there in British service. And he had brought back not only what any other European brought back with him, carvings, textiles, and little idols manufactured for sale to tourists, but something of a feeling, which he had never lost, for the mysterious, bizarre glimmerings of esoteric Buddhism. Whatever he had picked up there, and had come to know more of from his later reading, he had passed on to his son, even from the boy's early childhood.

For the rest, his attitude to reading was an odd one. He was a cavalry officer and was not at all fond of books in general. Novels and philosophy he despised equally. When he read, he did not want to reflect on opinions and controversies, but, from the very instant of opening the book, to enter as through a secret portal into the midst of some very exclusive knowledge. Books that he read had to be such that the mere possession of them was as it were a secret sign of initiation and a pledge of more than earthly revelations. And this he found only in books of Indian philosophy, which to him seemed to be not merely books, but revelations, something real—keys such as were the alchemical and magical books of the Middle Ages.

With them this healthy, energetic man, who observed his duties strictly and exercised his three horses himself almost every day, would usually shut himself up for the evening.

Then he would pick out a passage at random and meditate on it, in the hope that this time it would reveal its inmost secret meaning to him. Nor was he ever disappointed, however often he had to admit that he had not yet advanced beyond the forecourts of the sacred temple.

Thus it was that round this sinewy, tanned, open-air man there hovered something like the nimbus of an esoteric mystery. His conviction of being daily on the eve of receiving some overpoweringly great illumination gave him an air of reserve and superiority. His eyes were not dreamy, but calm and hard. The habit of reading books in which no single word could be shifted from its place without disturbing the secret significance, the careful, scrupulous weighing of every single sentence for its meaning and counter-meaning, its possible ambiguities, had brought that look into those eyes.

Only occasionally did his thoughts lose themselves in a twilit state of agreeable melancholy. This happened when he thought of the esoteric cult bound up with the originals of the writings open before him, of the miracles that had emanated from them, stirring thousands, thousands of human beings who now, because of the vast distance separating him from them, appeared to him like brothers, while he despised the people round about him, whom he saw in all their detail. At such hours he grew despondent. He was depressed by the thought that he was condemned to spend his life far away from the sources of those holy powers and that his efforts were perhaps doomed in the end to be frustrated by these unfavourable conditions. But then, after he had been sitting gloomily over his books for a while, he would begin to have a strange feeling. True, his melancholy lost nothing of its oppressiveness—on the contrary, the sadness of it was still further intensified—but it no longer oppressed him. He would then feel more forlorn than ever, and as though defending a lost position; but in this mournfulness there lay a subtle relish, a pride in doing something utterly alien to the people about him, serving a divinity uncomprehended by the rest. And then it was that, fleetingly, something would flare up in his eyes that was like the ravishment of religious ecstasy.

*   *   *

Beineberg had talked himself to a standstill. In him the image of his eccentric father lived on in a kind of distorted magnification. Every feature was preserved; but what in the other had originally, perhaps, been no more than a mood that was conserved and intensified for the sake of its exclusiveness had in him grown hugely into a fantastic hope. That peculiarity of his father's, which for the older man was at bottom perhaps really no more than that last refuge for individuality which every human being—and even if it is only through his choice of clothes—must provide himself with in order to have something to distinguish him from others, had in him turned into the firm belief that he could achieve dominion over people by means of more than ordinary spiritual powers.

Törless knew this talk by heart. It passed away over him, leaving him almost quite unmoved.

He had now turned slightly from the window and was observing Beineberg, who was rolling himself a cigarette. And again he felt the queer repugnance, the dislike of Beineberg, that would at times rise up in him. These slim, dark hands, which were now so deftly rolling the tobacco into the paper, were really—come to think of it—beautiful. Thin fingers, oval, beautifully curved nails: there was a touch of breeding, of elegance, about them. So there was too in the dark brown eyes. It was there also in the long-drawn lankiness of the whole body. To be sure, the ears did stick out more than would quite do, the face was small and irregular, and the sum total of the head's expression was reminiscent of a bat's. Nevertheless— Törless felt this quite clearly as he weighed the details against each other in the balance—it was not the ugly, it was precisely the more attractive features that made him so peculiarly uneasy.

The thinness of the body—Beineberg was in the habit of lauding the steely, slender legs of Homeric champion runners as the ideal— did not at all have this effect on him. Törless had never yet tried to give himself an account of this, and for the moment he could not think of any satisfactory comparison. He would have liked to scrutinise Beineberg more closely, but then Beineberg would have noticed what he was thinking and he would have had to strike up some sort of conversation. Yet it was precisely thus—half looking at him, half filling the picture out in his imagination—that he was struck by the difference. If he thought the clothes away from the body, it became quite impossible to hold on to the notion of calm slenderness; what happened then, instantly, was that in his mind's eye he saw restless, writhing movements, a twisting of limbs and a bending of the spine such as are to be found in all pictures of martyrs' deaths, or in the grotesque performances of acrobats and 'rubber men' at fairs.

And the hands, too, which he could certainly just as well have pictured in some beautifully expressive gesture, he could not imagine otherwise than in motion, with flickering fingers. And it was precisely on these hands, which were really Beineberg's most attractive feature, that his greatest repugnance was concentrated. There was something prurient about them. That no doubt, was, what it amounted to. And there was for him something prurient, too, about the body, which he could not help associating with dislocated movements. But it was in the hands that this seemed to accumulate, and it seemed to radiate from them like a hint of some touch that was yet to come, sending a thrill of disgust coursing over Törless's skin. He himself was astonished at the notion, and faintly shocked. For this was now the second time today that something sexual had without warning, and irrelevantly, thrust its way in among his thoughts.

Beineberg had taken up a newspaper, and now Törless could consider him closely.

There was in reality scarcely anything to be found in his appearance that could have even remotely justified this sudden association of ideas in Törless's mind.

And for all that, in spite of the lack of justification for it, his sense of discomfort grew ever more intense. The silence between them had lasted scarcely ten minutes, and yet Törless felt his repugnance gradually increasing to the utmost degree. A fundamental mood, a fundamental relationship between himself and Beineberg, seemed in this way to be manifesting itself for the first time; a mistrust that had always been lurking somewhere in the depths seemed all at once to have loomed up into the realm of conscious feeling.

The atmosphere became more and more acutely uncomfortable. Törless was invaded by an urge to utter insults, but he could find no adequate words. He was uneasy with a sort of shame, as though something had actually happened between himself and Beineberg. His fingers began to drum restlessly on the table.

*   *   *

Finally, in order to escape from this strange state of mind, he looked out of the window again.

Now Beineberg glanced up from the newspaper. Then he read a paragraph aloud, laid the paper aside, and yawned.

With the breaking of the silence the spell that had bound Törless was also broken. Casual words began to flow over the awkward moment, blotting it out. There had been a momentary alertness, but now the old indifference was there again. . . .

"How long have we still got?" Törless asked.

"Two and a half hours."

Suddenly shivering, Törless hunched up his shoulders. Once again he felt the paralysing weight of the constriction he was about to re-enter, the school time-table, the daily companionship of his friends. Even that dislike of Beineberg would cease which seemed, for an instant, to have created a new situation.

". . . What's for supper tonight?"

"I don't know."

"What have we got tomorrow?"

"Mathematics."

"Oh. Was there something to prepare?"

"Yes. A few new trigonometry theorems. But you needn't worry about them, they're not difficult."

"And what else?"

"Divinity."

"Divinity. . . . Oh, well. That's something to look forward to. . . . I think when I really get going I could just as easily prove that twice two is five as that there can be only one God. . . ."

Beineberg glanced up at Törless mockingly. "It's quite funny how you go on about that. It strikes me almost as if you really enjoyed it. Anyway, there's a positive glare of enthusiasm in your eyes. . . ."

"And why not? Don't you think it's fun? There's always a point you get to where you stop knowing whether you're just making it all up or if what you've made up is truer than you are yourself."

"How do you mean?"

"Well, I don't mean literally, of course. Naturally, you always know you *are* making it up. But all the same, every now and then the whole thing strikes you as being so credible that you're brought up standing, in a way, in the grip of your own ideas."

"Well, but what is it about it you enjoy, then?"

"Just that: you get a sort of jerk in your head, a sort of dizziness, a shock . . ."

"Oh, I say, shut up! That's all foolery."

"Well, I didn't say it wasn't. But still, so far as I'm concerned, it's more interesting than anything else at school."

"It's just a way of doing gymnastics with your brain. But it doesn't get you anywhere, all the same."

"No," Törless said, looking out into the garden again. Behind his back—as though from a long way off—he heard the buzzing of the gas-lights. He was preoccupied by an emotion rising up in him, mournfully and like a mist.

"It doesn't get you anywhere. You're right about that. But it doesn't do to tell yourself that. How much of all the things we spend our whole time in school doing is really going to get anyone anywhere? What do we get anything out of? I mean for ourselves— you see what I mean? In the evening you know you've lived another day, you've learnt this and that, you've kept up with the time-table, but still, you're empty—inwardly, I mean. Right inside, you're still hungry, so to speak . . ."

Beineberg muttered something about exercising the mind by way of preparation—not yet being able to start on anything—later on . . .

"Preparation? Exercise? What *for*? Have you got any definite idea of it? I dare say you're hoping for something, but it's just as vague to you as it is to me. It's like this: everlastingly waiting for something you don't know anything about except that you're wait-ing for it. . . . It's so boring. . . ."

"Boring . . ." Beineberg drawled in mimicry, wagging his head.

Törless was still gazing out into the garden. He thought he could hear the rustling of the withered leaves being blown into drifts by the wind. Then came that moment of utter stillness which always occurs a little while before the descent of complete darkness. The shapes of things, which had been sinking ever more deeply into the dusk, and the blurring, dissolving colours of things—for an instant it all seemed to pause, to hover, as it were with a holding of the breath . . .

"You know, Beineberg," Törless said, without turning round, "when it's getting dark there always seem to be a few moments that are sort of different. Every time I watch it happening I remember the same thing: once when I was quite small I was playing in the woods at this time of evening. My nursemaid had wandered off somewhere. I didn't know she had, and so I still felt as if she were nearby. Suddenly something made me look up. I could feel I was alone. It was suddenly all so quiet. And when I looked around it was as though the trees were standing in a circle round me, all silent, and looking at me. I began to cry. I felt the grownups had deserted me and abandoned me to inanimate beings. . . . What is it? I still often get it. What's this sudden silence that's like a language we can't hear?"

"I don't know the thing you mean. But why shouldn't things have a language of their own? After all, there are no definite grounds for asserting that they haven't a soul!"

Törless did not answer. He did not care for Beineberg's speculative view of the matter.

But after a while Beineberg went on: "Why do you keep on staring out of the window? What is there to be seen?"

"I'm still wondering what it can be." But actually he had gone on to thinking about something else, which he did not want to speak of. That high tension, that harkening as if some solemn mystery might become audible, and the burden of gazing right into the midst of the still undefined relationships of things—all this was something he had been able to endure only for a moment. Then he had once again been overcome by the sense of solitude and forlornness which always followed this excessive demand upon his resources. He felt: there's something in this that's still too difficult for me. And his thoughts took refuge in something else, which was also implicit in it all, but which, as it were, lay only in the background and biding its time: loneliness.

From the deserted garden a leaf now and then fluttered up against the lit window, tearing a streak of brightness into the darkness behind it. Then the darkness seemed to shrink and withdraw, only in the next instant to advance again and stand motionless as a wall outside the window. This darkness was a world apart. It had descended upon the earth like a horde of black enemies, slaughtering or banishing human beings, or, whatever it did, blotting out all trace of them.

And it seemed to Törless that he was glad of this. At this moment he had no liking for human beings—for all who were adults. He never liked them when it was dark. He was in the habit then of cancelling them out of his thoughts. After that the world seemed to him like a sombre, empty house, and in his breast there was a sense of awe and horror, as though he must now search room after room—dark rooms where he did not know what the corners might conceal—groping his way across thresholds that no human foot would ever step on again, until—until in one room the doors would suddenly slam behind him and before him and he would stand confronting the mistress of the black hordes herself. And at the same instant the locks would snap shut in all the doors through which he had come; and only far beyond, outside the walls, would the shades of darkness stand on guard like black eunuchs, warding off any human approach.

This was his kind of loneliness since he had been left in the lurch that time—in the woods, where he had wept so bitterly. It held for him the lure of woman and of something monstrous. He felt it as a woman, but its breath was only a gasping in his chest, its face a whirling forgetfulness of all human faces, and the movements of its hands a shuddering all through his body. . . .

He feared this fantasy, for he was aware of the perverted lust in the secrecy of it, and he was disturbed by the thought that such imaginings might gain more and more power over him. But they would overwhelm him just when he believed himself to be most serious and most pure. It happened, perhaps, as a reaction to those moments when he had an inkling of another emotional awareness, which, though it was already implicit in him, was as yet beyond his years. For there is, in the development of every fine moral energy, such an early point where it weakens the soul whose most daring experience it will perhaps be some day—just as if it had first to send down its roots, gropingly, to disturb the ground that they will afterwards hold together; and it is for this reason that boys with a great future ahead of them usually go through a period abounding in humiliations.

Törless's taste for certain moods was the first hint of a psychological development that was later to manifest itself as a strong sense of wonder. The fact was that later he was to have—and indeed to be dominated by—a peculiar ability: he could not help frequently experiencing events, people, things, and even himself, in such a way as to feel that in it all there was at once some insoluble enigma and some inexplicable kinship for which he could never quite produce any evidence. Then these things would seem tangibly comprehensible, and yet he could never entirely resolve them into words and ideas. Between events and himself, indeed between his own feelings and some inmost self that craved understanding of them, there always remained a dividing-line, which receded before his desire, like a horizon, the closer he tried to come to it. Indeed, the more accurately he circumscribed his feelings with thoughts, and the more familiar they became to him, the stranger and more incomprehensible did they seem to become, in equal measure; so that it no longer even seemed as though they were retreating before him, but as though he himself were withdrawing from them, and yet without being able to shake off the illusion of coming closer to them.

This queer antithesis, which was so difficult for him to grasp, later occupied an important phase of his spiritual development; it was something that tore at his soul, as though to rend it apart, and for a long time it was his soul's chief problem and the chief threat to it.

For the present, however, the severity of these struggles was indicated only by a frequent sudden lassitude, alarming him, as it were, from a long way off, when ever some ambiguous, odd mood—such as this just now—brought him a foreboding of it. Then he would seem to himself as powerless as a captive, as one who had been abandoned and shut away as much from himself as from others. At such times he could have screamed with desperation and the horror of emptiness; but instead of doing anything of the kind he would avert himself from this solemn and expectant, tormented, wearied being within himself and—still aghast at his abrupt renunciation—would begin to listen, more and more enchanted by their warm, sinful breath, to the whispering voices of his solitude.

*   *   *

Törless suddenly proposed that they should pay and go. A look of understanding gleamed in Beineberg's eyes: he knew and shared the mood. Törless was revolted by this concord, and his dislike of Beineberg quickened again; he felt himself degraded by their having anything in common.

But that had by now practically become part of it all. Degradation is but one solitude more and yet another dark wall.

And so, without speaking to each other, they set out on a certain road.

There must have been a light shower of rain a few minutes earlier—the air was moist and heavy, a misty halo trembled round the street-lamps, and here and there the pavement glimmered.

Törless's sword clattered on the stones, and he drew it closer to his side. But there was still the sound of his heels on the pavement, and even that sent a queer shiver through him.

After a while, leaving the pavements of the town behind them, they had soft ground underfoot and were walking along wide village streets towards the river.

The water rolled along, black and sluggish, and with deep gurgling sounds under the wooden bridge. There was a single lamp there, with broken, dusty glass. Now and then the gleam of the light, which was blown uneasily hither and thither by the gusts of wind, would fall on a rippling wave below and dissolve on its crest. The rounded foot-planks of the bridge yielded under every step . . . revolving forward, then back again. . . .

Beineberg stopped. The farther bank was thickly wooded, and along the road, which turned at a right-angle on the other side and continued along the river, the trees had the menacing look of a black, impenetrable wall. Only if one looked carefully did one discover a narrow, hidden path leading straight on and into it. As, they went on their way through the thick, rank undergrowth, which brushed against their clothes, they were continually showered with drops. After a while they had to stop again and strike a match. It was very quiet now; even the gurgling of the river could not be heard. Suddenly from the distance there came a vague, broken sound. It was like a cry or a warning. Or perhaps it was merely like a call from some inarticulate creature that, somewhere ahead, was breaking its way through the bushes, like themselves. They walked on towards this sound, stopped again, and again walked on. All in all it was perhaps a quarter of an hour before, with a long breath of relief, they recognized loud voices and the notes of a concertina.

Now the trees grew more sparsely, and a few paces further they found themselves standing on the edge of a clearing, in the midst of which there was a squat, square building, two storeys high.

It was the old pump-room. In former times it had been used by the people of the little town and peasants from the neighbouring countryside for taking the waters; but for years now it had been almost empty. Only the ground floor was still used, as a tavern, and one that was of ill repute.

The two boys stopped for a moment, listening.

Törless was just taking a step forward, about to issue forth from the thicket, when there was a sound of heavy boots tramping on the floor-boards inside the house and a drunken man came staggering out of the door. Behind him, in the shadow of the doorway, stood a woman, and they could hear her whispering hurriedly and angrily, as though demanding something from the man. He merely laughed, swaying on his feet. Then it seemed that the woman was pleading, but again the words were indistinguishable; all that could be made out was the coaxing, cajoling tone of the voice. Now she advanced further and laid a hand on the man's shoulder. The moon shone upon her, lighting up her petticoat, her jacket, her pleading smile. The man stared straight ahead of him, shook his head, and kept his hands firmly in his pockets. Then he spat and pushed the woman away, perhaps because of something she had said. Now their voices were raised and what they said could be understood.

"—so you won't pay up, eh? You—!"

"You just take yourself off upstairs, you dirty slut!"

"The cheek! You peasant clod, you!"

By way of answer the drunken man bent down, with a clumsy movement, and picked up a stone. "If you don't clear off, you silly bitch, I'll knock your block off!", and he raised his arm, preparing to throw the stone at her. Törless heard the woman running up the steps with a last cry of abuse.

The man stood still for a moment, irresolutely holding the stone in his hand. He laughed, glanced up at the sky, where the moon floated, wine-yellow, among black clouds, and then stared at the dark mass of the thicket, as though he were wondering whether to go that way. Warily Törless drew his foot back; he could feel his heart hammering in his throat. Finally, however, the drunken man seemed to reach a decision. The stone dropped from his hand. With a raucous, triumphant laugh he shouted an obscenity up at the window; then he disappeared round the corner.

The two boys stood motionless a while longer. "Did you recognise her?" Beineberg whispered. "It was Božena." Törless did not answer; he was listening, trying to make sure that the drunken man was not coming back again. Then Beineberg gave him a push forward. In swift, wary dashes—avoiding the wedge of light from the ground-floor window—they crossed the clearing and entered the dark house. A wooden staircase, narrow and twisting, led up to the first floor. Here their footsteps must have been heard, or perhaps the clatter of their swords against the woodwork, for the door of the tavern room opened and someone came out to see who was in the house; at the same time the concertina ceased playing, and there was a momentary hush in the talk, a pause of suspense.

Startled, Törless pressed close to the staircase wall. But in spite of the darkness it seemed he had been seen, for he heard the barmaid's jeering voice as the door was shut again, and whatever she said was followed by guffaws of laughter.

On the first-floor landing it was pitch-dark. They hardly dared to take another step for fear of knocking something over and making a noise. Fumbling excitedly, they felt their way along towards the door-handle.

* * *

As a peasant girl Božena had gone to the capital, where she went into service and in time became a lady's maid.

At first she did quite well. Her peasant ways, which she never entirely lost any more than her plodding, firm-footed walk, inspired confidence in her mistresses, who liked the whiff of the cow-shed about her and the simplicity they associated with it; it also inspired amorous desires in her masters, who liked the whiff of the cow-shed for other reasons. Perhaps from caprice, and perhaps too from discontent and a vague yearning for passion, she gave up this quiet, orderly life. She took a job as a waitress, fell ill, found employment in a house of public resort, one of the smarter kind, and in the course of time, in the same measure as her debauched life wore her down, drifted further and further out into the provinces again.

And finally here, where she had now been living for several years, not far from her native village, she helped in the tavern during the day and spent the evenings reading cheap novels, smoking cigarettes, and occasionally having a man in her room.

She had not yet become actually ugly, but her face was strikingly lacking in any sort of charm, and she evidently went to some trouble to emphasise this by her general air and behaviour. She liked to convey that she was well acquainted with the smartness and the manners of the stylish world, but that she had got beyond all that sort of thing. She was fond of declaring that she did not care a snap of the fingers for that, or for herself, or indeed for anything whatsoever. On this account, and in spite of her blowsiness, she enjoyed a certain degree of respect among the peasant lads of the neighbourhood. True, they spat when they spoke of her, and felt obliged to treat her with even more coarseness than other girls, but at bottom they were really mightily proud of this 'damned slut' who had issued from their own midst and who had so thoroughly seen through the veneer of the world. Singly and furtively, it is true, but ever and again they came to see her. Thus Božena found a residue of pride and self-justification in her life. But what gave her perhaps even greater satisfaction was the young gentlemen from 'the college'. For their benefit she deliberately displayed her crudest and most repellent qualities, because—as she was in the habit of putting it— in spite of that they still came creeping along to her just the same.

When the two friends came in she was, as usual, lying on her bed, smoking and reading.

Even as he hesitated in the doorway, Törless was greedily devouring her with his eyes.

"Bless my soul, look at the pretty boys that have come!" she called out in scornful greeting, surveying them with a shade of contempt. "Well, young Baron? What'll Mamma say to this, eh?" This was the sort of welcome to be expected from her.

"Oh, shut up!" Beineberg muttered, sitting down on the bed beside her. Törless sat down at some distance; he was annoyed with Božena for taking no notice of him and pretending she did not know him.

Visits to this woman had recently become his sole and secret delight. Towards the end of the week he would become restless, scarcely able to wait for Sunday, when he would steal off to her in the evening. It was chiefly this necessary stealth that preoccupied him. What, for instance, if the drunken yokels in the bar-room just now had taken it into their heads to pursue him? Say for the sheer pleasure of taking a swipe at the vicious young gentleman. . . . He was no coward, but he knew he was defenceless here. By comparison with those big fists his dainty sword was a mockery. And apart from that, the disgrace and the punishment that would follow! There would be nothing for it but to run, or to plead for mercy. Or to let himself be protected by Božena. The thought went shuddering through him. But that was it! That was just it! Nothing else! This fear, this self-abandonment, was what seduced him anew every time. This stepping out of his privileged position and going among common people—among them? no, lower than them!

He was not vicious. When it came to the point his repugnance always had the upper hand, and together with it his fear of possible consequences. It was only his imagination that had taken an unhealthy turn. When the days of the week began to lay themselves, leaden, one by one, upon his life, these searing lures began to work upon him. The memories of these visits gradually took on the character of a peculiar temptation. Božena appeared to him as a creature of monstrous degradation, and his relationship to her, with the sensations it evoked in him, was like a cruel rite of self-sacrifice. It fascinated him to have to break the bounds of his ordinary life, leaving behind his privileged position, the ideas and feelings with which he was, as it were, being injected, all those things that gave him nothing and only oppressed him. It fascinated him to throw everything to the winds and, shorn of it all, to go racing off crazily and take his refuge with this woman.

This was no different from the way it is with such young people generally. Had Božena been pure and beautiful and had he been capable of love at that time, he would perhaps have sunk his teeth in her flesh, so heightening their lust to the pitch of pain. For the awakening boy's first passion is not love for the one, but hatred for all. The feeling of not being understood and of not understanding the world is no mere accompaniment of first passion, but its sole non-accidental cause. And the passion itself is a panic-stricken flight in which being together with the other means only a doubled solitude.

Almost every first passion is of short duration and leaves a bitter after-taste. It is a mistake, a disappointment. Afterwards one cannot understand how one could ever have felt it, and does not know what to blame for it all. That is because the characters in this drama are to a large extent accidental to each other: chance companions on some wild flight. When everything has calmed down, they no longer recognise each other. They become aware of discordant elements in each other, since they are no longer aware of any concord.

With Törless it was different only because he was alone. The ageing and degraded prostitute could not release all the forces in him. Yet she was woman enough to, as it were, bring to the surface, prematurely, particles of his innermost being, of all that still lay dormant in him waiting for the moment of fulfilment.

Such, then, were his weird imaginings and fantastic temptations. But at times he was almost as ready to fling himself on the ground, screaming with desperation.

*   *   *

Božena was still taking no notice of Törless. She seemed to be behaving in this way out of spite, merely in order to annoy him. Suddenly she broke the talk off by saying: "Give me some money, you boys, I'll fetch tea and gin."

Törless gave her one of the silver coins that had been a present from his mother that afternoon.

She took a battered spirit-lamp from the window-sill and lit it. Then she went out, slowly shuffling down the stairs.

Beineberg nudged Törless. "Why are you being such a bore? She'll think you're scared."

"Leave me out of it," Törless said. "I'm not in the mood. You go ahead and have your fun with her. By the way, why does she keep on about your mother like that?"

"Since she's known my name she insists she was once in service with my aunt and knew my mother. I dare say there's some truth in it, but I'm sure the rest is a lie—she *likes* lying. Anyway, I can't quite see what the joke is."

Törless blushed. A strange thought had just occurred to him. But at that moment Božena came back with the gin and sat down on the bed again beside Beineberg. And she at once took the conversation up where it had been dropped.

"Yes, your Mamma was a good-looking girl. You don't take after her very much, really, with those ears of yours sticking out like that. She was a gay one, too. There were plenty of men after her, I dare say. How right she was."

After a pause, something particularly amusing seemed to occur to her. "You know your uncle, the dragoon officer . . . Karl was his name, I think, he was a cousin of your mother's. How he did pay court to her! But on Sundays, when the ladies were in church, he was after me. Every few minutes I had to be bringing something to his room for him. A stylish chap he was, I remember him well, but he didn't beat around the bush much, I must say . . ." And she laughed insinuatingly. Then she continued elaborating this theme, which apparently afforded her particular pleasure. Her manner of speech was impertinently familiar, and her tone was even more scurrilous than her words. ". . . It's my guess your mother had a liking for him too. If she'd only known about the goings-on! I dare say your aunt would have had to kick me out of the house, and him too. That's the way fine ladies are, and all the more when they haven't got a man yet. Dear Božena here and dear Božena there— that's the way it went all day long. But when the cook got in the family way, my word, you should have heard them! I'm sure what they think about the like of us is that we only wash our feet once a year. Not that they said a word to the cook, but I heard plenty when I happened to be in the room and they happened to be talking about it. Your mother looked as if she felt like drinking nothing but eau-de-Cologne. And for all that it wasn't so long before your aunt herself had a belly on her so big it nearly touched her nose. . . ."

While Božena was talking, Törless felt almost totally defenceless against her coarse innuendos.

He could see vividly before his eyes what she was describing. Beineberg's mother turned into his own. He remembered the bright rooms at home; the well-cared-for, immaculate, unapproachable faces that often inspired him with a certain awe when his parents gave dinner-parties; the cultivated, cool hands that seemed to lose none of their dignity even while handling knife and fork. Many such details came back to his mind, and he was ashamed of being here in a malodorous little room, trembling whenever he replied to the humiliating words uttered by a prostitute. His memory of the perfected manners of that society, which never for an instant allowed itself any slip out of its own style, had a stronger effect on him than any moral considerations. The upheaval of his dark passions suddenly seemed ridiculous. With visionary intensity he saw the cool gesture of rejection, the shocked smile, with which those people would brush him off, like a small, unclean animal. Nevertheless he remained sitting where he was, as though transfixed.

For with every detail that he remembered not only the shame grew greater in him, but with it a chain of ugly thoughts. It had begun when Beineberg explained what Božena was talking about and Törless had blushed.

At that moment he had suddenly found himself thinking of his own mother, and this now held him in its grip and he could not shake it off. At first it had simply shot across the frontiers of his consciousness—a mere flash of something, too far away to be recognised, on the very edge of his mind—something that could scarcely be called a thought at all. And immediately it had been followed by a series of questions that were meant to cover it up: 'What is it that makes it possible for this woman Božena to bring her debased existence into proximity with my mother's existence? To squeeze up against her in the narrow space of one and the same thought? Why does she not bow down and touch the ground with her forehead when she speaks of her, if she must speak of her at all? Why isn't it as plain as if there were an abyss between them that they have nothing whatsoever in common? How *can* it be like this?— this woman, who is for me a maze of all sexual lust, and my mother, who up to now moved through my life like a star, beyond the reach of all desire, in some cloudless distance, clear and without depths . . .'

But all these questions were not the core of the matter. They scarcely touched it. They were something secondary, something that occurred to Törless only afterwards. They multiplied only because none of them pointed to the real thing. They were only ways of dodging the real problem, circumlocutions for the fact that, all at once, preconsciously, instinctively, an association of feelings had come about that was an inimical answer to the questions even before they were formulated. Törless devoured Božena with his eyes, and at the same time was unable to put his mother out of his mind. It was his being that linked them one with another, inextricably; everything else was only a writhing under this convolution of ideas. This was the sole fact. But because he was unable to shake himself free of its tyranny, it assumed a terrible, vague significance that hovered over all his efforts like a perfidious smile.

*   *   *

Törless looked around the room, trying to rid himself of these thoughts. But by now everything had taken on the one aspect. The little iron stove with the patches of rust on the lid, the bed with the rickety posts and the paint peeling off the wooden frame, the dirty blankets showing through holes in the worn counterpane; Božena with her shift slipping off one shoulder, the common, glaring red of her petticoat, and her broad, cackling laughter; and finally Beineberg, whose behaviour by contrast with other times struck Törless as like that of a lecherous priest who had taken leave of his senses and was weaving equivocal words into the solemn formulae of a prayer: all this was urgent in one and the same direction, invading him and violently turning his thoughts back again and again.

Only at one place did his gaze, which fled nervously from one thing to another, find rest. That was above the little curtain over the lower half of the window. There the sky looked in, with the clouds travelling across it, and the unmoving moon.

Then he felt as if he had suddenly stepped out of doors into the fresh, calm air of the night. For a while all his thoughts grew still. A pleasant memory came back to him: that of the house they had taken in the country the previous summer . . . nights in the silent grounds . . . a velvety dark firmament tremulous with stars . . . his mother's voice from the depths of the garden, where she was strolling on the faintly glimmering gravel paths, together with his father . . . songs that she hummed quietly to herself . . . But at once— a cold shudder went through him—there was again this tormenting comparison. What must the two of them have been feeling then? Love? The thought came to him now for the first time. But no, that was something entirely different. That was nothing for grown-up people, and least of all for his parents. Sitting at the open window at night and feeling abandoned by everyone, feeling different from the grown-ups, misunderstood by every laugh and every mocking glance, being unable to explain to anybody what one already felt

oneself to be, and yearning for *her*, the one who would understand—that was love! But in order to feel that one must be young
and lonely. With them it must have been something different, something calm and composed. Mamma simply hummed a little song
there in the evening, in the dark garden, and was cheerful. . . .
But that was the very thing Törless could not understand. The
patient plans that for the adult imperceptibly link the days into
months and years were still beyond his ken. And so too was that
blunting of perception which makes it cease to be anything of a
problem when yet another day draws to its close. His life was
focused on each single day. For him each night meant a void, a
grave, extinction. The capacity to lay oneself down to die at the
end of every day, without thinking anything of it, was something
he had not yet acquired.

That was why he had always supposed there was something
behind it that they were keeping from him. The nights seemed to
him like dark gateways to mysterious joys that were kept a secret
from him, so that his life remained empty and unhappy.

He recalled the peculiar ring of his mother's laughter and how,
as he had observed on one of those evenings, she had clung more
tightly, as though jokingly, to her husband's arm. There seemed to
be no doubt. There must be a gate leading hither even out of the
world of those calm and irreproachable beings. And now, since he
knew, he could think of it only with that special smile of his,
expressing the malicious mistrust against which he struggled in
vain . . .

Meanwhile Božena had gone on talking. Törless began to listen
with half an ear. She was talking about somebody who also came
almost every Sunday. "Let me see now, what's his name? He's in
your class."

"Reiting?"

"No."

"What does he look like?"

"He's about as tall as him over there," Božena said with a jerk
of her head in Törless's direction, "only his head is a bit too big."

"Oh, Basini?"

"Yes, that's right, that's what he said his name was. He's really
comical. And quite the fine gentleman, drinks nothing but wine.

But he's stupid. It costs him a pretty penny, and he never does anything but tell me stories. He boasts about the love-affairs he says he has at home. What does he get out of it? I can see quite plainly it's the first time in his life he's been with a woman. You're only a young lad too, but you've got a nerve. But he's clumsy and frightened of it, and that's why he spins his long-winded stories about how to treat women if you're a sensualist—yes, that's what he calls himself. He says women don't deserve anything else. How do the like of you know that so soon, I wonder?"

By way of answer Beineberg grinned at her mockingly.

"Oh all right, laugh if you like!" Božena flung at him in amusement. "One time I asked him if he wouldn't be ashamed for his mother to know. 'Mother? Mother?' he said. 'What's that? There's no such thing now. I left that at home, before I came to see you. . . .' Yes, you may well prick up your big ears, that's what you boys are like! Good little sons you are, you fine young gentlemen! It almost makes me sorry for your mothers!"

At these words Törless recalled his former notion of himself, realising how he was leaving everything behind him and betraying the image of his parents. And now he had to admit to himself that in this he was not even doing something unique and terrible; it was really quite commonplace. He was ashamed. But the other thoughts were there again too. They do it too! They betray you! You have secret accomplices! Perhaps it is somehow different with them, but this one thing must be the same: a secret, frightful joy. Something in which one can drown oneself and all one's fear of the monotony of the days . . . Perhaps indeed they know more? . . . something quite extraordinary? For in the daytime they are so calm . . . And that laughter of his mother's? . . . as though she were going, with quiet steps, to shut all the doors . . .

In this conflict there came a moment when Törless abandoned himself, letting the tempest rage over his suffocating heart.

And at that very moment Božena got up and came over to him.

"Why is our little boy not talking? Miserable, eh?"

Beineberg whispered something and smiled spitefully.

"Homesick, eh? Mamma's gone away, has she? And the moment she's gone the naughty boy comes running to the like of me!"

Božena dug her fingers caressingly into his hair.

"Come on, don't be silly. Give me a kiss, that's right. You fine gentry are only made of flesh and blood, after all, the same as everyone else," and she bent his head back.

Törless wanted to say something, to pull himself together and utter some crude joke, for he felt that everything now depended on his being able to speak some indifferent word that would not betray him. But he could not utter a sound. With a stony smile he gazed into the depraved face, the blank eyes looking down into his own, and then the outer world began to shrink, to withdraw further and further. . . . For a moment there loomed before him the image of the peasant who had picked up the stone, and it seemed to jeer at him. Then he was quite alone.

"I say," Reiting whispered, "I've got him."

"Who?"

"The chap who's been stealing from the lockers!"

Törless had just come in, together with Beineberg. It was only a short time till supper, and the usher on duty had already left. Groups of chattering boys had formed between the green baize tables, and the whole large room hummed and whirred with warm life.

It was the usual classroom with whitewashed walls, a big black crucifix, and portraits of the Emperor and Empress on each side of the blackboard. Beside the large iron stove, which was not yet lighted, the boys sat—some of them on the platform, some of them on overturned chairs—among them those who had been at the railway station that afternoon to see Törless's parents off. Apart from Reiting they were the tall Hofmeier and Dschjusch, a little Polish count who was known by this nickname.

Törless felt a certain curiosity.

The lockers, which were at the back of the room, were long cupboards subdivided into compartments that could be locked, and in them the boys kept their letters, books, money, and all their little pet possessions.

For some time now various boys had been complaining that they had missed small sums of money, but none of them had anything definite to go on.

Beineberg was the first to be able to say with certainty that the previous week he had been robbed of a considerable sum of money. But only Reiting and Törless knew of it.

They suspected the servants.

"Go on, tell us!" Törless urged.

But Reiting made a swift sign to him. "Sssh! Later. Nobody knows anything about it yet."

"Servant?" Törless whispered.

"No."

"Well, give us some idea, anyway. Who?"

Reiting turned away from the others and said in a low voice: "B." No one else had heard anything of this whispered conversation. Törless was thunderstruck at what he had learnt. B.? That could only be Basini. And surely that wasn't possible! His mother was a wealthy woman, and his guardian an 'Excellency'. Törless could not bring himself to believe it, and yet time and again the story Božena had told came to his mind.

He could scarcely wait for the moment when the others went in to supper. Beineberg and Reiting remained behind, on the pretext of having had so much to eat that afternoon.

Reiting suggested that it would be better to go 'upstairs' and talk about it there.

They went out into the corridor, which stretched endlessly in each direction outside the classroom. The flickering gaslight lit it only in patches, and their footsteps echoed from recess to recess, howeverly lightly they walked. . . .

About fifty yards from the door there was a staircase leading up to the second floor, where the natural science 'specimen' room was, and other collections that were used in teaching. There were also a large number of empty rooms.

From there on the stairs became narrow and went up, in short flights at right-angles to each other, to the attics. And—as old buildings are often whimsical in plan, with an abundance of nooks and crannies and unmotivated steps—this staircase actually went a considerable way above the level of the attics, so that on the other side of the heavy, iron, locked door, which blocked the way further, it was necessary to go down again, by a flight of wooden steps, in order to reach the floor of the attic.

What this meant was that on this side of the attic door was waste space some yards high, reaching up into the rafters. In this place, which hardly anybody ever entered, old stage-scenery had been stored, dating from school theatricals in the remote past.

Even at brightest noon the daylight on this staircase was reduced to a twilight, which was choked with dust, for this way into the attic, lying as it did in a remote wing of the enormous building, was almost never used.

From the top landing Beineberg swung himself over the bannister and, still holding on to the bars, let himself drop between the pieces of scenery. Reiting and Törless followed him. There they got a footing on a crate that had been specially dragged along for that purpose, and from there jumped to the floor.

Even if the eye of someone standing on the stairs had become accustomed to the darkness, that person could not possibly have seen anything there but an irregular and indistinct jumble of variously shaped pieces of stage-scenery all piled up together.

But when Beineberg shifted one of these pieces of scenery slightly to one side, a narrow tunnel opened up before the boys.

They hid the crate that had aided them in their descent, and entered the tunnel.

Here it became completely dark, and one had to know one's way very well in order to make progress. Now and then one of the big pieces of canvas scenery rustled, when they brushed against it; there was a scurrying on the floors as of startled mice; and their nostrils were filled with a musty smell as though from long-unopened trunks.

The three boys, who knew the way well, nevertheless went along very cautiously, step for step, careful to avoid tripping on any of the ropes pulled tight across the floor as traps and alarm-signals.

It was some time before they reached a little door on their right, only a short distance from the wall separating this place from the attic.

When Beineberg opened this door they found themselves in a narrow room under the top landing. It looked fantastic enough in the light of a small, flickering oil-lamp, which Beineberg had lit.

The ceiling was horizontal only where it was directly under the landing, and even here only just high enough for one to be able to stand upright. Towards the back it sloped away, following the line of the stairs, until it ended in an acute angle. The thin partition-wall at the opposite side of the room divided the attic from the staircase, and the third wall was formed by the brickwork on which the stairs rested. It was only the fourth wall, in which the door was, that seemed to have been added specially. Doubtless it had been built with the intention of making a small room here to keep tools in, unless perhaps it owed its existence only to a whim on the part of the architect, in whom this dark nook had inspired the medieval notion of walling it up to make a hiding-place.

However that might be, apart from these three boys there was doubtless scarcely anyone in the whole school who knew of its existence, and still less anyone who thought of putting it to any use.

And so they had been free to furnish it entirely according to their own fantastic notions.

The walls were completely draped with some blood-red bunting that Reiting and Beineberg had purloined from one of the storerooms, and the floor was covered with a double layer of thick woolly horse-blanket, of the kind that was used in the dormitories as an extra blanket in winter. In the front part of the room stood some low boxes, covered with material, which served as seats; at the back, in the acute angle formed by the sloping ceiling and the floor, a sort of bed had been made, large enough for three or four people, and this part could be darkened by the drawing of a curtain, separating it from the rest of the room.

On the wall by the door hung a loaded revolver.

Törless did not like this room. True, the constriction and isolation it afforded appealed to him; it was like being deep inside a mountain, and the smell of the dusty old stage-scenery gave rise to all sorts of vague sensations in him. But the concealment, those trip-ropes to give the alert, and this revolver, which was meant to provide the utmost illusion of defiance and secrecy, struck him as ridiculous. It was as though they were trying to pretend they were leading the life of bandits.

Actually the only reason why Törless joined in was that he did not want to lag behind the other two. Beineberg and Reiting themselves took the whole thing very seriously indeed. Törless knew that. He also knew that Beineberg had skeleton keys that would open the doors of all the cellars and attics in the school building, and that he often slipped away from lessons for several hours in order to sit somewhere—high up in the rafters of the roof, or underground in one of the many semiruinous, labyrinthine vaults— by the light of a little lamp, which he always carried about with him, reading adventure stories or thinking his thoughts about supernatural things.

He knew similar things of Reiting, who also had his hidden retreats, where he kept secret diaries; and these diaries were filled with audacious plans for the future and with exact records of the origin, staging, and course of the numerous intrigues that he instigated among the other boys. For Reiting knew no greater pleasure than to set people against each other, subduing one with the aid of the other and revelling in favours and flatteries obtained by extortion, in which he could still sense the resistance of his victim's hate.

"I'm practising," was the only excuse he gave, and he gave it with an affable laugh. It was also by way of practising that almost daily he would box in some out-of-the-way place, against a wall, a tree, or a table, to strengthen his arms and harden his hands with callouses.

Törless knew about all this, but he could understand it only up to a certain point. He had several times accompanied both Reiting and Beineberg on their singular paths. The fantastic element in it all did in fact appeal to him. And what he also liked was afterwards coming back into the daylight, walking among the other boys, and being back in the midst of their jollity, while he could still feel the excitements of solitude and the hallucinations of darkness trembling in his eyes and ears. But when Beineberg or Reiting, for the sake of having someone to talk to about themselves, on such occasions expounded what impelled them to all this, his understanding failed. He even considered Reiting somewhat overstrung. For Reiting was particularly fond of talking about how his father, who had one day disappeared, had been a strangely unsettled person. His name was, as a matter of fact, supposed to be only an incognito, concealing that of a very exalted family. He expected that his mother would make him acquainted with far-reaching claims that he would in due course put forward; he had day-dreams of *coups d'état* and high politics, and hence intended to be an officer.

Törless simply could not take such ambitions seriously. The centuries of revolutions seemed to him past and gone once and for all. Nevertheless Reiting was quite capable of putting his ideas into practice, though for the present only on a small scale. He was a tyrant, inexorable in his treatment of anyone who opposed him. His supporters changed from day to day, but he always managed to have the majority on his side. This was his great gift. A couple of years earlier he had waged a great war against Beineberg, which ended in the defeat of the latter. Finally Beineberg had been pretty well isolated, and this although in his judgment of people, his coolness and his capacity for arousing antipathy against those who incurred his disfavour, he was scarcely less formidable than his opponent. But he lacked Reiting's charm and winning ways. His composure and his unctuous philosophic pose filled almost everyone with mistrust. One could not help suspecting something excessive and unsavoury at the bottom of his personality. Nevertheless he had caused Reiting great difficulties, and Reiting's victory had been little more than a matter of luck. Since that time they found it profitable to combine forces.

Törless, by contrast, remained indifferent to these things. Hence also he had no skill in them. Nevertheless he too was enclosed in this world and every day could see for himself what it meant to play the leading part in a State—for in such a school each class constituted a small State in itself. Thus he had a certain diffident respect for his two friends. The urge he sometimes felt to emulate them, however, always remained a matter of dilettante experiment. Hence, and also because he was the younger, his relationship to them was that of a disciple or assistant. He enjoyed their protection, and they for their part would gladly listen to his advice. For Törless's mind was the most subtle. Once he was set on a trail, he was extremely ingenious in thinking of the most abstruse combinations. Nor was anyone else so exact as he in foreseeing the various possible reactions to be expected of a person in a given situation. Only when it was a matter of reaching a decision, of accepting one of these psychological possibilities as the definite probability and taking the risk of acting on it, did he fail, losing both interest and energy. Still, he enjoyed his role of secret chief of staff, and this all the more since it was practically the only thing that set him going, stirring him out of his state of deep inner boredom.

Sometimes, however, he did realise how much he was losing as a result of this psychological dependence. He was aware that everything he did was merely a game, merely something to help him over this time at school, this larval period of his existence. It was without relation to his real personality, which would emerge only later, at some time still a long way off in the future.

For when on certain occasions he saw how very seriously his two friends took these things, he felt quite unable to understand them.

He would have liked to make fun of them, but still he could not help being afraid that there might be more truth behind their fantastic notions than he was capable of admitting to himself. He felt as though torn between two worlds: one was the solid everyday world of respectable citizens, in which all that went on was well regulated and rational, and which he knew from home, and the other was a world of adventure, full of darkness, mystery, blood, and undreamt-of surprises. It seemed then as though one excluded the other. A mocking smile, which he would have liked to keep always on his lips, and a shudder that ran down his spine cut across each other. What came about then was an incandescent flickering of his thoughts. . . .

Then he would yearn to feel something firm in himself at long last, to feel definite needs that would distinguish between good and bad, between what he could make use of and what was useless, and to know he himself was making the choice, even though wrongly—for even that would be better than being so excessively receptive that he simply soaked up everything. . . .

When he entered the little room this inner dichotomy had asserted itself in him again, as it always did here.

Meanwhile Reiting had begun telling what he had discovered.

Basini had owed him money and had kept on promising to pay and putting it off, each time giving his word of honour that he was really going to pay the next time.

"Well, I didn't particularly mind that," Reiting commented. "The longer it went on, the more he was in my power. I mean, after all, breaking one's word three or four times is no joke, is it? But in the end I needed my money myself. I pointed this out to him, and he gave me his solemn oath. And of course didn't stick to it that time either. So then I told him I'd report him. He asked for two days' grace, as he was expecting supplies from his guardian. In the meantime, however, I did some investigating into his circumstances. I wanted to find out if he was in anyone else's power as well. After all, one must know what one has to reckon with.

"I wasn't particularly pleased with what I discovered. He was in debt to Dschjusch and to several of the others as well. He'd paid back some of it, and of course out of the money he still owed me. It was the others he felt it most urgent to pay. That annoyed me. I wasn't going to have him thinking I was the easy-going one of the lot. I could scarcely have put up with that. But I thought to myself: 'Let's just wait and see. Sooner or later there'll be an opportunity to knock *that* sort of idea out of his head.' Once he mentioned the actual amount he was expecting, sort of casually, you know, to put my mind at rest by showing me it was more than what he owed me. So I checked up with the others and found out that the total amount he owed was far more than what he said he was expecting. 'Aha,' I thought to myself, 'so now I suppose he'll try it on yet once again.'

"And, sure enough, he came along to me, all confidentially, and asked me to give him a little more time, as the others were pressing him so hard. But this time I was dead cold with him. 'Beg off from the others,' I said to him, 'I'm not in the habit of taking a back seat.' So he said: 'I know you better, I trust you more.' 'You'll bring me the money tomorrow,' I said to him, 'or you'll have to comply with my terms. That's my last word.' 'What terms?' he wanted to know. Oh, you should have heard him! As if he were prepared to sell his soul. 'What terms? Oho! You'll have to act as my vassal in all my enterprises.' 'Oh, if that's all, I'll do that all right, I'm *glad* to be on your side.' 'Oh no, not just when *you* happen to like it. You'll have to do everything I tell you to do—in blind obedience!' So now he squinted at me in a way that was half grinning and half embarrassed. He didn't know how far he ought to go, what he was letting himself in for, or how serious I was. Probably he would have promised me anything, but of course he couldn't help being afraid I was only putting him to the test. So in the end he got very red and said, 'I'll bring you the money.' I was getting my fun out of him, he'd turned out to be a fellow like that and I'd never taken any notice of him before, among the fifty others. I mean, he never sort of counted at all, did he? And now suddenly he'd come so close to me that I could see right into him, down to the last detail. I knew for a certainty the fellow was ready to sell himself—and without making much fuss about it, only so long as he could keep people from finding out. It was a real surprise, and there's no nicer sight than that: when a fellow is suddenly laid bare before you, and suddenly his way of living, which you've never troubled to notice before, is exposed to your gaze like the worm-holes you see when a piece of timber splits open. . . .

"Right enough, the next day he brought me the money. And that wasn't all, either. He actually invited me to have a drink with him down town. He ordered wine, cake, and cigarettes, and pressed it all on me—out of 'gratitude', because I'd been so patient. The only thing about it I didn't like was how awfully innocent and friendly he acted. Just as if there'd never been an offensive word said between us. I said as much. But that only made him more cordial than ever. It was as if he wanted to wriggle out of my grip and get on equal terms with me again. He behaved as if it were all over and done with, and every other word he uttered was to assure me of his friendship. Only there was something in his eyes that was a sort of clutching at me as though he were afraid of losing this feeling of intimacy he had artificially worked up. In the end I was revolted by him. I thought to myself: 'Does he really think I'm going to put up with this?' and I began to think how I could take him down a peg or two. What I wanted was something that would really get under his skin. So then it struck me Beineberg had told me that morning that some of his money had been stolen. It just occurred to me by the way. But it kept coming back into my mind. And it made me feel quite tight about the throat. 'It *would* turn out wonderfully handy,' I thought to myself, and in a casual way I asked him how much money he had left. When he told me, I added it up and got the right answer. I laughed and asked him: 'Who on earth was so stupid as to lend you money again after all this?' 'Hofmeier,' he said.

"I simply shook with joy. The fact is, Hofmeier had come to me two hours before that, asking me to lend *him* some money. So what had shot into my head a few minutes ago suddenly turned out to be true. Just the way you think to yourself, merely as a joke: 'Now that house over there ought to go on fire,' and the next moment there are flames shooting out of it, yards high. . . .

"I quickly ran over all the possibilities in my mind once again. Admittedly there wasn't any way of making dead certain, but my instinct was good enough for me. So I leaned over towards him and said in the most amiable way you can imagine, just as if I were gently driving a little thin, pointed stick into his brain: 'Look here, my dear Basini, why do you insist on trying to deceive me?' At that his eyes seemed to swim in his head with fear. And I went on: 'I dare say there are plenty of people you can take in, but I don't happen to be the right person. You know, don't you, that Beine-

berg . . .' He didn't turn red or white, it was as if he were waiting
for some misunderstanding to be cleared up. 'Well, to cut a long
story short,' I said, 'the money from which you've paid me back
what you owed me is the money you took out of Beineberg's locker
last night.''

"I leaned back to study the effect it had on him. He went as red
as a tomato. He began spluttering and slavering, as though choked
by his own words. Finally he managed to get it out. There were
torrents of reproaches and accusations against me. He wanted to
know how I could dare to make such an assertion and what faintest
justification there was for such an abominable conjecture. He said
I was only trying to pick a quarrel with him because he was the
weaker and that I was only doing it out of annoyance because now
that he had paid his debts he was out of my power, and that he
would appeal to the class—the ushers—the Head—and that God
would bear witness to his innocence, and so on and on ad infinitum.
I really began to be quite worried that I had done him wrong and
hurt his feelings for nothing, he looked so sweet with his face all
red. He looked just like a tormented, defenceless little animal, you
know. Still, I couldn't bring myself to let it go at that quite so easily.
So I kept up a jeering smile—almost only out of embarrassment,
actually—as I went on listening to his talk. Now and then I wagged
my head and said calmly: 'Yes, but I *know* you did.'

"After a while then he quieted down. I kept on smiling. I felt as
though simply by smiling at him like that I could make a thief of
him, even if he weren't one already. 'And as for putting it right
again,' I thought to myself, 'there's always plenty of time for that
later.'

"And then after a while, when he had kept on glancing at me
furtively, he suddenly got quite white. A queer change came over
his face. The innocent and delightful look that had beautified him
vanished out of his face, so to speak together with the colour. It
turned quite green, cheesy, and puffy. I've only seen anything like
it once before—once in the street when I came along just as they
were arresting a murderer. *He'd* been going around among people
too, without anyone's noticing anything queer about him. But when
the policeman put his hand on his shoulder, he was suddenly changed
into a different person. His face altered and his eyes popped with

terror and looked around, searching for some way of escaping—a thoroughgoing gallow's-bird he looked.

"That came back to my mind when the change came over Basini's face. Then I knew it all, and only had to bide my time. . . .

"And then it all came out. Without my having to say anything, Basini—worn out by my silence—began to blubber and implore me for mercy. He said he'd only taken the money because he was in a fix, and if I hadn't found him out he would have put it back before anyone noticed. He said I shouldn't say he'd *stolen* it. He'd only taken it as a secret loan. . . . By that time he was blubbering too much to say any more.

"Afterwards he began pleading with me again. He said he would do my will in everything, he would do whatever I wanted, if only I wouldn't give him away. At this price he positively offered to be my slave, and the mixture of cunning and greed and fear that wriggled in his eyes was simply disgusting. So to get it all done with I told him I'd think it over and decide what was to to be done with him, but I also told him that primarily it was Beineberg's affair. Well now, what do you chaps think we should do with him?"

While Reiting told his story Törless listened in silence, with his eyes shut. From time to time a shiver went through him, right to his finger-tips, and in his head the thoughts rose to the surface, wildly and chaotically, like bubbles in boiling water. It is said to be thus with one who for the first time sets eyes on the woman who is destined to involve him in a passion that will be his undoing. It is said that between two human beings there can be a moment of bending down, of drawing strength from deep within, of holding breath—a moment of utmost inner tension under a surface of silence. No one can say what happens in this moment. It is, as it were, the shadow that coming passion casts ahead of it. This is an organic shadow; it is a loosening of all previous tensions and at the same time a state of sudden, new bondage in which the whole future is already implicit; it is an incubation so concentrated that it is sharp as the prick of a needle . . .And then again it is a mere nothing, a vague, dull feeling, a weakness, a faint dread . . .

That was how Törless felt it all. Reiting's story seemed to him, when he put it to himself squarely, to be of no importance in itself: a reckless misdeed, a mean and cowardly act, on Basini's side, and now, without doubt, some cruel whim of Reiting's would follow. On the other hand, however, he felt something like an anxious premonition that events had now taken a quite personal turn against himself and that there was in the incident some sharp menace directed against him, like a pointed weapon.

He could not help imagining Basini together with Božena, and he glanced around the narrow room. The walls seemed to threaten him, to be closing in on him, to be reaching out for him with blood-stained hands, and the revolver seemed to swing to and fro where it hung. . . .

Now for the first time it was as though something had fallen, like a stone, into the vague solitude of his dreamy imaginings. It was there. There was nothing to be done about it. It was a reality. Yesterday Basini had been the same as himself. Now a trap-door had opened and Basini had plunged into the depths. It was precisely as Reiting had described it: a sudden change, and the person had become someone else. . . .

And once again this somehow linked up with Božena. He had committed blasphemy in his thoughts. The rotten, sweet smell rising from them had made him dizzy. And this profound humiliation, this self-abandonment, this state of being covered with the heavy, pale, poisonous leaves of infamy, this state that had moved through his dreams like a bodiless, far-off reflection of himself, all this had now suddenly *happened* to Basini.

So it was something one must really reckon with, something one must be on one's guard against, which could suddenly leap out of the silent mirrors in one's mind?

But then everything else was possible too. Then Reiting and Beineberg were possible. Then this narrow little room was possible . . . Then it was also possible that from the bright diurnal world, which was all he had known hitherto, there was a door leading into another world, where all was muffled, seething, passionate, naked, and loaded with destruction—and that between those people whose lives moved in an orderly way between the office and the family, as though in a transparent and yet solid structure, a building all of glass and iron, and the others, the outcasts, the blood-stained, the debauched and filthy, those who wandered in labyrinthine passages full of roaring voices, there was some bridge—and not only that, but that the frontiers of their lives secretly marched together and the line could be crossed at any moment. . . .

And the only other question that remained was: how is it possible? What happens at such a moment? What then shoots screaming up into the air and is suddenly extinguished?

These were the questions that this incident set stirring in Törless. They loomed up, obscurely, tight-lipped, cloaked in some vague, dull feeling . . . weakness . . . a faint dread . . .

And yet as though from a long way off, raggedly, at random, many of their words rang out within him, filling him with anxious foreboding.

It was at this moment that Reiting put his query.

Törless at once began to talk. In doing so he was obeying a sudden impulse, a rush of bewildered feeling. It seemed to him that something decisive was imminent, and he was startled to the approach of it, whatever it was, and wanted to dodge it, to gain time. . . . Even as he talked he could feel that he had nothing but irrelevant points to bring up, and that his words were without any inner substance, having nothing to do with his real opinion . . .

What he said was: "Basini is a thief." And the firm, hard ring of the last word pleased him so much that he repeated it twice. "A thief. And a thief gets punished—everywhere in the world. He must be reported. He must be expelled. If he reforms afterwards, that's his affair, but he doesn't belong here any more!"

But Reiting, with a look of being unpleasantly disconcerted, said: "No, no, why go and rush to extremes?"

"Why? But isn't it a matter of course?"

"Not at all. You're coming on exactly as if fire and brimstone would be called down upon us all if we kept Basini in our midst a minute longer. It's not as if what he'd done were so very frightful, after all."

"How can you talk like that! Do you really mean to sit, and eat, and sleep in the same room, day in, day out, with a creature who has stolen money and who's then gone and offered himself to you as your servant, your slave? I simply fail to understand you. After all, we're being brought up together because we belong together socially. Will it be all the same to you if some day you find yourself in the same regiment with him, or working together in the same government office, if you meet him at the houses of people you know—supposing he were to pay court to your sister?"

"Here, I say, you *are* exaggerating!" Reiting said with a laugh. "Anyone would think we'd joined a fraternity for life! Do you really think we shall go round for ever wearing a badge: 'Educated at W. College for the Sons of Gentlemen—has special privileges and obligations'—? Afterwards each of us will go his own way, and everyone will become whatever he's entitled to become. There isn't only one society. So I don't think we need to worry about the future. And as for the present, I didn't say we've got to be dear friends with Basini. There'll be some way of managing all right so that a proper distance is kept. We've got Basini in the hollow of our hand, we can do whatever we like with him, for all I care you can spit at him twice a day. So long as he'll put up with it, what's to bother us about having him among us? And if he rebels, there's always time to show him who's master. . . . You've only got to drop the idea that there's any relationship between us and Basini other than the pleasure we get out of what a rotten swine he is!"

Although Törless was far from being convinced of his own line of argument, he pressed on with it. "Look here, Reiting, why are you so keen to defend Basini?"

"Keen to defend him? Not that I know of. I've no particular reason to defend him at all. The whole thing leaves me stone-cold from A to Z. I'm only annoyed at the way you exaggerate. What's the bee in your bonnet? Seems to be some kind of idealism. Enthusiasm for the sacred cause of the school, or for justice. You've no idea how boring and virtuous it sounds. Or perhaps"—and Reiting narrowed his eyes in suspicion—"you have some other reason for wanting Basini kicked out and only don't want to admit what you're up to. Some old score to settle, eh? Well, come on, out with it! If there's enough in it we might really turn it to account."

Törless looked at Beineberg. But Beineberg only grinned. He sat there, cross-legged in Oriental style, sucking at a long chibouk, and with his protruding ears in this deceptive light he looked like a grotesque idol. "For all I care," he said, between puffs, "you chaps can do what you like. I'm not interested in the money, nor in justice either. In India they would drive a pointed bamboo pole through his guts. There'd be some fun in that, anyway. He's stupid and cowardly, so he would be no loss, and anyway it's always been a matter of the utmost indifference to me what happens to such people. They themselves are nothing, and what may yet become of their souls, we don't know. May Allah bestow his grace upon your verdict!"

Törless made no reply to this. After Reiting had disagreed with him and Beineberg had refused to take sides in the matter, leaving the decision to the two of them, he had no more to say. He did not feel capable of arguing further; indeed, he felt he no longer had any desire to do anything in order to prevent whatever was imminent.

And so a proposal that Reiting now put forward was accepted. It was resolved that for the present they should keep Basini under surveillance, appointing themselves, as it were, his guardians, in order to give him a chance to make good what he had done. His income and expenditure were from now on to be strictly checked and his relations with the rest of the boys to depend on permission from the three guardians.

This decision had the air of being very correct and benevolent. But this time Reiting did not say it was 'boring and virtuous'. For, without admitting it even to themselves, each of them was aware that this was to constitute only a sort of interim state. Reiting would have been reluctant to renounce any chance of carrying the affair further, since he got such pleasure out of it; on the other hand, however, he could not yet see clearly what turn he should give it next. And Törless was as though paralysed by the mere thought that from now on he would be in close touch with Basini every day.

When he had uttered the word 'thief' a short time earlier, for a moment he had felt easier. It had been like a turning out, a pushing away from himself, of the things that were causing such upheaval in him.

But the problems that instantly rose up again could not be solved by the use of this simple word. They had become more distinct, now that there was no longer any question of dodging them.

Törless glanced from Reiting to Beineberg, shut his eyes, repeated to himself the resolve that had just been made, and looked up again. . . . He himself no longer knew whether it was only his imagination that was like a gigantic distorting-glass between him and everything, or whether it was true and everything was really the way it uncannily loomed before him. And was it then only Beineberg and Reiting who knew nothing of these problems—and this although it was precisely the two of them who had from the beginning been so at home in this world that now all at once, for the first time, seemed so strange to him?

Törless felt afraid of them. But he felt afraid only as one might feel afraid of a giant whom one knew to be blind and stupid.

One thing, however, was settled: he was much further ahead now than he had been only a quarter of an hour earlier. There was no longer any possibility of turning back. A faint curiosity rose in him about what was to come, since he was held fast against his will. All that was stirring within him still lay in darkness, and yet he already felt a desire to gaze into the darkness, with all the shapes that populated it, which the others did not notice. There was a thin prickling chill mingled with this desire. It was as though over his life there would now always be nothing but a grey, veiled sky— great clouds, monstrous, changing forms, and the ever-renewed question: Are they monsters? Are they merely clouds?

And this question was for him alone! A secret, strange territory forbidden to the others. . . .

So it was that Basini for the first time began to assume that significance which he was later to have for Törless.

The next day Basini was put under surveillance.

It was done not without ceremony. It was in the morning, when they had slipped away from gymnastics, which were performed on a large lawn in the school grounds.

Reiting delivered a sort of speech. It was not exactly short. He pointed out to Basini that he had forfeited his right to exist, that he actually ought to be reported, and that it was only thanks to their extraordinary mercifulness that for the present they were sparing him the disgrace of expulsion.

Then he was informed of the particular conditions. Reiting took it upon himself to see that they were kept.

During the whole scene Basini was very pale, but did not utter a word, and his face revealed nothing of what was going on in him.

Törless found the scene alternately in very bad taste and of very great significance.

Beineberg's attention was focused on Reiting more than on Basini.

During the following days the affair seemed to be practically forgotten. Reiting was scarcely to be seen at all, except in class and at meals, Beineberg was more taciturn than ever, and Törless continually put off thinking about the matter.

Basini went around among the other boys just as if nothing had ever happened.

*　　*　　*

He was a little taller than Törless, but very slight in build, with slack, indolent movements and effeminate features. He was not very intelligent, and he was one of the worst at fencing and gymnastics, but he had a pleasing manner, a rather coquettish way of making himself agreeable.

His visits to Božena had begun only because he wanted to play the man. Backward he was in his development, it was scarcely to be supposed that he was impelled by any real craving. What he felt was perhaps only a compulsion, a sort of obligation, lest he should be noticeably lacking in the aura of one who has had his experiences in gallantry. He was always glad when he left her, having got that behind him; all that mattered to him was to have the memory of it.

Occasionally, too, he lied—out of vanity. After every holiday, for instance, he came back with souvenirs of little affairs—ribbons, locks of hair, tiny *billets-doux*. But once, when he had brought back in his trunk a dear little scented, sky-blue garter, and it subsequently turned out to belong to none other than his own twelve-year-old sister, he was exposed to a great deal of jeering on account of his ridiculous boasting.

The moral inferiority that was apparent in him and his stupidity both had a single origin. He had no power of resisting anything that occurred to him and was always surprised by the consequences. In this he resembled the kind of woman, with pretty little curls on her forehead, who introduces doses of poison into her husband's food at every meal and then is amazed and horror-struck at the strange, harsh words of the public prosecutor and the death-sentence pronounced on her.

*   *   *

Törless avoided Basini. So there was a gradual fading of that profound inmost shock that had in the first instant gone to the roots of his thoughts, shaking his whole being. Things around him became rational again; his sense of bewilderment left him and with each passing day the whole thing became more unreal, like vestiges of a dream, something that could not assert its existence in the real, solid world on which the sun shone.

In order to make still more sure of this condition, he wrote a letter all about it to his parents. The only thing he passed over in silence was what he himself had felt at the time.

He had now regained the point of view that it was after all best to get Basini expelled from school at the next opportunity. He simply could not imagine that his parents would think differently. What he expected from them was disgusted condemnation of Basini, a gesture of horror at his being in their son's proximity, something like the flick of the fingertips with which one brushed off an unclean insect.

There was nothing of this kind in the letter he received by way of answer. His parents had been conscientious and painstaking about the matter, weighing up all the circumstances like sensible people, in so far as they could form a picture of it all from the rather incoherent and hasty letter he had written them. What appeared was that they inclined to the most indulgent and reserved judgment, and this all the more since they saw the need to allow for a certain element of exaggeration in their son's account, born of youthful indignation. Hence they approved of the decision to give Basini a chance to reform, and suggested that a person's career should not be ruined at the outset because of one minor offence, especially—and this, as was proper, they particularly emphasised—since those concerned were not mature adults, but at a stage when their characters were still unformed and undergoing development. It was doubtless best, of course, to treat Basini in a strict and serious way, but at the same time one should be charitable in one's attitude to him and try to reform him.

They reinforced this by a whole series of examples, which were familiar to Törless. He distinctly remembered that in the junior classes, where the authorities favoured Draconic measures and kept pocket-money within strict limits, many of the little boys, in their natural greed for sweets and delicacies, often could not resist begging the fortunate possessor of a ham sandwich, or the like, for a piece of it. He himself had not always been proof against this temptation, even if, ashamed of it as he was, he tried to cover it up by abuse of the wicked, unkind school regulations. And he owed it not only to the passing of the years, but also to his parents' admonitions, as kindly as they were serious, that he had gradually learnt to have his pride and not to give in to such weaknesses.

But now all this failed to have any effect.

He could not help seeing that his parents were in many ways right, and he also knew that it was scarcely possible to judge quite accurately from such a distance; yet something much more important seemed to be missing from their letter.

What was missing was an appreciation of the fact that something irrevocable had happened, something that ought never to happen among people in a certain stratum of society. What was missing was any sign of their being surprised and shocked. They treated it as though it were quite a normal thing, which must be handled with tact but without much ado, merely as a blemish, as something that was no more beautiful, but also no more avoidable, than the relief of one's natural needs. In their whole letter there was as little trace of any more personal feelings or dismay as there was in the attitude of Beineberg and Reiting.

Törless might usefully have taken some note of this too. Instead, however, he tore the letter into shreds and burnt it. It was the first time in his life that he committed such an act of disrespect towards his parents.

The effect on him was the opposite of what had been intended. In contrast with the plain view that had been set before him he was again suddenly filled with awareness of all that was problematic and ambiguous in Basini's crime. Shaking his head, he told himself that it still needed thinking about, although he could not give himself any exact account of the reason for this attitude.

It was queerest of all when he pursued the matter dreamily rather than with conscious thought. Then at one moment Basini seemed to him comprehensible, commonplace, and clear-cut, just as his parents and his friends seemed to see him: and the next moment this Basini would vanish, only to come again, and yet again, as a small and even smaller figure, tiny and sometimes luminous against a deep, very deep background. . . .

A nd then one night—it was very late and everyone was asleep—
Törless was waked by someone shaking him.

Beineberg was sitting on the edge of his bed. This was so unusual
that he at once realised something extraordinary must be afoot.

"Get up. Don't make a noise, we don't want anyone to notice.
I want you to come upstairs, I've got something to tell you."

Törless quickly put some clothes on, got into his slippers, and
threw his coat round his shoulders.

When they were up in their lair, Beineberg put all the obstacles
back in their places with special care. Then he made tea.

Törless, who was still heavy with sleep, relaxed in enjoyment of
the golden-yellow, aromatic warmth pervading him. He leaned back
in a corner and curled up; he was expecting a surprise.

At last Beineberg said: "Reiting is up to something behind our
backs."

Törless felt no astonishment; he accepted it as a matter of course
that the affair must necessarily develop in some such way, and he
felt almost as though he had been waiting for this. Involuntarily he
said: "I thought as much."

"Oh? You thought so, did you? But I don't suppose you noticed
anything? That wouldn't be at all like you."

"That's true, there wasn't anything special that struck me. And
I haven't been racking my brains about the whole thing."

"But I've been keeping a good look-out. I didn't trust Reiting
from the very beginning. I suppose you know Basini's paid me back
my money. And where do you think he got it? D'you think it was
his own? No."

"And so you think Reiting has been up to something?"

"Definitely."

For a moment all Törless could imagine was that now Reiting had got entangled in a similar way himself.

"So you think Reiting has done what———?"

"What an idea! Reiting simply gave Basini some of his own money, so that he could settle his debt to me."

"But I can't see any good reason why he should do that."

"Neither could I for a long time. Still, it must have struck you too how Reiting stood up for Basini right from the start. You were quite right then. It would really have been the most natural thing to have had the fellow chucked out. But I knew what I was doing. I didn't take your side at the time, because I thought to myself: I must get to the bottom of this, I must see what he's up to. Frankly, I can't say for certain whether he had it all worked out quite clearly at that stage or whether he only wanted to wait and see what would come of it once he made completely sure of Basini. Anyway, I know how things stand now."

"Well?"

"Wait, the whole story isn't so simple. I take it you know about what happened in the school four years ago?"

"What do you mean?"

"Well—that affair!"

"Vaguely. I only know there was a great row about some swinishness that had been going on, and quite a number of chaps got expelled."

"Yes, that's what I mean. Once in the holidays I found out some more about it from one of the chaps in that class. It was all because of a pretty boy there was in the class, that a lot of them were in love with. You know that sort of thing, it happens every few years. But *they* went a bit too far."

"How do you mean?"

"Well—how! Don't ask such silly questions! And that's what Reiting's doing with Basini!"

Törless suddenly understood what he meant, and he felt a choking in his throat as if it were full of sand.

"I wouldn't have thought that of Reiting." He did not know what else to say.

Beineberg shrugged his shoulders. "He thinks he can take us in."

"Is he in love with him?"

"Not a bit of it. He's not such a fool. It amuses him; at the most he gets some sort of excitement out of it."

"And how about Basini?"

"Oh, him! Hasn't it struck you how uppish he's become recently? He hardly takes anything from me at all now. It's always Reiting, Reiting, with him—as if Reiting were his private patron saint. He probably decided it was better to put up with everything from one than with a bit from everyone. And I dare say Reiting's promised to look after him as long as he does whatever Reiting wants of him. But they'll find out they've made a mistake, and I'm going to knock such ideas out of Basini's head!"

"How did you find out?"

"I followed them once."

"Where to?"

"In there, in the attic. Reiting had my key to the other door. Then I came up here, carefully opened up the gap and crept up to them."

The fact was that in the thin partition-wall dividing the cubby-hole from the attics they had broken open a gap just wide enough to allow one to wriggle through. It was intended to serve as an emergency exit in the event of their being surprised, and it was generally kept closed with loose bricks.

Now there was a long pause, in which all that could be heard was the faint hiss when the tips of their cigarettes glowed.

Törless was incapable of thinking; he simply saw . . . Behind his shut eyelids there was all at once a wild vortex of happenings . . . people, people moving in a glare, with bright lights and shifting, deep-etched shadows . . . faces . . . one face . . . a smile . . . an upward look . . . a shivering of the skin . . . He saw people in a way he had never seen them before, never felt them before. But he saw them without seeing, without images, without forms, as if only his soul saw them; and yet they were so distinct that he was pierced through and through by their intensity. Only, as though they halted at a threshold they could not cross, they escaped him the moment he sought for words to grasp them with.

He could not stop himself from asking more. His voice shook. "And—did you see?"

"Yes."

"And—did Basini—was he—?"

But Beineberg remained silent, and once again there was nothing to be heard but, now and then, the vaguely disturbing hiss of the cigarettes. Only after a long time did Beineberg begin to talk again.

"I've considered the whole thing from all points of view, and, as you know, I have my own way of thinking about such things. First of all, as far as Basini goes, it's my view he's no loss in any case. It makes no difference whether we go and report him, or give him a beating, or even if we torture him to death, just for the fun of it. Personally, I can't imagine that a creature like that can have any meaning in the wonderful mechanism of the universe. He strikes me as being merely accidental, as it were a random creation outside the order of things. That's to say—even he must of course mean something, but certainly only something as undefined as, say, a worm or a stone on the road, the sort of things you never know whether to walk round or step on. In other words, they're practically nothing. For if the spirit of the universe wants one of its parts to be preserved, it manifests its will more clearly. In such a case it says 'no' and creates a resistance, it makes us walk round the worm and makes the stone so hard that we can't smash it without tools. And before we can get the tools, it has had time to interpolate resistances in the form of all sorts of tough little scruples, and if we get the better of them, well, that just shows that the whole thing has had another meaning all along.

"With a human being, it puts this hardness into his character, into his consciousness as a human being, into the sense of responsibility he has as a part of the spirit of the universe. And if a human being loses this consciousness, he loses himself. But if a human being has lost himself, abandoned himself, he has lost the special and peculiar purpose for which Nature created him as a human being. And this is the case in which one can be perfectly certain that one is dealing with something unnecessary, an empty form, something that has already long been deserted by the spirit of the universe."

Törless felt no inclination to argue. He was not even listening very attentively. He himself had never felt the need to go in for such a metaphysical train of thought, nor had he ever wondered how anyone of Beineberg's intellect could indulge in such notions. The whole problem had simply not yet risen over the horizon of his life.

Thus he made no effort to enquire into the possible meaning, or lack of meaning, of Beineberg's remarks. He only half listened.

One thing he did not understand, and that was how anyone could approach this matter in such a longwinded way. Everything in him quivered, and the elaborate formality with which Beineberg produced his ideas—wherever he got them from—seemed to him ridiculous and out of place; it irritated him.

But Beineberg continued calmly: "Where Reiting is concerned, on the other hand, it's all very different. He has also put himself in my power by doing what he has done, but his fate is certainly not so much a matter of indifference to me as Basini's is. You know his mother is not very well off. So if he gets expelled, it'll be all up with his plans. If he stays here, he may get somewhere. If not, there's not likely to be much chance for him. And Reiting never liked me—see what I mean?—he's always hated me. He used to try to damage me wherever he could. I think he would still be glad if he could get rid of me. Now do you see what an immense amount I can make out of what I've discovered?"

Törless was startled—and it was strangely as if Reiting's fate affected him personally, were almost his own. He looked at Beineberg in dismay. Beineberg had narrowed his eyes to a mere slit, and to Törless he looked like a great, weird spider quietly lurking in its web. His last words rang in Törless's ears with the coldness and clarity of an ultimatum.

Törless had not been following, had only known: Beineberg is talking about his ideas again, and they have nothing at all to do with the matter in hand . . .And now all at once he did not know how it had reached this point.

The web, which had, after all, been begun somewhere far off in a realm of abstractions, as he vaguely remembered, seemed to have contracted suddenly and with miraculous speed. For all at once it was there, concrete, real, alive, and there was a head twitching in it—choking.

He was far from having any liking for Reiting, but he now recalled the agreeable, impudent, carefree way in which he set about all his intrigues, and in contrast Beineberg seemed infamous as he sat there, calm and grinning, pulling his many-threaded, grey, abominable web of thoughts tight around the other.

Involuntarily Törless burst out: "You mustn't turn it to account against him!" What impelled him to the exclamation was perhaps partly his constant secret repugnance for Beineberg. But after a few minutes' reflection Beineberg said of his own accord: "What good would it do, anyway? Where he is concerned it would really be a pity. From now on in any case he's no danger to me, and after all he's not so worthless that one should trip him up over a silly thing of this kind." And so that aspect of the affair was settled. But Beineberg went on talking, now again turning his attention to Basini's fate.

"Do you still thing we ought to report Basini?"

But Törless gave no answer. Now he wanted Beineberg to go on talking, to hear his words sounding like the hollow echoing of footsteps over a vault; he wanted to savour the situation to the full.

Beineberg went on expounding his ideas. "I think for the present we'll keep him in our own hands and punish him ourselves. He certainly must be punished—if only for his presumption. All the school would do would be to send him home and write his uncle a long letter about it. Surely you know more or less how automatically that sort of thing works. Your Excellency, your nephew has so far forgotten himself . . . bad influence . . . restore him to your care . . . hope you will be successful . . . road towards improvement . . . for the present, however, impossible among the others . . . and so on and so forth. You don't suppose, do you, that such a case has any interest or value in their eyes?"

"And what sort of value can it have for us?"

"What sort of value? None for you, perhaps, for you're going to be a government official some day, or perhaps you'll write poems— all in all you don't need that kind of thing, and perhaps you're even frightened of it. But I picture my life rather differently."

Now Törless really began to listen.

"For me Basini has some value—very great value indeed. Look, it's like this—you would simply let him go and would be quite satisfied with the thought that he was a bad person." Here Törless suppressed a smile. "That's all it amounts to for you, because you have no talent or interest in training yourself by means of such a case. But *I* have that interest. Anyone with my road ahead of him must take quite a different view of human beings. That's why I want to save Basini up for myself—as something to learn from."

"But how do you mean to punish him?"

Beineberg withheld his answer for a moment, as though considering the effect he expected it to have. Then he said, cautiously and with some hesitation: "You're wrong if you think I'm so very much concerned with the idea of punishment. Of course ultimately it will be possible to look at it as a punishment for him too. But to cut a long story short, I've got something different in mind, what I want to do with him is—well, let's call it tormenting him."

Törless took good care to say nothing. He was still far from seeing the whole thing clearly, but he could feel that it was all working out as—inwardly—it must work out for him.

Beineberg, who could not gather what effect his words had had, continued: "You needn't be shocked, it's not as bad as all that. First of all, as I've already explained to you, there's no cause to consider Basini's feelings at all. Whether we decide to torment him or perhaps let him off depends solely on whether we feel the need of the one or the other. It depends on our own inner reasons. Have you got any? All that stuff about morality and society and the rest of it, which you brought up before, doesn't count at all, of course. I should be sorry to think you ever believed in it yourself. So I assume you to be indifferent. But however it may be, you can still withdraw from the whole affair if you don't want to take any risks.

"My own road, however, leads not back or around, but straight ahead and through the middle of it. It has to be like that. Reiting won't leave off either, for in his case too there's a special value in having a human being in the hollow of his hand so that he can use him for the purpose of training himself, learning to handle him like a tool. He wants to exercise power, and he would treat you just the same as Basini if he ever happened to get the chance. But for me it's a matter of something more than that. It's almost a duty to myself. Now, how am I to make clear to you exactly what this difference is between him and me? You know how Reiting venerates Napoleon. Now contrast that with the fact that the sort of person who most appeals to me is more like a philosopher or a holy man in India. Reiting would sacrifice Basini and feel nothing but a certain interest in the process. He would dissect him morally in order to find out what one has to expect from such operations. And, as I said before, it could be you or me just as well as Basini, and it would be all the same to him. On the other hand, I have this certain feeling, just as you have, that Basini is, after all, in the last resort a human being too. There's something in me too that is upset by any act of cruelty. But that's just the point! The point is the sacrifice! You see, there are two threads fastened to me too. The first is an obscure one that, in contrast with my clear conviction, ties me to the inaction that comes from pity. But there is the second, too, which leads straight to my soul, to the most profound inner knowledge, and links me to the universe. People like Basini, as I told you before, signify nothing—they are empty, accidental forms. True human beings are only those who can penetrate into themselves, cosmic beings that are capable of that meditation which reveals to them their relationship to the great universal process. These people do miracles with their eyes shut, because they know how to make use of the totality of forces in the universe, which are within them just as they are also outside them. But hitherto everyone who has followed up the second thread, has had to tear the first. I've read about appalling acts of penance done by illumined monks, and the means used by Indian ascetics are, I imagine, not entirely unknown to you either. All the cruel things that are done in this way have only one aim, to kill the miserable desires directed towards the external world, which, whether they are vanity or hunger, joy or pity, only take away something from the fire that everyone can kindle in himself.

"Reiting knows only the outward thread, but I follow the second. For the present he has got ahead of me in everybody else's eyes, for my road is slower and more uncertain. But I can overtake him with one stride, just as if he were a worm. You see, they say the universe is governed by mechanical laws that are unshakable. That's all wrong! That's only what the school-books say! The external world is stubborn, I dare say, and to some extent its so-called laws stand firm, but there have been people who succeeded in bending them to their will. It's written about in sacred books that have stood the test of time and of which most people know nothing. From these books I know there have been people who could move stones and air and water merely by means of their will, and whose prayers were stronger than any earthly power. But even these are only the external triumphs of the spirit. For him who *entirely* succeeds in beholding his own soul, physical life, which is only an accidental thing, dissolves. It is written in the books that such beings enter directly into a higher spiritual realm."

Beineberg spoke with entire seriousness and with suppressed excitement. Törless still kept his eyes shut almost all the time; he could feel Beineberg's breath like something touching him and drew it into himself like a suffocating narcotic. And so Beineberg concluded his harangue:

"Well, you can see what I am concerned with. What tells me to let Basini off is something of low, external origin. You can obey it if you like. For me it is a prejudice from which I have to cut myself loose as from everything else that would distract me from my inner way.

"The very fact that I find it hard to torture Basini—I mean, to humiliate him, debase him, and cast him away from me—is good. It requires a sacrifice. It will have a purifying effect. I owe it to myself to learn daily, with him as my material, that merely being human means nothing—it's a mockery, a mere external semblance."

Törless did not understand all of it. But once again it seemed to him as though an invisible noose had suddenly been tightened into a palpable and fatal knot. Beineberg's final words went on echoing in his mind: ". . . a mockery, a mere external semblance." It seemed to apply also to his own relation to Basini. Was it not in such fantasies that the queer fascination lay which Basini held for him? Was it not simply in the fact that he could not enter into Basini's mind and so always experienced him only in vague images? Just now, when he had tried to picture Basini to himself, had there not been behind his face a second one, blurred and shadowy and yet on a tangible likeness, though it was impossible to say what it was a likeness of?

So it came about that, instead of thinking over Beineberg's very odd intentions, being bemused as he was by these new and unfamiliar impressions, Törless was engaged in trying to become clear about himself. He remembered the afternoon before he had heard about Basini's offence. Come to think of it, these fantasies had been there even then. There had always been something that his thoughts could not get the better of, something that seemed at once so simple and so strange. There had been pictures in his mind that were not really pictures at all. It had been like that passing the cottages on the road back from the station, and also when he was sitting in the cake-shop with Beineberg.

They were likenesses and yet at the same time unlikenesses, unsurmountable. And the toying with it all, this secret, entirely private perspective, had excited him.

And now a human being took possession of this. Now it was all embodied in a human being; it had become real. Thus all the queerness of it attached itself to that human being. Thus it shifted out of the imagination into life itself and became a menace.

All this agitation had tired Törless; his thoughts were now but loosely linked together.

The only thing he could really hold on to was the thought that he must not let go of this Basini, that Basini was destined to play an important part in his life too, one that he already recognised, although as yet unclearly.

And yet, recalling Beineberg's words, he could not help shaking his head in amazement. Was it the same with him . . . ?

'It can't be that he is after the same things as I am, and yet it was he who found the right words for it . . . '

Törless was dreaming rather than thinking. He was no longer capable of distinguishing his own inner problem from Beineberg's flights of fancy. In the end nothing remained but the one feeling: a vast noose tightening, tightening round everything . . .

No more was said between them. They put out the light and crept warily back to their dormitory.

The next days brought no decision. There was a great deal of school work, Reiting was careful not to find himself alone with either of them, and Beineberg too avoided any reopening of their last discussion.

So it happened, in the days that followed, that the thought of the affair went deeper into Törless, like a river forced underground, and set his imagination moving irrevocably in one particular direction.

This put a definite end to any intention of getting rid of Basini. Now for the first time Törless felt he was focused exclusively on himself, and was incapable of thinking of anything else. Božena too had become a matter of indifference to him. What he had felt about her now became a mere fantastic memory; it had been replaced by something really serious.

Admittedly, this really serious matter seemed no less fantastic.

*   *   *

Absorbed in his thoughts, Törless had gone for a walk alone in the park. It was noon, and in the light of the late autumn sun the lawns and paths shone as though with the wan gleam of memory. Since in his restlessness he felt no inclination to go far, he merely walked round the building and then threw himself down on the pale, rustling grass at the foot of an almost windowless sidewall. The sky above him was a vault—of that faded, ailing blue which is peculiar to autumn, and there were little white puffs of cloud scudding across it.

Lying flat on his back, he blinked, vaguely and dreamily, looking up between the tops of two trees in front of him, now almost leafless.

He thought about Beineberg. What a strange fellow that was! His way of talking would not have been out of place in some crumbling Indian temple, among uncanny idols, where wizard serpents lay hidden in deep crannies. But what place had such talk in broad daylight, in this school, in modern Europe? And yet those words of his, after trailing on and on, like an endless road of a thousand meanderings, leading no one knew where, had seemed suddenly to arrive at a tangible goal . . .

And suddenly—and it seemed to him as if it had happened for the very first time—Törless became aware of how incredibly high the sky was.

It was almost a shock. Straight above him, shining between the clouds, was a small, blue hole, fathomlessly deep.

He felt it must be possible, if only one had a long, long ladder, to climb up and into it. But the further he penetrated, raising himself on his gaze, the further the blue, shining depth receded. And still it was as though some time it must be reached, as though by sheer gazing one must be able to stop it and hold it. The desire to do this became agonisingly intense.

It was as if, straining to the utmost, his power of vision were shooting glances like arrows between the clouds; and yet, the further and further it aimed, still they always fell just a little short.

Now Törless began to think about this, making an effort to be as calm and rational as he could. "Of course there *is* no end," he said to himself, "it just keeps going on and on for ever, into infinity." He kept his eyes fixed on the sky, saying this aloud to himself as though he were testing the power of a magical formula. But it was no use; the words meant nothing, or rather, they meant something quite different, as if, while dealing with the same subject, they were taking it from another side, one that was strange, unfamiliar and irrelevant.

"Infinity!" Törless had often heard the word in mathematics lessons. It had never meant anything in particular to him. The term kept on recurring; somebody had once invented it, and since then it had become possible to calculate with it as surely as with anything real and solid. It was whatever it stood for in the calculation; and beyond that Törless had never sought to understand it.

But now it flashed through him, with startling clarity, that there was something terribly disturbing about this word. It seemed to him like a concept that had been tamed and with which he himself had been daily going through his little circus tricks; and now all of a sudden it had broken loose. Something surpassing all comprehension, something wild and annihilating, that once had been put to sleep by some ingenious operation, had suddenly leapt awake and was there again in all its terrifying strength. There, in the sky, it was standing over him, alive and threatening and sneering.

At last he shut his eyes, the sight of it was such anguish to him.

* * *

When a little later he was aroused by a gust of wind rustling through the withered grass, he could scarcely feel his own body: there was a pleasant coolness streaming upwards from his feet, enfolding his limbs in gentle numbness. Now a kind of mild exhaustion mingled with his dismay. He still felt the sky as something vastly and silently staring down at him, but now he remembered how often before he had felt the same thing; and in a state between waking and dreaming he went back through all those memories, feeling how they spun their threads round him, wrapping him up in ever further meanings and associations, as in a cocoon.

There was, first of all, that childhood memory of the trees standing there as solemn and silent as if they were really people under an enchantment. Even then he must have felt this thing that was later to happen to him again and again. There had been something of this even behind those thoughts he had had in Božena's room, something special, something of a larger premonition, that was more than the thoughts themselves. And that moment in the cakeshop when everything had grown quiet outside the window, in the garden just before the dark veils of sensuality sank about him, yes, that too had been the same. And often, for the fraction of a thought, Beineberg and Reiting would turn into something strange, unfamiliar, unreal. And what about Basini? The thought of what was happening to Basini had rent Törless in two. At one moment this thought was rational and commonplace; at another it was vested in the same silence, flashing with sudden mental images, which was common to all these impressions,which had been steadily seeping through into Törless's conscious mind and which now all at once was asserting its claim to be treated as something real and living: just as the idea of infinity had, a while earlier.

Törless now felt it enclosing him on all sides. Like some far-off, obscure force it had probably been threatening from the very beginning, but he had instinctively shrunk from it, only now and then giving it a shy, fleeting glance. But now a chance happening had made him alert to it, forced him to attend to it, and, as at a signal, it came rushing at him from all directions: a torrent of immense perplexity that spread out further and further with every instant.

Törless was assailed by a sort of madness that made him experience things, processes, people, all as something equivocal: as something that by some ingenious operation had been fettered to a harmless explanatory word and which nevertheless was something entirely strange, which might break loose from its fetters at any moment now.

True, there is a simple, natural explanation for everything, and Törless knew it too; but to his dismayed astonishment it seemed only to tear off an outer husk, without getting anywhere near laying bare what was within—that other, further thing which now, as with a gaze that had grown unnaturally penetrating, he could always see glimmering underneath.

So he lay there, all wrapped up in memories, out of which strange notions grew like exotic flowers. Those moments that nobody forgets, when there is a failure of that power of association which generally causes our life to be faultlessly reflected in our understanding, as though life and understanding ran parallel to each other and at equal speed—those moments formed a bewilderingly close-knit mesh around him.

In his memory that dreadfully still, sad-coloured silence of certain evenings alternated abruptly with the hot, quivering uneasiness of a summer noon—an uneasiness that had once rippled over his soul, in blazing heat and as with the light flitting feet of innumerable iridescent lizards.

Then suddenly he recalled that little prince—his smile, the glance, the movement—with which, at the time when they had reached the end of their relationship, he had gently freed himself from all the associations that Törless had involved him in, and moved off into some distance—new and alien and, as it were, concentrated in the life of one ineffable instant—that had all at once opened out before him. Then again there came memories of the forest and from out in the fields. Then there was a silent scene in a darkening room at home, where he had suddenly felt reminded of his lost friend. Words of a poem came into his mind. . . .

And there are yet other things in which this incomparability reigns, somewhere between experience and comprehension. Yet it is always of such a nature that what in one moment we experience indivisibly, and without question, becomes unintelligible and confused as soon as we try to link it with chains of thought to the permanent store of what we know. And what looks grand and remote so long as our words are still reaching out towards it from a long way off, later, once it has entered the sphere of our everyday activities, becomes quite simple and loses all its disturbing quality.

*   *   *

And so it was that all these memories all at once had the same mystery in common. As though they all belonged together, they stood before him so distinctly that it seemed he could almost take hold of them.

In their own time they had been accompanied by an obscure emotion of which he had taken little notice.

And it was this that he was trying to get at now. It occurred to him that once, when he had been standing with his father, looking at one of those landscapes he had suddenly cried out: 'Oh, how beautiful it is!'—and then been embarrassed when his father was glad. For he might just as easily have said: 'How terribly sad it is.' It was the failure of language that caused him anguish, a half-awareness that the words were merely accidental, mere evasions, and never the feeling itself.

And today he recalled the scene, recalled the words—very distinctly recalled the sense he had had of falsehood, though without knowing why or in what way. In memory his eye went over it all again. But time and again it returned without bringing relief. A smile of delight in the wealth of the thoughts that came to him, a smile that had gradually become more and more absentminded, now slowly took on a just perceptible twist of pain. . . .

He felt the urge to search unceasingly for some bridge, some connection, some means of comparison, between himself and the wordless thing confronting his spirit.

But as often as he had put his mind at rest about any one idea, there would again be that incomprehensible objection: It's all a lie.

It was as if he must work out an unending sum in long division with a recurring decimal in it, or as if he were skinning his fingers in the frantic struggle to undo an endless knot.

And finally he gave up. It all closed tightly round him, and the memories grew large, weirdly distorted.

He had raised his eyes to the sky again—as though he might yet by some fluke snatch its secret from it and, that once gained, guess what perplexed him everywhere. But he grew tired, and a feeling of profound loneliness closed over him. The sky kept silent. And Törless felt that under that immovable, dumb vault he was quite alone, a tiny speck of life under that vast, transparent corpse.

But it hardly frightened him any more at all. It was like an old, familiar pain that had at last spread even to the last limb.

It seemed to him as if the light had now become milky and shimmering, dancing before his eyes like a pallid, cold mist.

Slowly and warily he turned his head and glanced about him to see if everything had really changed. His glance happened to pass over the grey, windowless wall behind him: it seemed to have leaned forward over him and to be looking at him in silence. From time to time there was a faint rustling in it, the sound of uncanny life awakening in the bricks and mortar.

It was the same faint rustling he had often listened to in the lair upstairs, when Beineberg and Reiting had raised the curtain on their fantastic world, and he had rejoiced in it as in the queer incidental music to a grotesque play.

But now the bright day itself seemed to have turned into an unfathomable lair, and the living silence closed in on Törless from all sides.

He could not turn his head away. Beside him, in a damp, shady corner, the ground was overgrown with colt's-foot, its broad leaves making fantastic lurking-places for slugs and snails.

Törless could hear the beating of his own heart. Then again there was a faint, whispering rustle that came and faded away. . . . And these sounds were the only things alive in a timeless world of silence.

The next day Törless saw Beineberg and Reiting together, and he went and joined them.

"I've talked to Reiting," Beineberg said, "and it's all fixed. After all, you're not really interested in such things, are you?"

Törless felt something like anger and jealousy rising up in him at this sudden change; but he did not quite know whether to mention the nocturnal discussion in front of Reiting. "Well, you might have called me in on it," he remarked. "After all, I've as much say in the whole thing as you chaps have."

"Oh, we would have, my dear Törless," Reiting hastened to say, obviously wishing to have no unnecessary difficulties this time. "But you happened to have disappeared, and we assumed you'd agree. Well, and what do you think of Basini now?" (There was no word of excuse, just as if his own behaviour were entirely a matter of course.)

"If you want to know," Törless replied, in embarrassment, "I think he's a low skunk."

"Isn't he just? A thorough skunk."

"But you're going in for something a bit off-colour yourself!" And Törless smiled in a rather forced manner, for he was ashamed of not being more indignant with Reiting.

"Me?" Reiting shrugged his shoulders. "What harm does it do? One's got to have had all sorts of experiences, and if *he's* stupid and low enough . . . "

"Have you talked to him since?" Beineberg now interposed.

"Yes. He came to me yesterday evening, asking for money, because he's got into debt again and can't pay up."

"Did you give him any?"

"No, not yet."

"Excellent," Beineberg commented. "Then we've got just the opportunity we want for settling his hash. You might tell him to come along somewhere tonight."

"Where? The cubby-hole?"

"No, I don't think so. He doesn't need to know about that yet. But make him come up to the attic where you took him before."

"What time?"

"Let's say—eleven."

"Right.—D'you want to come for a bit of a walk now?"

"Yes. I expect Törless still has lots to do—haven't you, Törless?"

He actually had no more work to do, but he could feel that the other two were up to something together that they wanted to keep a secret from him. He was annoyed with himself for being too stiff to push his way in whether they wanted him or not.

So he watched them go, jealously, and racked his brains about what they might be planning in secret.

And as he watched them it struck him how much innocent grace and charm there was in Reiting's erect carriage and supple walk— just as there was in his way of talking. By contrast he tried to imagine what Reiting must have been like—inwardly, in his emotions—that other night. It must have been like some long, slow sinking of two souls with a mortal stranglehold on each other, and then depths as of some subterranean realm—and, in between, a moment in which the sounds of the world, far, far above, faded and died out.

Could a human being really be so gay and easy-going again after such an experience? Surely then it could not mean so much to him. Törless would have liked to ask him. And instead of that, now, in his childish timidity, he had left him with that spidery creature Beineberg!

At a quarter to eleven Törless saw Beineberg and Reiting slip out of their beds, and he also got up and began dressing.

"Ssh! I say, wait, can't you? Somebody'll notice if the three of us all go out together."

Törless got back under the bed-clothes.

A little while later they all met in the passage, and with their usual caution they went on upstairs to the attics.

"Where's Basini?" Törless asked.

"He's coming up the other way. Reiting gave him the key."

They went all the way in darkness. Only when they reached the top, outside the big iron door, did Beineberg light his little hurricane-lamp.

The lock was stiff. It was rusty from years of disuse and would not answer to the skeleton key. Then at last it gave, with a loud snap. The heavy door scraped back reluntantly on its rusty hinges, yielding only inch by inch.

From inside the attic came a breath of warm, stale air, like that in small hothouses.

Beineberg shut the door after them.

They went down the little wooden staircase and then squatted on the floor beside a huge roof-beam.

On one side of them were some large water-tubs for use in case of fire. It was obvious that the water in them had not been changed for a very long time; it had a sweet, sickly smell.

The whole place was oppressive, with the hot, bad air under the roof and the criss-cross pattern on the huge beams and rafters, some of them vanishing into the darkness overhead, some of them reaching down to the floor, forming a ghostly network.

Beineberg shaded his lamp, and there they sat quite still in the dark, not speaking a word—for long, long minutes.

Then the door in the darkness at the other end of the attic creaked, faintly, hesitantly. It was a sound to make one's heart leap into one's mouth—the first sound of the approching prey.

Then came some unsure footsteps, a foot stumbling against wood, a dull sound as of a falling body . . . Silence . . . Then again hesitant footsteps . . . A pause . . . A faint voice asking: "Reiting?"

Now Beineberg removed the shade from his lamp, throwing a broad ray of light in the direction from which the voice had come.

Several immense wooden beams loomed up, casting deep shadows. Apart from that, there was nothing to be seen but the cone of light with dust whirling in it.

The footsteps grew steadier and came closer.

Then . . . and this time quite near . . . a foot banged against wood again, and the next moment . . . framed in the wide base of the cone of light . . . Basini's face appeared, ash-grey in that uncertain illumination.

*　　*　　*

Basini was smiling . . . sweetly, cloyingly. It was like the fixed smile of a portrait, hanging above them there in the frame of light.

Törless sat still, pressing himself tightly against the woodwork; he felt his eyelids twitching.

Now Beineberg recited the list of Basini's infamies—monotonously, in a hoarse voice.

Then came the question: "So you're not ashamed at all?" At that Basini looked at Reiting, and his glance seemed to say: 'Now I think it's time for you to help me.' And at that moment Reiting hit him in the face so that he staggered back, tripped over a beam, and fell. Beineberg and Reiting leapt upon him.

The lamp had been kicked sideways, and now its light flowed senselessly, idly, past Törless's feet, across the floor. . . .

From the sounds in the darkness Törless could tell that they were pulling Basini's clothes off and then that they were whipping him with something thin and pliant. Evidently they had had everything prepared. He heard Basini's whimpering and half-stifled cries of

pain as he went on pleading for mercy; and then finally he heard
nothing but a groaning, a suppressed howling, and at the same time
Beineberg cursing in a low voice and his heavy, excited breathing.
Törless had not stirred from where he sat. Right at the beginning,
indeed, he had been seized with a savage desire to leap up too and
join in the beating; but his feeling that he would come too late and
only be one too many had held him back. His limbs were encased
in paralysing rigidity, as though in the grip of some great hand.

In apparent indifference he sat staring at the floor. He did not
strain his ears to distinguish what the various sounds meant, and
his heart beat no faster than usual. His eyes followed the light that
spread out in a pool at his feet. Grains of dust gleamed in it, and
one ugly little cobweb. And the light seeped further, into the darkness under the beams, and peered out in dusty, murky gloom.

Törless could have sat there like that for an hour without noticing
the passing of time. He was thinking of nothing, and yet he was
inwardly very much preoccupied. At the same time he was observing
himself. And it was like gazing into a void and there seeing himself
as if out of the corner of his eye, in a vague, shapeless glimmer.
And then out of this vagueness—as though coming round the corner
of his mind—slowly, but ever more distinctly, a desire advanced
into clear consciousness.

Something made Törless smile at this. Then once again the desire
came more strongly, trying to draw him from his squatting position
down on to his knees, on to the floor. It was an urge to press his
body flat against the floorboards; and even now he could feel how
his eyes would grow larger, like a fish's eyes, and how through the
flesh and bones of his body his heart would slam against the wood.

Now there was indeed a wild excitement raging in Törless, and
he had to hold on tight to the beam beside him in an effort to fight
off the dizziness that was trying to draw him downwards.

Sweat pearled on his forehead, and he wondered anxiously what
all this could mean.

Startled quite out of his former indifference, he was now straining
his ears again to hear what the other three were doing in the darkness.

It had grown quiet over there. Only Basini could be heard groping
for his clothes and moaning softly to himself.

An agreeable sensation went through Törless when he heard this whimpering. A tickling shudder, like thin spidery legs, ran up and down his spine, then contracted between his shoulder blades, pulling his scalp tight as though with faint claws. He was disconcerted to realise that he was in a state of sexual excitement. He thought back, and though he could not remember when this had begun, he knew it had already been there when he felt that peculiar desire to press himself against the floor. He was ashamed of it; but it was like a tremendous surge of blood going through him, numbling his thoughts.

Beineberg and Reiting came groping their way back and sat down in silence beside him. Beineberg looked at the lamp.

At this moment Törless again felt drawn downward. It was something that came from his eyes—he could feel that now—a sort of hypnotic rigidity spreading from the eyes to the brain. It was a question, indeed, it was—no, it was a desperation—oh, it was something he knew already—the wall, that garden outside the window, the low-ceilinged cottages, that childhood memory—it was all the same thing! all the same! He glanced at Beineberg. 'Doesn't he feel anything?' he wondered. But Beineberg was bending down, about to put the lamp straight. Törless gripped his arm to stop him.

"Isn't it like an eye?" he said, pointing to the light streaming across the floor.

"Getting poetical now, are you?"

"No. But don't you yourself say there's something special about eyes? It's all in your own favourite ideas about hypnotism—how sometimes they send out a force different from anything we hear about in physics. And it's a fact you can often tell far more about someone from his eyes than from what he says . . . "

"Well—what of it?"

"This light seems like an eye to me—looking into a strange world. It makes me feel as if I had to guess something. Only I can't. I only could gulp it down—drink it."

"Well, so you really are getting poetical."

"No. I'm perfectly serious. It simply makes me frantic. Just look at it yourself and you'll see what I mean. It makes you sort of want to wallow in the pool of it—to crawl right into that dusty corner on all fours, as if that were the way to guess it . . . "

"My dear chap, these are idle fancies, all nonsense. That'll be enough of that sort of thing for the moment."

Beineberg now bent right down and restored the lamp to its

former position. But Törless felt a sudden spiteful satisfaction. He realised that, with some extra faculty he had, he got more out of these happenings than his companions did.

He was now waiting for Basini to re-appear, and with a secret shudder he noticed that his scalp was again tightening under those faint claws.

After all, he knew quite well by now that there was something in store for him, and the premonition of it was coming to him at ever shorter intervals, again and again: it was a sensation of which the others knew nothing, but which must evidently be of great importance for his future life.

Only he did not know what could be the meaning of this sexual excitement that was mingled with it. He did remember, however, that it had in fact been present each time when things began to be queer—though only to him—and to torture him because he could find no reason for the queerness.

And he resolved that at the next opportunity he would think hard about this. For the moment he gave himself up entirely to the shudder of excitement with which he looked for Basini's re-appearance.

Since Beineberg had replaced the lamp, the rays of light once again cut out a circle in the darkness, like an empty frame.

And all at once there was Basini's face again, just as it had been the first time, with the same fixed, sweet, cloying smile—as though nothing had happened in the meantime—only now, over his upper lip, mouth, and chin, slowly, drops of blood were making a red, wriggling line, like a worm.

* * *

"Sit down over there!" Reiting ordered, pointing to the great beam. When Basini had obeyed, Reiting launched out: "I suppose you were thinking you'd got yourself nicely out of the whole thing, eh? I suppose you thought I was going to help you? Well, that's just where you were wrong. What I've been doing with you was only to see exactly *how* much of a skunk you are."

Basini made a gesture of protest, at which Reiting moved as though to leap at him again. Then Basini said: "But look, for heaven's sake, there wasn't anything else I could do!"

"Shut up!" Reiting barked at him. "We're sick and tired of your excuses! We know now, once and for all, just where we stand with you, and we shall act accordingly."

There was a brief silence. Then suddenly Törless said quietly, almost amiably: "Come on, say 'I'm a thief'."

Basini stared at him with wide, startled eyes. Beineberg laughed approvingly.

But Basini said nothing. Then Beineberg hit him in the ribs and ordered sharply: "Can't you hear? You've been told to say you're a thief. Get on and *say* it!"

Once again there was a short, scarcely perceptible pause. Then in a low voice, in a single breath, and with as little expression as possible, Basini murmured: "I'm a thief."

Beineberg and Reiting laughed delightedly, turning to Törless: "That was a good idea of yours, laddie." And then to Basini: "And now get on with it and say: I'm a beast, a pilfering, dishonest beast, *your* pilfering, dishonest, filthy beast."

And Basini said it, all in one breath, with his eyes shut.

But Törless had leaned back into the darkness again. The scene sickened him, and he was ashamed of having delivered up his idea to the others.

During the mathematics period Törless was suddenly struck by an idea.

For some days past he had been following lessons with special interest, thinking to himself: 'If this is really supposed to be preparation for life, as they say, it must surely contain some clue to what I am looking for, too.'

It was actually of mathematics that he had been thinking, and this even before he had had those thoughts about infinity.

And now, right in the middle of the lesson, it had shot into his head with searing intensity. As soon as the class was dismissed he sat down beside Beineberg, who was the only person he could talk to about such things.

"I say, did you really understand all that stuff?"

"What stuff?"

"All that about imaginary numbers."

"Yes. It's not particularly difficult, is it? All you have to do is remember that the square root of minus one is the basic unit you work with."

"But that's just it. I mean, there's no such thing. The square of every number, whether it's positive or negative, produces a positive quantity. So there *can't* be any real number that could be the square root of a minus quantity."

"Quite so. But why shouldn't one try to perform the operation of working out the square root of a minus quantity, all the same? Of course it can't produce any real value, and so that's why one calls the result an imaginary one. It's as though one were to say: someone always used to sit here, so let's put a chair ready for him today too, and even if he has died in the meantime, we shall go on behaving as if he were coming."

"But how can you when you know with certainty, with mathematical certainty, that it's impossible?"

"Well, you just go on behaving as if it weren't so, in spite of everything. It'll probably produce some sort of result. And after all, where is this so different from irrational numbers—division that is never finished, a fraction of which the value will never, never, never be finally arrived at, no matter how long you may go on calculating away at it? And what can you imagine from being told that parallel lines intersect at infinity? It seems to me if one were to be over-conscientious there wouldn't be any such thing as mathematics at all."

"You're quite right about that. If one pictures it that way, it's queer enough. But what is actually so odd is that you *can really* go through quite ordinary operations with imaginary or other impossible quantities, all the same, and come out at the end with a tangible result!"

"Well, yes, the imaginary factors must cancel each other out in the course of the operation just so that does happen."

"Yes, yes, I know all that just as well as you do. But isn't there still something very odd indeed about the whole thing? I don't quite know how to put it. Look, think of it like this: in a calculation like that you begin with ordinary solid numbers, representing measures of length or weight or something else that's quite tangible—at any rate, they're real numbers. And at the end you have real numbers. But these two lots of real numbers are connected by something that simply doesn't exist. Isn't that like a bridge where the piles are there only at the beginning and at the end, with none in the middle, and yet one crosses it just as surely and safely as if the whole of it were there? That sort of operation makes me feel a bit giddy, as if it led part of the way God knows where. But what I really feel is so uncanny is the force that lies in a problem like that, which keeps such a firm hold on you that in the end you land safely on the other side."

Beineberg grinned. "You're starting to talk almost like the chaplain, aren't you? You see an apple—that's light-waves and the eye and so forth—and you stretch out your hand to steal it—that's the muscles and the nerves that set them in action—but between these two there lies something else that produces one out of the other, and that is the immortal soul, which in doing so has committed a sin . . . ah yes, indeed, none of your actions can be explained without the soul, which plays upon you as upon the keys of a piano . . ." And he imitated the cadences in which the chaplain was in the habit of producing this old simile. "Not that I find all that stuff particularly interesting."

"I thought you were the very person who would find it interesting. Anyway, it made me think of you at once because—if it's really impossible to explain it—it almost amounts to a piece of evidence for what you believe."

"Why shouldn't it be impossible to explain? I'm inclined to think it's quite likely that in this case the inventors of mathematics have tripped over their own feet. Why, after all, shouldn't something that lies beyond the limits of our intellect have played a little joke on the intellect? But I'm not going to rack my brains about it: these things never get anyone anywhere."

That same day Törless asked the mathematics master for permission to call on him, in order to discuss some points in the last lesson.

The next day, during the noon break, he went upstairs to the master's little apartment.

He had gained an entirely new respect for mathematics, for now it seemed all of a sudden to have ceased to be a dead school subject and to have turned into something very much alive. And arising out of this respect he felt something like envy of the master, who must be on familiar terms with all these processes and relationships and who carried the knowledge of them about with him always, like the key to a locked garden. But above and beyond this Törless was also impelled by curiosity, though it was, to be sure, rather diffident curiosity. He had never before been in the room of a grown-up young man, and there was a certain titillation in wondering what things looked like in the life of such a person, a different person, one who knew things and yet was composed and calm, at least so far as one could tell from the external objects surrounding him.

He had always been shy and withdrawn in his relations with his teachers and believed that as a result he was not particularly well liked by them. Hence his request, as he now paused in agitation outside the door, seemed to him an act of daring in which the main object was less to get some further light on his difficulties—for at the back of his mind he had already begun to doubt that he would get any—than to cast a glance, as it were, past the master and into this man's daily cohabitation with mathematics.

He was shown into the study. It was a long narrow room with a single window; near the window was a desk spattered with ink-blots, and against the wall was a sofa covered in some scratchy green ribbed material, with tassels. Over this sofa a faded student's cap hung on the wall, together with a number of photographs, the size of visiting-cards, brown and now grown dark with age, dating from the master's university days. On the oval table with the knock-kneed legs, which were of a would-be grace and prettiness that had somehow gone wrong, there lay a pipe and some leafy, crude-cut tobacco. The whole room was permeated with the smell of cheap tobacco-smoke.

Törless had scarcely had time to make these observations and note a trace of discomfort in himself, as on contact with something unsavoury, when the master came in.

He was a fair, nervous young man of no more than thirty, and quite a sound mathematician, who had already submitted several important papers to the academy.

He at once sat down at his desk, rummaged about a little among the papers strewn upon it (later it struck Törless that he had positively taken refuge there), then, crossing his legs, he began to polish his *pince-nez* with his handkerchief, and fixed an expectant gaze on Törless.

Meanwhile Törless had been scrutinising him too. He observed a pair of thick white woollen socks and saw that over them the bands of the underpants had been rubbed black by the blacking on the boots.

In contrast the handkerchief peeping out of the breast pocket was all white and dainty, and though the tie was a made-up one, it counterbalanced this by being as magnificently gaudy as a painter's palette.

Törless could not help feeling further repelled by these little observations; he scarcely found it in him to go on hoping that this man was really in possession of significant knowledge, when there was nothing whatsoever about either his person or his surroundings to suggest that it might be so. He had been secretly imagining a mathematician's study quite differently and as somehow expressive of the awe-inspiring matters that were excogitated there. The ordinariness of what he saw affronted him; he projected this on to mathematics, and his respect began to give way before a mistrustful reluctance.

And since the master was now shifting impatiently on his chair, not knowing what to make of this long silence and this scrutinising gaze, even at this stage there was already an atmosphere of misunderstanding between the two people in the room.

"And now let us . . . now you . . . I shall be pleased to tell you whatever you want to know," the master began at last.

Törless then came out with his difficulties, exerting himself to make clear what they meant to him. But he felt as though he were talking through a dense and gloomy fog, and his best words died away in his throat.

The master smiled, now and then gave a little fidgety cough, said: "If you don't mind," and lit a cigarette, at which he took hasty puffs. The cigarette-paper—and this was yet another thing that Törless noticed and found incredibly sordid—at each puff became greasy and crumpled up, crackling a little. The master took off his *pince-nez*, put it on again, nodded . . . And finally he cut Törless short. "I am delighted, my dear Törless, yes, I am indeed delighted," he said, interrupting him, "your qualms are indications of a seriousness and a readiness to think for yourself, of a . . . h'm . . . but it is not at all easy to give you the explanation you want. . . . Now, you must not misunderstand what I am going to say.

"It is like this, you see—you have been speaking of the intervention of transcendent, h'm, yes—of what are called *transcendent* factors. . . .

"Now of course I don't know what you feel about this. It's always a very delicate matter dealing with the suprasensual and all that lies beyond the strict limits of reason. I am not really qualified to intervene there in any way. It doesn't come into my field. One may hold this view or that, and I should greatly wish to avoid entering into any sort of controversy with anyone . . . But as regards mathematics," and he stressed the word 'mathematics' as though he were slamming some fateful door once and for all, "yes, as regards mathematics, we can be quite definite that here the relationships also work out in a natural and purely mathematical way.

"Only I should really—in order to be strictly scientific—I should really have to begin by posing certain preliminary hypotheses that you would scarcely grasp, at your stage. And apart from that, we have not the time.

"You know, I am quite prepared to admit that, for instance, these imaginary numbers, these quantities that have no real existence whatsoever, ha-ha, are no easy nut for a young student to crack. You must accept the fact that such mathematical concepts are nothing more or less than concepts inherent in the nature of purely mathematical thought. You must bear in mind that to anyone at the elementary stage at which you still are it is very difficult to give the right explanation of many things that have to be touched upon. Fortunately, very few boys at your stage feel this, but if one does really come along, as you have today—and of course, as I said before, I am delighted—really all one can say is: My dear young friend, you must simply take it on trust. Some day, when you know ten times as much mathematics as you do today, you will understand—but for the present: believe!

"There is nothing else for it, my dear Törless. Mathematics is a whole world in itself and one has to have lived in it for quite a while in order to feel all that essentially pertains to it."

Törless was glad when the master stopped talking. Since he had heard that door slam it had seemed to him that the words were moving farther and farther away from him . . . towards that other, indifferent realm where all correct and yet utterly irrelevent explanations lie.

But he was dazed by the torrent of words and the failure, and did not instantly grasp the fact that now he should get up and go.

So, in order to put an end to it once and for all, the master looked for one last, convincing argument.

On a little table lay a volume of Kant, the sort of volume that lies about for the sake of appearances. This the master took up and held out to Törless.

"You see this book. Here is philosophy. It treats of the grounds determining our actions. And if you could fathom this, if you could feel your way into the depths of this, you would come up against nothing but just such principles, which are inherent in the nature of thought and do in fact determine everything, although they themselves cannot be understood immediately and without more ado. It is very similar to the case with mathematics. And nevertheless we continually act on these principles. There you have the proof of how important these things are. But," he said, smiling, as he saw Törless actually opening the book and turning the pages, "that is something you may well leave on one side for the present. I only wanted to give you an example which you may remember some day, later on. For the present I think it would still be a little beyond you."

All the rest of that day Törless was in a state of inward upheaval. The fact that he had had the volume of Kant in his hand— this quite haphazard circumstance, to which he had paid little attention at the time—now worked mightily within him. The name of Kant was familiar enough to him, though only as a name, and its currency value for him was that which it had generally among those who even remotely occupied themselves with things of the mind—it was the last word in philosophy. And this authority it had was indeed part of the reason why Törless had hitherto spent so little time on serious reading.

For very young people, once they have got over the stage of wanting to be cab-drivers, gardeners or confectioners when they grow up, in their imaginings are inclined to set their ambitions for life in whatever field seems to hold out most chance for them to distinguish themselves. If they say they want to be doctors, it is sure to be because some time, somewhere, they have seen a well-furnished waiting-room crowded with patients, or a glass case containing mysterious and alarming surgical instruments, or the like; if they dream of a diplomatic career, it is because they are thinking of the urbane glamour of cosmopolitan drawing-rooms; in short, they choose their occupation according to the milieu in which they would most like to see themselves, and according to the pose in which they like themselves best.

Now, in Törless's hearing the name Kant had never been uttered except in passing and then in the tone in which one refers to some awe-inspiring holy man. And Törless could not think anything but that with Kant the problems of philosophy had been finally solved, so that since then it had become futile for anyone to concern himself with the subject, just as he also believed there was no longer any point in writing poetry since Schiller and Goethe.

At home these men's works were kept in the book-case with the green glass panes in Papa's study, and Törless knew this book-case was never opened except to display its contents to a visitor. It was like the shrine of some divinity to which one does not readily draw nigh and which one venerates only because one is glad that thanks to its existence there are certain things one need no longer bother about.

This distorted relationship to philosophy and literature in due course had its unhappy effect on Törless's development, and to it he owed many of these miserable hours. For in this way his ambition was diverted from the subjects to which he was really most inclined; and while, being deprived of his natural goal, he was searching for another, his ambition fell under the coarse and resolute influence of his companions at school. His inclinations re-asserted themselves only occasionally and shamefacedly, each time leaving him with a sense of having done something useless and ridiculous. Nevertheless they were so strong that he did not succeed in getting rid of them entirely; and it was this unceasing conflict that left his personality without firm lines, without straightforward drive.

Today, however, this relationship seemed to have entered a new phase. The thoughts that had just caused him to seek in vain for enlightenment were no longer the baseless concatenations produced by the random play of his fantasy; on the contrary, they created upheaval in him, holding him in their grip, and with his whole body he could feel that behind them there pulsed an element of his life. This was something quite new for him. There was within him now something definite, a certainty that he had never known in himself before. It was something mysterious, almost like a dream. It must, he thought to himself, have been very quietly developing under the various influences he had been exposed to in these last weeks, and now suddenly it was like imperious knuckles rapping at a door within him. His mood was that of a woman who for the first time feels the assertive stirring of the growing child within her.

He spent an afternoon full of wonderful enjoyment.

He got out of his locker all the poetical scribblings that he had stored away there. Taking them with him, he sat down by the stove, where he remained quite alone and unseen behind the huge screen. He went through one copy-book after another, afterwards slowly tearing each into small shreds and throwing the pieces into the fire one by one, each time relishing the exquisite pathos of farewell.

In this way he meant to cast away all the impedimenta he had brought with him from earlier days, just as though he must now travel light, giving all his attention to the steps that had to be taken, on into the future.

At last he got up and went to join the others. He felt free, able to look at everything squarely. What he had done had actually been done only in a quite instinctive way; there was no surety that he would really be capable of being a new person now, none at all unless the sheer existence of that impulse was surety. 'Tomorrow,' he said to himself, 'tomorrow I shall go over everything very carefully, and I shall get a clear view of things all right somehow.'

He strolled about the room, between the separate desks, glanced into copy-books lying open, at the fingers moving swiftly and busily along in the act of writing on that glaring white paper, each finger drawing along after it its own little brown shadow—he watched all this like someone who had suddenly waked up, with eyes for which everything seemed now to be of graver import.

But the very next day brought a bad disappointment. What happened was that first thing in the morning Törless bought himself the cheap paper-bound edition of the book he had seen in his mathematics master's room, and made use of the first break between lessons to begin reading it. But with all its parentheses and footnotes it was incomprehensible to him, and when he conscientiously went along the sentences with his eyes, it was as if some aged, bony hand were twisting and screwing his brain out of his head.

When after perhaps half an hour he stopped, exhausted, he had reached only the second page, and there was sweat on his forehead.

But then he clenched his teeth and read on, and he got to the end of one more page before the break was over.

That evening, however, he could not bring himself even to touch the book again. Was it dread? Disgust? He did not rightly know. Only one thing tormented him, with burning intensity: the mathematics master, that man who looked so thoroughly insignificant, quite openly had the book lying about in his room as if it were his daily entertainment.

He was in this mood when Beineberg came upon him.

"Well, Törless, how was it yesterday with the maths crammer?" They were sitting alone in a window-bay and had pushed the long clothes-stand, on which all the coats hung, across in front of them, so that all they heard and saw of the class was the rising and falling hum of voices and the reflection of the lamps on the ceiling. Törless fiddled absent-mindedly with one of the coats hanging in front of him.

"I say, are you asleep? He must have given you some answer, I suppose? Though I must say I can imagine it got him in quite a fix, didn't it?"

"Why?"

"Well, I dare say he wasn't prepared for a silly question like that."

"It wasn't a silly question at all. I haven't done with it yet."

"Oh, I didn't mean it like that, I only meant it must have seemed silly to him. They learn their stuff off by heart just the way the chaplain can reel off the catechism, and if you go and ask them anything out of turn it always gets them in a fix."

"Oh, he wasn't at a loss for the answer. He didn't even let me finish saying what I wanted to say, he had it all so pat."

"And how did he explain the thing?"

"Actually he didn't explain it at all. He said I wouldn't be able to understand it yet, these things were principles inherent in the mode of thought, and only become clear to someone who has gone on deeper into the subject."

"There you are, you see, there's the swindle of it! They simply can't put their stuff across to someone who just has his brains and nothing else. It only works after he's spent ten years going through the mill. But up to then he's done thousands of calculations on the basis of the thing and erected huge constructions that always worked out to the last dot. What it means is he then simply believes in it the way a Catholic believes in revelation—it's always worked so nicely. And where's the difficulty, then afterwards, in getting such people to believe in the proof as well? On the contrary, nobody would be capable of persuading them that though their construction stands, each single brick in it evaporates into thin air as soon as you try to get hold of it!"

Beineberg's exaggeration made Törless feel uncomfortable.

"I don't think it's quite so bad as you make out. I've never doubted that mathematics is right—after all, the results show that it is—the only thing that seemed queer to me was that every now and then it all seems to go against reason. And after all it's quite possible that that only seems to be so."

"Well, you can wait and see at the end of ten years, and perhaps by then your brain will be properly softened up and receptive to it. But I've been thinking about it too since we talked the other day, and I'm perfectly convinced there's a catch in it somewhere. Come to think of it, you talked about it quite differently then from the way you're talking today."

"Oh no. It still seems pretty dubious to me even now, only I'm not going to rush off into exaggerations the way you do. It certainly *is* thoroughly queer. The idea of the irrational, the imaginary, the lines that are parallel and yet meet at infinity—in other words, they do meet *somewhere*—it all simply staggers me! When I start thinking about it, I feel stunned, as though I'd been hit on the head." Törless leaned forward, right into the shadows, and his voice was low and husky. "Everything was all so clear and plain in my head before. But now it's as if my thoughts were like clouds, and when I come to these particular things, it's like a sort of gap you look through into an infinite, indefinable distance. Mathematics is probably right. But what is this thing in my head, and what about all the others? Don't they feel it at all? How does it look to all of them? Or doesn't it look like anything?"

"It seems to me you could see that from how your maths master reacted. When *you* hit on a thing like that, you always take a look round and wonder: now how does this fit in with everything else in me? *They've* bored a track through their brains, with thousands of spiral whorls in it, and they can only see as far as the last turning, whenever they look back to see if the thread they spin out behind them is still holding. That's why it gets them in a fix when you come along with that sort of question. None of *them* ever finds the way back. And anyway, how can you say I'm exaggerating? These people who've grown up and become so very clever have just spun themselves up completely in a web, with each mesh of it keeping the next in place, so that the whole thing looks as large as life and twice as natural. But there's nobody who knows where the first mesh is that keeps all the rest in place.

"The two of us have never talked seriously about this before— after all one doesn't paricularly care to make a lot of fuss about such things—but now you can see for yourself what a feeble point of view these people have and how they come to terms with their world. It's all delusion, it's all swindle, mere feebleness of mind! It's anemic! Their intellect takes them just far enough for them to think their scientific explanation out of their heads—but once it's outside it freezes up, see what I mean? Ha ha! All these fine points, these extreme fine points that the masters tell us are so fine and sharp that we're not capable of touching them yet—they're all dead—frozen—d'you see what I mean? There are these admired icy points sticking out in all directions, and there isn't anyone who can do anything with them, they're so dead!"

For some time now Törless had been leaning back again. Beineberg's hot breath was caught up among the coats and made the little corner warm. And as always when he was excited, Beineberg made a disagreeable impression on Törless. It was especially so now when he thrust up close, so close that his unwinking, staring eyes were like two greenish stones straight in front of Törless's own eyes, while his hands darted this way and that in the half-darkness with a peculiarly repellent nimbleness.

"Everything they assert is quite uncertain. They say everything works by a natural law. When a stone falls, that's the force of gravity. But why shouldn't it be the Will of God? And why should someone in whom God is well pleased not some time be liberated from sharing the fate of the stone? Still, why am I saying such things to you? You'll never be more than half a human being, anyway! Discovering a little bit of something queer, shaking your head a little, being horrified a little—that's your way. Beyond that you just don't dare to go. Not that it's any loss to me."

"But it is to me, you think? Yet it isn't as if your own statements were by any means so certain."

"How can you say such a thing! They're the only thing that *is* certain. Anyway, why should I quarrel with you about it? You'll see all right some day, my dear Törless. I'd even be prepared to bet that the day will come when you'll be quite confoundedly interested in the way it is with these things. For instance, when things with Basini turn out as I—"

"I don't want to hear about that," Törless cut him short. "I don't want that mixed up with it just now."

"Oh, and why not?"

"Just like that. I don't want to, that's all. I don't care for it. Basini and this are two different things for me. This is one thing, and Basini is an entirely different kettle of fish."

Beineberg grimaced in annoyance at this unaccustomed decisiveness, indeed roughness, on the part of his younger friend. But Törless himself realised that the mere mention of Basini had undermined all the confidence he had been displaying, and in order to conceal this he talked himself into annoyance too.

"Anyway you make these sweeping statements with a certainty that's positively mad. Hasn't it occurred to you that your theories may be just as much without a solid basis as anyone else's? The spiral whorls in your own head go a lot deeper and call for a whole lot more good will."

Remarkably enough, Beineberg did not lose his temper. He only smiled—though rather twistedly, and his eyes gleamed more restlessly than ever—and he said over and over again: "You'll see for yourself, you'll see for yourself . . ."

"Well, what shall I see? Oh, all right then, I'll see, I'll see. But I don't give a damn about it, Beineberg! It doesn't interest me. You don't understand me. You simply don't know what interests me. If mathematics torments me and if"—but he instantly thought better of it and said nothing about Basini—"if mathematics torments me, it's because I'm looking for something quite different behind it from what you're looking for. What I'm after isn't anything supernatural at all. It's precisely the natural—don't you see? nothing outside myself at all—it's something in me I'm looking for! something natural, but, all the same, something I don't understand! Only you have just as little feeling for it as any maths master in the world. Oh, leave me in peace—I've had enough of your speculations!"

Törless was trembling with agitation when he stood up.

And Beineberg was saying over and over again: "Well, we shall see, we shall see . . ."

When Törless was in bed that night he could not sleep. The quarters of the hours crept away like nurses tiptoeing from a sick-bed; his feet were icy cold, and the blankets merely lay heavy on him without warming him.

In the dormitory there was nothing to be heard but the calm and regular breathing of the boys, all sunk in their healthy, animal sleep after their lessons, gymnastics, and running about in the open air.

Törless listened to the sleepers' breathing. There was Beineberg's, Reiting's, Basini's breathing—which was which? He did not know. But each was one of the many regular, equally calm, equally steady sounds of breathing that rose and fell like the working of some mechanism.

One of the linen blinds had jammed half-way down, and under it the clear night shone into the room, making out a pale, motionless rectangle on the floor. The cord must have got stuck at the top, or it had slipped off the roller, and now it hung down, hideously twisted, and its shadow crept like a worm across the bright rectangle on the floor.

It was all grotesquely, frighteningly hideous.

Törless tried to think of something pleasant. Beineberg came into his mind. Had he not taken him down a peg today? Dealt a blow to his sense of superiority? Had he today not succeeded for the first time in asserting his individuality against him? In making it apparent in such a way that the other must have felt the infinite difference in the fineness of sensibility distinguishing their two views of things? Had there been anything left for Beineberg to say? Yes or no?

But this 'yes or no?' swelled up inside his head like a great bubble rising, and burst . . . and 'yes or no?' swelled, ceaselessly, in a stamping rhythm like the clatter of a railway train running over the rails, like the nodding of flowers on excessively long stems, like the thudding of a hammer that could be heard through many thin walls, in a silent house . . . This insistent, complacent 'yes or no?' disgusted Törless. His pleasure was not quite genuine, it hopped about so ridiculously.

And finally, when he started up, it seemed to be his own head that was nodding, lolling about on his shoulders, or thudding up and down like a hammer . . .

In the end all grew quiet in him. Before his eyes there was only a great circular plain spreading out in all directions.

Then . . . right from the very edge . . . there came two tiny, wobbling figures . . . tiny figures approaching obliquely across the table. Evidently they were his parents. But they were so small that he could not feel anything about them.

At the far rim they vanished again.

Then came another two—but look, there was somebody running up behind them and past them—with strides twice as long as his body—and an instant later he had vanished over the edge of the table. Had it not been Beineberg? Now for the two—wasn't one of them the mathematics master? Törless recognised him by the handkerchief coyly peeping out of his breast-pocket. But the other? The one with the very, very thick book under his arm, which was half as big as himself, so that he could only just manage to trudge along with it? . . . At every third step they stopped and set the book down on the ground. And Törless heard his teacher say in a squeaky little voice: 'If that is really so, we shall find the right answer on page twelve, page twelve refers us then to page fifty-two, but then we must also bear in mind what is pointed out on page thirty-one, and on this supposition . . .' As he spoke they were stooping over the book and plunging their hands into it, making the pages fly. After a while then they straightened up, and the other stroked the master's cheek five or six times. Then once more they went on a few paces, and after that Törless yet again heard the voice, just as if it were unravelling the long skein of some theorem in a mathematics lesson; and this went on until the other again stroked the master's cheek.

This other . . . ? Törless frowned in the effort to see more clearly.

Was he not wearing a peruke? And rather old-fashioned clothes? Very old-fashioned indeed? In fact, silk knee-breeches? Wasn't it—? Oh! And Törless woke up with a cry: "Kant!"

The next moment he smiled. All was quiet around him; the sleepers' breathing was very quiet now. He too had been asleep. And meanwhile his bed had grown warm. He stretched luxuriously under the bed-clothes.

'So I've been dreaming about Kant,' he thought to himself. 'Why didn't it last longer? Perhaps he would have let me into some of the secret . . .' For he remembered that once recently when he had not done his history preparation he had all night long dreamt of the persons and events concerned, so vividly that the next day he had been able to recount it all just as though he had been there, and he had passed the test with distinction. And now he thought of Beineberg again, Beineberg and Kant—their discussion the previous day.

Slowly the dream receded—slowly, like a silk cover slipping off the skin of a naked body, but without ever coming to an end.

Yet soon his smile faded again; he felt a queer uneasiness. Had he really come a single step forward in his thoughts? Could he really get anything, anything at all, out of this book that was supposed to contain the solution to all the riddles? And his victory? Oh, it was probably only his unexpected energy that had made Beineberg fall silent. . . .

And now again he was overwhelmed by profound discontent and a positively physical feeling of nausea. So he lay for long minutes, hollowed out by disgust.

But then again suddenly he became conscious of how his body was lapped by the mild, warm linen. Warily, quite slowly and warily, Törless turned his head. Sure enough, there the pale rectangle still lay on the floor—the sides of it now slanting rather differently, it was true, but still with that wormy shadow twisting across it. It was as if there some danger lay bound in chains, something that he could contemplate from here in his bed, as though protected by the bars of a cage, with the calm knowledge that he was in safety.

In his skin, all over his body, there awoke a sensation that suddenly turned into an image in his memory. When he was quite small—yes, yes, that was it—when he was still in pinafores and had not yet begun to go to kindergarten, there had been times when he had had a quite unspeakable longing to be a little girl. And this longing too had not been in his head—oh no—nor in his heart either—it had tingled all over his body and gone racing round under his skin. Yes, there had been moments when he so vividly felt himself a little girl that he believed it simply could not be otherwise. For at that time he still knew nothing of the significant bodily differences between the sexes, and did not understand why they all told him he must just put up with being a boy once and for all. And when he was asked why then he thought he would rather be a girl, he had not known how to say what he meant. . . .

Today for the first time he felt something similar again—again that longing, that tingling under the skin.

It was something that seemed to partake simultaneously of body and soul. It was a multifold racing and hurrying of something beating against his body, like the velvety antennae of butterflies. And mingled with it there was that defiance with which little girls run away when they feel that the grown-ups simply do not understand them, the arrogance with which they then giggle about the grown-ups, that timid arrogance which is always, as it were, poised for flight and which feels that at any instant it can withdraw into some terribly deep hiding-place inside its own little body. . . .

Törless laughed quietly to himself, and once again he stretched luxuriously under the bed-clothes.

How feverishly that quaint little mannikin he had dreamt of had gone leafing through the book! And the rectangle down there on the floor? Ha ha. Had such clever little mannikins ever in their lives noticed anything of that sort? He felt vastly secure now, safe from those clever persons, and for the first time felt that in his sensuality— for he had long known that this was what it was—he had something that none of them could take away from him, and which none of them could imitate, either, something that was like a very high and very secret wall protecting him against all the cleverness of the outside world.

Had such clever little mannikins ever in their lives—he went on wondering—lain at the foot of a solitary wall and felt terror at every rustle inside the bricks and mortar, which was as though something dead were trying to find words that it might speak to them? Had they ever felt the music that the breeze kindled among the autumn leaves, and felt it through and through, so that suddenly there was terror looming behind it—terror that slowly, slowly turned into lust? But into such strange lust, more like running away from something, and then like laughter and mockery. Oh, it is easy to be clever if one does not know all these questions. . . .

In the meantime, however, the mannikin every now and then grew to gigantic size, his face inexorably stern; and each time this happened something like an electric shock ran agonisingly from Törless's brain all through his body. Then once again all his anguish at still being left to stand outside a locked door—the very thing that only an instant earlier had been flooded away by the warm waves of his pulsing blood—awoke in him again, and a wordless lament streamed through his spirit, like a dog's howling in the night, tremulous over an expanse of dark fields.

So he fell asleep. And even as he dropped off he looked across once or twice to the patch under the window, like someone mechanically reaching out for a supporting rope, to feel whether it is still taut. Then vaguely a resolution loomed up in his mind: the next day he would again do some hard thinking about himself . . . it would be best to do it with pen and paper . . . and then, last of all, there was only the pleasant warmth that lapped him . . . like a bath and a stirring of the senses . . . but no longer conscious to him as that, only in some utterly unrecognisable but very definite way being linked with Basini.

Then he slept soundly and dreamlessly.

And yet this was the first thing in his mind when he woke the next morning. Now he intensely wished he could know what it had really been that he had half thought, half dreamt, about Basini as he fell asleep; but he could not manage to recollect it.

So all that remained was a tender mood such as reigns in a house at Christmas-time, when the children know the presents are already there, though locked away behind the mysterious door, and all that can be glimpsed now and then is a glow of light through the chinks.

In the evening Törless stayed in the classroom. Beineberg and Reiting had disappeared; probably they had gone off to the lair by the attics. Basini was sitting in his place in front, hunched over a book, his head supported on both hands.

Törless had bought himself a copy-book and now carefully set out his pen and ink. Then, after some hesitation, he wrote on the first page: De natura hominum. The Latin title was, he thought, the philosophic subject's due. Then he drew a large artistic curlicue round the title and leaned back in his chair to wait until it dried.

But it had been dry for a long time, and still he had not picked up his pen again. Something held him fast, kept him motionless. It was the hypnotic atmosphere of the big, hot lamps, and the animal warmth emanating from all the living bodies in the crowded room. He had always been susceptible to such an atmosphere, and this state was one that could rise to such a pitch of intensity that he became physically feverish, which again was always associated with an extraordinary heightening of mental perceptiveness. So it was today too. He had worked out, during the course of the day, what it actually was he wanted to make notes about: the whole series of those particular experiences from the evening with Božena on, culminating in that vague sensual state which had recently been coming over him. Once that was all put down, fact for fact, then—or so he hoped—the real intellectual pattern of it would emerge of its own accord, just as an encompassing line stands out distinctly and gives form to a tangled composition of hundreds of intersecting curves. And more than that he did not want. But so far he had fared like a fisherman who can feel by the jerking of his net that he has got a heavy haul and yet in spite of all his straining cannot manage to get it up into the light.

And now Törless did begin to write after all, but rapidly and without paying any attention to the form. "I feel something in me," he wrote, "and don't quite know what it is." Then, however, he hastily crossed this line out and wrote instead: "I must be ill—insane!" At this a shudder went through him, for the word was pleasantly melodramatic. "Insane—else what is it that makes things seem so odd to me that are quite ordinary for the others? And why does this oddness of things torment me? And why does this oddness cause me lusts of the flesh?"—he deliberately used this Biblical and unctuous expression because it struck him as more obscure and laden with implication. "Before, I used to have the same attitude to this as any of the others here—" but then he came to a halt. 'Is that really true?' he wondered. 'For instance, even that time at Božena's it was all so queer. So when did it actually begin? . . . Oh well.' he thought, 'it doesn't matter. Some time, anyway.' But he left his sentence unfinished.

"What are the things that seem odd to me? The most trivial. Mostly inanimate objects. What is it about them that seems odd? Something about them that I don't know about. But that's just it! Where on earth do I get this 'something' notion from? I feel it's there, it exists. It has an effect on me, just as if it were trying to lip-read from the twisted mouth of someone who's paralysed, and simply not being able to do it. It's as if I had one extra sense, one more than the others have, but not completely developed, a sense that's there and makes itself noticed, but doesn't function. For me the world is full of soundless voices. Does this mean I'm a seer or that I have hallucinations?

"But it's not only inanimate objects that have this effect on me.

What makes me so much more doubtful about it all is that people do it too. Up to a certain point in time I saw them the way they see themselves. Beineberg and Reiting, for instance—they have their lair, a perfectly ordinary secret cubby-hole, because they enjoy having a place like that to retreat to. And they do one thing because they're furious with one fellow, they do another thing because they want to prevent someone else from having any influence on the others. All quite sensible, obvious reasons. But nowadays they sometimes appear to me as if I were having a dream and they were only people in it. It's not only what they say or what they do—everything about them, bound up with their physical presence, sometimes has the same sort of effect on me as inanimate objects have. And all the same, I still hear them talking exactly the same way as before, I see how what they do and say still follows the same old patterns . . . This really goes to show all the time that there's nothing extraordinary happening at all, and at the same time something in me still goes on protesting that it isn't like that. So far as I can remember exactly, this change began with Basini's—' "

Here Törless involuntarily glanced over at Basini himself.

Basini was still sitting hunched over his book in the same attitude, apparently memorising something. At the sight of him sitting there like that, Törless's thoughts came to a standstill, and now he had a chance to feel once more the workings of the seductive torments that he had just been describing. For as soon as he became aware of how quietly and harmlessly Basini was sitting there before him, in no way differentiated from the others to right and to left, he vividly recalled the humiliations that Basini had undergone. They sprang to life in his mind: that is to say, he was far from thinking of them with the kind of indulgence which goes with the moral reflection that it is in every one's nature to try, after having suffered humiliations, to regain at least an outward air of casualness and unembarrassment as quickly as possible. On the contrary, something instantly began in him that was like the crazy whirling of a top, immediately compressing Basini's image into the most fantastically dislocated attitudes and then tearing it asunder in incredible distortions, so that he himself grew dizzy. True, these were only figures of speech that he found for it afterwards. At the moment he merely had the feeling of something in his tightened breast whirling upwards into his head, like a wildly spinning top, and this was the dizziness. Into the midst of it, like sparks, like dots of colour, there sprang those same feelings that he had had at various times about Basini.

Actually it had always been one and the same feeling. And more accurately, it was not a feeling at all, but more like a tremor deep down within him, causing no perceptible waves and nevertheless making his soul shudder quietly and yet so violently that in comparison the surges of even the stormiest feelings were like harmless ripples on the surface.

If this one 'feeling' was one that had at different times seemed different to him, it was because all he had to help him in interpreting this tide of emotion that would flood through his whole being was the images it cast up into his consciousness—as if all that could be seen of a swell stretching endlessly far away into the darkness were single, separate droplets of foam flung high against the cliffs of some lighted shore and, all force spent, immediately falling away again, out of the circle of light.

So these impressions were unstable, varying, and accompanied by an awareness of their random nature. Törless could never hold on to them; and when he looked more closely, he could feel that these incidents on the surface were in no proportion to the force of the dark mass, deep down, of which they seemed to be the manifestations.

He never at any time 'saw' Basini in any sort of physically plastic and living attitude; never did any of all this amount to a real vision. It was always only the illusion of one, as it were only the vision of his visions. For within him it was always as if a picture had just flashed across the mysterious screen, and he never succeeded in catching hold of it in the very instant that this happened. Hence there was all the time a restlessness and uneasiness in him such as one feels when watching cinematographic pictures, when, for all the illusion the whole thing creates, one is nevertheless unable to shake off a vague awareness that behind the image one perceives there are hundreds of other images flashing past, and each of them utterly different from the picture as a whole.

But he did not know where in himself to search for this power of creating illusion—illusion that was, moreover, by an immeasurably slight degree always just insufficient. He simply had an obscure inkling that it was connected with that enigmatic quality his spirit had of being assailed at times even by inanimate objects, by mere things, as by hundreds of mutely questioning eyes.

And so Törless sat quite still, transfixed, staring across at Basini, wholly involved in the seething whirl within him. And ever and again the same question rose up before him: What is this special quality I have? Gradually he ceased to see Basini any longer, or the hot glaring lamps, ceased to feel the animal warmth surrounding him, or to hear the buzzing and humming that goes up from a crowd of human beings even if they are only whispering. It all merged into one hot, darkly glowing mass that swung in a circle round him. His ears were burning, and his finger-tips were icy cold. He was in that state of more psychic than bodily fever which he loved. The mood went on intensifying, and now and then impulses of tenderness mingled with it. Previously, when in this state, he had enjoyed abandoning himself to those memories that are left in a young soul when for the first time it has been touched by the warm breath of a woman. And today too he felt that indolent warmth. A memory came to him . . . It was on a journey . . . in a little town in Italy . . . his parents and he were staying in a hotel not far from the theatre. Every evening the same opera was performed there, and every evening he heard every word and every note of it wafted over to him. He had no knowledge of the language; but for all that he spent his evenings sitting at the open window, listening. So it came about that he fell in love with one of the singers, without ever having set eyes on her. He was never again so moved by the theatre as at that time; the passion of those arias was for him like the wing-beats of great dark birds, and it was as though he could feel the lines that their flight traced in his soul. These were no longer human passions that he heard; no, they were passions that had escaped out of the human hearts, taking flight as out of cages that were too cramped, too commonplace, for them. In that state of excitement he could never think of the people who were over there—invisible— acting out those passions. If he did try to picture them, on the instant dark flames shot up before his eyes—or undreamt-of gigantic dimensions opened up, as in the darkness people's bodies grow and people's eyes shine like the mirroring surface of deep wells. This lurid conflagration, these eyes in the dark, these black wing-beats, were what he at that time loved under the name of the singer he had never seen.

And who had composed the opera? He did not know. Perhaps the libretto was some dreary sentimental romance. Had its creator ever felt that once set to music it would be transformed into something else?

A sudden thought made his whole body grow tense. Are even older people like that? Is the world like that? Is it a universal law that there's something in us stronger, bigger, more beautiful, more passionate and darker than ourselves? Something we have so little power over that all we can do is aimlessly strew thousands of seeds, until suddenly out of one seed it shoots up like a dark flame and grows away out over our heads? . . . And every nerve in his body quivered with the impatient answer: Yes.

Törless glanced about him with blazing eyes. It was all still there, the lamps, warmth, and light, the boys busily at work. But here in the midst of it he seemed to himself as one elect—like a saint, having heavenly visions. For the intuition of great artists was something of which he did not know.

Hurriedly, with the hastiness of nervous dread, he snatched up his pen and made some notes on his discovery. Once again there seemed to be a light within him scattering its sparks in all directions . . . then an ash-grey shower of rain fell over his gaze, and the glory in his spirit was quenched.

The Kant episode was now practically over and done with. By day Törless had quite ceased to think of it; the conviction that he himself was very close to the answer to his riddles was much too strong for him to go on bothering about anyone else's way of dealing with such problems. Since the last evening it was as if he had already felt in his hand the knob of the door that would open into the further realm, and then it had slipped from his grasp. But since he had realised that he must manage without the aid of philosophic books, and since he put no real trust in them anyway, he was rather at a loss as to how he was to find that knob again. He several times made an attempt to continue his notes; but the written words remained lifeless, a series, it seemed, of irksome and all too familiar question-marks, and there was no re-awakening of that moment in which he had gazed through them as into a vault illumined by flickering candle-flames.

Therefore he resolved that as often as possible, and ever and again, he would seek those situations which had that for him so peculiar meaning. And especially often did his gaze rest on Basini, when the latter, having no sense of being watched, went about among the others as if nothing at all were wrong. 'Sooner or later,' Törless thought to himself, 'it'll come to life again, and then perhaps more intensely and clearly than before.' And he was quite relieved at the thought that where such things were concerned one was simply in a dark room and there was nothing else one could do, once the fingers had slipped from the right place, but keep on groping and groping at random over the walls in the dark.

Yet at night this thought lost some of its conviction, and he would be overtaken by something like shame at having shied away from his original resolve to seek in the book his teacher had shown him the explanation that it might, after all, contain. This happened when he was lying still and listening for the sound of breathing from Basini, whose outraged body drew breath as tranquilly as those of all the others. He would lie still like a stalker in his hiding-place, with the feeling that he only had to wait and the time so spent would surely bring its reward. And then the thought of the book would come into his mind, and at once a fine-toothed doubt would begin to gnaw in him, disturbing this stillness—a foreboding that he was wasting his time, a hesitant admission that he had suffered a defeat.

As soon as this vague feeling asserted itself, his attentiveness lost the comfortable quality of watching the development of a scientific experiment. It seemed then that some physical influence emanated from Basini, a fascination such as comes from sleeping near a woman and knowing one can at any instant pull the covers off her body. It was a tingling in the brain, which started from the awareness of only having to stretch out one's hand. It was the same thing that often drives young couples into orgies of sensuality far beyond the bodies' real demands.

*   *   *

According to the intensity with which it struck him that his enterprise would perhaps seem ridiculous even to himself if he knew all that Kant knew, all that his mathematics master knew, and all that those people knew who had got to the end of their studies— according to the varying force of this qualm in him there was a weakening or an intensification of those sensual impulses that often kept his burning eyes wide open, in spite of the stillness all round him, where everyone else was asleep. At times, indeed, these impulses overwhelmed all other thoughts. When at such moments he abandoned himself, half willingly, half despairingly, to their insinuations, it was with him only as it is with all those people who, after all, never so much incline to a mad outburst of soul-rending, wantonly destructive debauchery as when they have suffered some failure that upsets the balance of their self-confidence. . . .

Then, when at last, after midnight, he was drifting into an uneasy sleep, it several times seemed to him that someone got up, over where Reiting's and Beineberg's beds were, and took his coat and went across to Basini. Then they left the dormitory . . . But it might equally well have been imagination. . . .

There came two public holidays; and since they fell on a Monday and Tuesday, the headmaster gave the boys Saturday off as well, so that they had four days free. For Törless this was still too short a time to make the long journey home worth while; and he had therefore hoped that at any rate his parents would come and see him. However, his father was kept by urgent affairs at his government office, and his mother did not feel well enough to face the strain of travelling alone.

But when Törless received his parents' letter, in which they told him they could not come, and added many affectionate words of comfort, he suddenly realised that this actually suited him very well. He knew now that it would have been almost an interruption—at least it would have embarrassed him considerably—if he had had to face his parents just at this stage.

Many of the boys had invitations to estates in the district. Dschjusch, whose parents owned a fine property at the distance of a day's drive from the little town, was one of those who went away, and with him went Beineberg, Reiting, and Hofmeier. Basini had also been asked, but Reiting had bidden him refuse. Törless excused himself on the grounds that he did not know for certain whether his parents might not come after all; he felt totally disinclined for innocent, cheerful frolics and amusements.

By noon on Saturday the great building was silent and almost quite deserted.

When Törless walked through the empty corridors, they echoed from end to end. There was nobody to bother about him, for most of the masters had also gone away for a few days' shooting or the like. It was only at meals, which were now served in a small room next to the deserted refectory, that the few remaining boys saw each other. When they left the table they once more took their separate ways through the many corridors and class-rooms; it was as if the silence of the building had swallowed them up, and whatever life they led in these intervals seemed to be of no more interest to anyone than that of the spiders and centipedes in the cellars and attics.

Of Törless's class the only two left were himself and Basini, with the exception of a few boys in the sick-bay. When leaving, Reiting had exchanged a few words in private with Törless in the matter of Basini, for he was afraid that Basini might make use of the opportunity to seek protection from one of the masters; he had therefore impressed it on Törless to keep a sharp eye on him.

However, there was no need of that to concentrate Törless's attention on Basini.

Scarcely had the uproar faded away—the carriages driving to the door, the servants carrying valises, the boys joking and shouting good-bye to each other—when the consciousness of being alone with Basini took complete possession of Törless's mind.

It was after the first midday meal. Basini sat in his place in front, writing a letter. Törless had gone to a corner right at the back of the room and was trying to read.

It was for the first time again the volume of Kant, and the situation was just as he had pictured it: in front there sat Basini, at the back himself, holding Basini with his gaze, boring holes into him with his eyes. And it was like this that he wanted to read: penetrating deeper into Basini at the end of every page. That was how it must be; in this way he must find the truth without losing grip on life, living, complicated, ambiguous life. . . .

But it would not work. This was what always happened when he had thought something out all too carefully in advance. It was too unspontaneous, and his mood swiftly lapsed into a dense, gluey boredom, which stuck odiously to every one of his all too deliberate attempts to get on with his reading.

In a fury, Törless threw the book on the floor. Basini looked round with a start, but at once turned away again and hurriedly went on writing.

So the hours crept on towards dusk. Törless sat there in a stupor.

The only thing that struck clearly into his awareness—out of a muffled, buzzing, whirring state of generalised sensation—was the ticking of his pocket-watch. It was like a little tail wagging on the sluggish body of the creeping hours. The room became blurred . . . Surely Basini could no longer be writing . . . 'Aha, he probably doesn't dare to light a lamp,' Törless thought to himself. But was he still sitting over there in his place at all? Törless had been gazing out into the bleak, twilit landscape and now had to accustom his eyes again to the darkness of the room. Oh yes, there he was. There, that motionless shadow, that would be Basini all right. And now he even heaved a sigh—once, twice. He hadn't gone to sleep, had he?

A servant came in and lit the lamps. Basini started up and rubbed his eyes. Then he took a book out of his desk and began to apply himself to it.

Törless could hardly prevent himself from speaking to him, and in order to avoid that he hurried out of the room.

In the night Törless was not far from falling upon Basini, such a murderous lust had awakened in him after the anguish of that senseless, stupefying day. By good fortune sleep overtook him just in time.

The next day passed. It brought nothing but the same bleak and barren quietness. The silence and suspense worked on Törless's overwrought nerves; the ceaseless strain on his attention consumed all his mental powers, so that he was incapable of framing any thought at all.

Disappointed, dissatisfied with himself to the point of the most extreme doubt, he felt utterly mangled. He went to bed early.

He had for a long time been lying in an uneasy, feverishly hot half-sleep when he heard Basini coming.

Lying motionless, with his eyes he followed the dark figure walking past the end of his bed. He heard the other undressing, and then the rustling of the blankets being pulled over the body.

He held his breath, but he could not manage to hear any more. Nevertheless he did not lose the feeling that Basini was not asleep either, but was straining to hear through the darkness, just like himself.

So the quarter-hours passed . . . hours passed. Only now and then the stillness was broken by the faint sound of the bodies stirring, each in its bed.

Törless was in a queer state that kept him awake. Yesterday it had been sensual pictures in his imagination that had made him feverish. Only right at the end had they taken a turn towards Basini, as it were rearing up under the inexorable hand of sleep, which then blotted them out; and it was precisely of this that he had the vaguest and most shadowy memory. But tonight it had from the very beginning been nothing other than an impelling urge to get up and go over to Basini. So long as he had had the feeling that Basini was awake and listening for whatever sounds he might make, it had been scarcely endurable; and now that Basini was apparently asleep, it was even worse, for there was a cruel excitement in the thought of falling upon the sleeper as upon a prey.

Törless could already feel the movements of rising up and getting out of bed twitching in all his muscles. But still he could not yet shake off his immobility.

'And what am I going to do, anyway, if I do go over to him?' he wondered, in his panic almost speaking the words aloud. And he had to admit to himself that the cruelty and lust in him had no real object. He would have been at a loss if he had now really set upon Basini. Surely he did not want to beat him? God forbid! Well then, in what way was his wild sensual excitement to get fulfilment from Basini? Instinctively he revolted at the thought of the various little vices that boys went in for. Expose himself to another person like that? Never!

But in the same measure as this revulsion grew the urge to go over to Basini also became stronger. Finally Törless was completely penetrated with the sense of how absurd such an act was, and yet a positively physical compulsion seemed to be drawing him out of bed as on a rope. And while his mind grew blank and he merely kept on telling himself, over and over again, that it would be best to go to sleep now if he could, he was mechanically rising up in the bed. Very slowly—and he could feel how the emotional urge was gaining, inch by inch, over the resistance in him—he began to sit up. First one arm moved . . . then he propped himself on one elbow, then pushed one knee out from under the bedclothes . . . and then . . . suddenly he was racing, barefoot, on tip-toe, over to Basini, and sat down on the edge of Basini's bed.

Basini was asleep.

He looked as if he were having pleasant dreams.

Törless was still not in control of his actions. For a moment he sat still, staring into the sleeper's face. Through his brain there jerked those short, ragged thoughts which do no more, it seems, than record what a situation is, those flashes of thought one has when losing one's balance, or falling from a height, or when some object is torn from one's grasp. And without knowing what he was doing he gripped Basini by the shoulder and shook him out of his sleep.

Basini stretched indolently a few times. Then he started up and gazed at Törless with sleepy, stupefied eyes.

A shock went through Törless. He was utterly confused; now all at once he realised what he had done, and he did not know what he was to do next. He was frightfully ashamed. His heart thudded loudly. Words of explanation and excuse hovered on the tip of his tongue. He would ask Basini if he had any matches, if he could tell him the time . . .

Basini was still goggling at him with uncomprehending eyes.

Now, without having uttered a word, Törless withdrew his arm, now he slid off the bed and was about to creep back soundlessly to his own bed—and at this moment Basini seemed to grasp the situation and sat bolt upright.

Törless stopped irresolutely at the foot of the bed.

Basini glanced at him once more, questioningly, searchingly, and then got out of bed, slipped into coat and slippers and went padding off towards the door. And in a flash Törless became sure of what he had long suspected: that this had happened to Basini many times before.

In passing his bed, Törless took the key to the cubbyhole, which he had been keeping hidden under his pillow.

Basini walked straight on ahead of him, up to the attics. He seemed in the meantime to have become thoroughly familiar with the way that had once been kept so secret from him. He steadied the crate while Törless stepped down on to it, he cleared the scenery to one side, carefully, with gingerly movements, like a well-trained flunkey.

Törless unlocked the door, and they went in. With his back to Basini, he lit the little lamp.

When he turned around, Basini was standing there naked.

Involuntarily Törless fell back a step. The sudden sight of this naked snow-white body, with the red of the walls dark as blood behind it, dazzled and bewildered him. Basini was beautifully built; his body, lacking almost any sign of male development, was of a chaste, slender willowyness, like that of a young girl. And Törless felt this nakedness lighting up in his nerves, like hot white flames. He could not shake off the spell of this beauty. He had never known before what beauty was. For what was art to him at his age, what—after all—did he know of that? Up to a certain age, if one has grown up in the open air, art is simply unintelligible, a bore!

And here now it had come to him on the paths of sexuality . . . secretly, ambushing him . . . There was an infatuating warm exhalation coming from the bare skin, a soft, lecherous cajolery. And yet there was something about it that was so solemn and compelling as to make one almost clap one's hands in awe.

But after the first shock Törless was as ashamed of the one reaction as of the other. 'It's a man, damn it!' The thought enraged him, and yet it seemed to him as though a girl could not be different.

In his shame he spoke hectoringly to Basini: "What on earth d'you think you're doing? Get back into your things this minute!"

Now it was Basini who seemed taken aback. Hesitantly, and without shifting his gaze from Törless, he picked up his coat from the floor.

"Sit down—there!" Törless ordered. Basini obeyed. Törless leaned against the wall, with his arms crossed behind his back.

"Why did you undress? What did you want of me?"

"Well, I thought . . ."

He paused hesitantly.

"What did you think?"

"The others . . ."

"What about the others?"

"Beineberg and Reiting . . ."

"What about Beineberg and Reiting? What did they do? You've got to tell me everything! That's what I want. See? Although I've heard about it from them, of course." At this clumsy lie Törless blushed.

Basini bit his lips.

"Well? Get on with it!"

"No, don't make me tell! Please don't make me! I'll do anything you want me to. But don't make me tell about it. . . . Oh, you have such a special way of tormenting me . . . !" Hatred, fear, and an imploring plea for mercy were all mingled in Basini's gaze.

Törless involuntarily modified his attitude. "I don't want to torment you at all. I only mean to make you tell the whole truth yourself. Perhaps for your own good."

"But, look, I haven't done anything specially worth telling about."

"Oh, haven't you? So why did you undress, then?"

"That's what they wanted."

"And why did you do what they wanted? So you're a coward, eh? A miserable coward?"

"No, I'm not a coward! Don't say that!"

"Shut up! If you're afraid of being beaten by them, you might find being beaten by me was something to remember!"

"But it's not the beatings they give me that I'm afraid of!"

"Oh? What is it then?"

By now Törless was speaking calmly again. He was already annoyed at his crude threat. But it had escaped him involuntarily, solely because it seemed to him that Basini stood up to him more than to the others.

"Well, if you're not afraid, as you say, what's the matter with you?"

"They say if I do whatever they tell me to, after some time I shall be forgiven everything."

"By the two of them?"

"No, altogether."

"How can they promise that? *I* have to be considered too!"

"They say they'll manage that all right."

This gave Törless a shock. Beineberg's words about Reiting's dealing with him, if he got the chance, in exactly the same way as with Basini now came back to him. And if it really came to a plot against him, how was he to cope with it? He was no match for the two of them in that sort of thing. How far would they go? The same as with Basini? . . . Everything in him revolted at the perfidious idea.

Minutes passed between him and Basini. He knew that he lacked the daring and endurance necessary for such intrigues, though of course only because he was too little interested in that sort of thing, only because he never felt his whole personality involved. He had always had more to lose than to gain there. But if it should ever happen to be the other way, there would, he felt, be quite a different kind of toughness and courage in him. Only one must know when it was time to stake everything.

"Did they say anything more about it—how they think they can do it? I mean, that about me."

"More? No. They only said they'd see to it all right."

And yet . . . there was danger now . . . somewhere lying in wait . . . lying in ambush for Törless . . . every step could run him into a gin-trap, every night might be the last before the fight. There was tremendous insecurity in this thought. Here was no more idle drifting along, no more toying with enigmatic visions—this had hard corners and was tangible reality.

Törless spoke again:

"And what do they do with you?"

Basini was silent.

"If you're serious about reforming, you have to tell me everything."

"They make me undress."

"Yes, yes, I see that for myself . . . And then?"

A little time passed, and then suddenly Basini said: "Various things." He said it with an effeminate, coy expression.

"So you're their—mi—mistress?"

"Oh no, I'm their friend!"

"How can you have the nerve to say that!"

"They say so themselves."

"What!"

"Yes, Reiting does."

"Oh, Reiting does?"

"Yes, he's very nice to me. Mostly I have to undress and read him something out of history-books—about Rome and the emperors, or the Borgias, or Timur Khan . . . oh well, you know, all that sort of big, bloody stuff. Then he's even affectionate to me. . . . And then afterwards he generally beats me."

"After what? Oh, I see!"

"Yes. He says, if he didn't beat me, he wouldn't be able to help thinking I was a man, and then he couldn't let himself be so soft and affectionate to me. But like that, he says, I'm his chattel, and so then he doesn't mind."

"And Beineberg?"

"Oh, Beineberg's beastly. Don't you think too his breath smells bad?"

"Shut up! What I think is no business of yours! Tell me what Beineberg does with you!"

"Well, the same as Reiting, only . . . But you mustn't go yelling at me again. . . ."

"Get on with it."

"Only . . . he goes about it differently. First of all he gives me long talks about my soul. He says I've sullied it, but so to speak only the outermost forecourt of it. In relation to the innermost, he says, this is something that doesn't matter at all, it's only external. But one must kill it. In that way many people have stopped being sinners and become saints. So from a higher point of view sin isn't so bad, only one must carry it to the extreme, so that it breaks off of its own accord, he says. He makes me sit and stare into a prism. . . ."

"He hypnotises you?"

"No, he says it's just that he must make all the things floating about on the surface of my soul go to sleep and become powerless. It's only then he can have intercourse with my soul itself."

"And how, may I ask, does he have intercourse with it?"

"That's an experiment he hasn't ever brought off yet. He sits there, and I have to lie on the ground so that he can put his feet on me. I have to get quite dull and drowsy from staring into the glass. Then suddenly he orders me to bark. He tells me exactly how to do it—quietly, more whimpering—the way a dog whines in its sleep."

"What's that good for?"

"Nobody knows what it's good for. And he also makes me grunt like a pig and keeps on and on telling me there's something of a pig about me, in me. But he doesn't mean it offensively, he just keeps on repeating it quite softly and nicely, in order—this is what he says—in order to imprint it firmly on my nerves. You see, he says it's possible one of my former lives was that of a pig and it must be lured out so as to render it harmless."

"And you believe all that stuff?"

"Good lord, no! I don't think he believes it himself. And then in the end he's always quite different, anyway. How on earth should I believe such things? Who believes in a soul these days anyway? And as for transmigration of souls—! I know quite well I slipped. But I've always hoped I'd be able to make up for it again. There isn't any hocus-pocus needed for that. Not that I spend any time racking my brains about how I ever came to go wrong. A thing like that comes on you so quickly, all by itself. It's only afterwards you notice that you've done something silly. But if he gets his fun out of looking for something supernatural behind it, let him, for all I care. For the present, after all, I've got to do what he wants. Only I wish he'd leave off sticking pins in me. . . ."

"What?"

"Pricking me with a pin—not hard, you know, only just to see how I react—to see if something doesn't manifest itself at some point or other on the body. But it does *hurt*. The fact is, he says the doctors don't understand anything about it. I don't remember now how he proves all this, all I remember is he talks a lot about fakirs and how when they see their souls they're supposed to be insensitive to physical pain."

"Oh yes, I know those ideas. But you yourself say that's not all."

"No, it certainly isn't all. But I also said I think this is just a way of going about it. Afterwards there are always long times—as much as a quarter of an hour—when he doesn't say anything and I don't know what's going on in him. But after that he suddenly breaks out and demands services from me—as if he were possessed—much worse than Reiting."

"And you do everything that's demanded of you?"

"What else can I do? I want to become a decent person again and be left in peace."

"But whatever happens in the meantime won't matter to you at all?"

"Well, I can't help it, can I?"

"Now pay attention to me and answer my questions. How could you steal?"

"How? Look, it's like this, I needed money urgently. I was in debt to the tuck-shop man, and he wouldn't wait any longer. Then I really did believe there was money coming for me just at that time. None of the other fellows would lend me any. Some of them hadn't got any themselves, and the saving ones are always just glad if someone who isn't like that gets short towards the end of the month. Honestly, I didn't want to cheat anyone. I only wanted to borrow it secretly. . . ."

"That's not what I mean," Törless said impatiently, interrupting this story, which it was obviously a relief for Basini to tell. "What I'm asking is *how*—how were you able to do it, what did you feel like? What went on in you at that moment?"

"Oh well—nothing, really. After all, it was only a moment, I didn't feel anything. I didn't think about anything, simply it had suddenly happened."

"But the first time with Reiting? The first time he demanded those things of you? You know what I mean. . . ."

"Oh, I didn't like it, of course. Because it had to be done just like that, being ordered to. Otherwise—well, just how many of the fellows do such things of their own accord, for the fun of it, without the others knowing anything? I dare say it's not so bad then."

"But you did it on being ordered to. You debased yourself. Just as if you had crawled into the muck because someone else wanted you to."

"Oh, I grant that. But I had to."

"No, you didn't have to."

"They would have beaten me and reported me. Think how I would have got into disgrace."

"All right then, let's leave that. There's something else I want to know. Listen. I know you've spent a lot of money with Božena. You've boasted to her and thrown your weight about and made out what a man you are. So you want to be a man? Not just boasting and pretending to be—but with your whole soul? Now look, then suddenly someone demands such a humiliating service from you, and in the same moment you feel you're too cowardly to say no—doesn't it make a split go through your whole being? A horror—something you can't describe—as though something unutterable had happened inside you?"

"Lord! I don't know what you mean. I don't know what you're getting at. I can't tell you anything—anything at all—about that."

"Now attend. I'm going to order you to get undressed again."

Basini smiled.

"And to lie down flat on the floor there in front of me. Don't laugh! I'm really ordering you to! D'you *hear* me? If you don't obey instantly, you'll see what you're in for when Reiting comes back! . . . That's right. So now you're lying naked on the ground in front of me. You're trembling, too. Are you cold? I could spit on your naked body now if I wanted to. Just press your head right on to the floor.

Doesn't the dust on the boards look queer? Like a landscape full of clouds and lumps of rock as big as houses? I could stick pins into you. There are still some over there in the corner, by the lamp. D'you feel them in your skin even now? . . . But I don't mean to do that. I could make you bark, the way Beineberg does, and make you eat dust like a pig, I could make you do movements—oh, you know—and at the same time you would have to sigh: 'Oh, my dear Moth——!' " But Törless broke off abruptly in the midst of this sacrilege. "But I don't mean to—don't mean to—do you understand?"

Basini wept. "You're tormenting me . . ."

"Yes, I'm tormenting you. But that's not what I'm after. There's just one thing I want to know: when I drive all that into you like knives, what goes on in you? What happens inside you? Does something burst in you? Tell me! Does it smash like a glass that suddenly flies into thousands of splinters before there's been even a little crack in it? Doesn't the picture you've made of yourself go out like a candle? Doesn't something else leap into its place, the way the pictures in the magic-lantern leap out of the darkness? Don't you *understand* what I mean? I can't explain it for you any better. You must tell me yourself . . . !"

Basini wept without stopping. His girlish shoulders jerked. All he could get out was to the same effect: "I don't know what you're after, I can't explain anything to you, it happens just in a moment, and then nothing different can happen, you'd do just the same as me."

Törless was silent. He remained leaning against the wall, exhausted, motionless, blankly staring straight in front of him.

'If you were in my situation, you would do just the same,' Basini had said. Seen thus, what had happened appeared a simple necessity, straightforward and uncomplicated.

Törless's self-awareness rebelled in blazing contempt against the mere suggestion. And yet this rebellion on the part of his whole being seemed to offer him no satisfactory guarantee . . . '. . . yes, *I* should have more character than he has, *I* shouldn't put up with such outrageous demands—but does it really matter? Does it matter that I should act differently, from firmness, from decency, from— oh, for all sorts of reasons that at the moment don't interest me in the least? No, what counts is not how I should act, but the fact that if I were ever really to act as Basini has done, I should have just as little sense of anything extraordinary about it as he has. This is the heart of the matter: my feeling about myself would be exactly as simple and clear of ambiguity as his feeling about himself . . .'

This thought—flashing through his mind in half-coherent snatches of sentences that ran over into each other and kept beginning all over again—added to his contempt for Basini a very private, quiet pain that touched his inmost balance at a much deeper point than any moral consideration could. It came from his awareness of a sensation he had briefly had before and which he could not get rid of. The fact was that when Basini's words revealed to him the danger potentially menacing him from Reiting and Beineberg, he had simply been startled. He had been startled as by a sudden assault, and without stopping to think had in a flash looked round for cover and a way of parrying the attack. That had been in the moment of a real danger; and the sensation it had caused him—those swift, unthinking impulses—exasperated and stimulated him. He tried, all in vain, to set them off again. But he knew they had immediately deprived the danger of all its peculiarity and ambiguity.

And yet it had been the same danger that he had had a foreboding of only some weeks previously, in this same place—that time when he had felt so oddly startled by the lair itself, which was like some forgotten scrap of the Middle Ages lying remote from the warm, bright-lit life of the class-rooms, and by Beineberg and Reiting, because they seemed to have changed from the people they were down there, suddenly turning into something else, something sinister, blood-thirsty, figures in some quite different sort of life. That had been a transformation, a leap, for Törless, as though the picture of his surroundings had suddenly loomed up before other eyes—eyes just awakened out of a hundred years of sleep.

And yet it had been the same danger. . . . He kept on repeating this to himself. And ever and again he tried to compare the memories of the two different sensations. . . .

Meanwhile Basini had got up. Observing his companion's blank, absent gaze, he quietly took his clothes and slipped away.

Törless saw it happening—as though through a mist—but he uttered no word and let it go at that.

His attention was wholly concentrated on this straining to re-discover the point in himself where the change of inner perspective had suddenly occurred.

But every time he came anywhere near it the same thing happened to him as happens to someone trying to compare the close-at-hand with the remote: he could never seize the memory images of the two feelings together. For each time something came in between. It was like a faint click in the mind, corresponding more or less to something that occurs in the physical realm—that scarcely percep-tible muscular sensation which is associated with the focusing of the gaze. And each time, precisely in the decisive moment, this would claim all his attention: the activity of making the comparison thrust itself before the objects to be compared, there was an almost unnoticeable jerk—and everything stopped.

So Törless kept on beginning all over again.

This mechanically regular operation lulled him into a rigid, wak-ing, ice-cold sleep, holding him transfixed where he was—and for an indefinite period.

Then an idea wakened him like the light touch of a warm hand. It was an idea apparently so obvious and natural that he marvelled at its not having occurred to him long ago.

It was an idea that did nothing at all beyond generalising the experience he had just had: what in the distance seems so great and mysterious comes up to us always as something plain and undis-torted, in natural, everyday proportions. It is as if there were an invisible frontier round every man . . . What originates outside and approaches from a long way off is like a misty sea full of gigantic, ever-changing forms; what comes right up to any man, and becomes action, and collides with his life, is clear and small, human in its dimensions and human in its outlines. And between the life one lives and the life one feels, the life one only has inklings and glimpses of, seeing it only from afar, there lies that invisible frontier, and in it the narrow gateway where all that ever happens, the images of things, must throng together and shrink so that they can enter into a man . . .

And yet, closely though this corresponded to his experience, Tör-less let his head sink, deep in thought.

It seemed a queer idea . . .

At last he was back in bed. He was not thinking of anything at all any more, for thinking came so hard and was so futile. What he had discovered about the secret contrivings of his friends did, it was true, go through his mind, but now as indifferently and lifelessly as an item of foreign news read in a newspaper.

There was nothing more to be hoped from Basini. Oh, there was still his problem! But that was so dubious, and he was so tired and mangled. An illusion perhaps—the whole thing.

Only the vision of Basini, of his bare, glimmering skin, left a fragrance, as of lilac, in that twilight of the sensations which comes just before sleep. Even the moral revulsion faded away. And at last Törless fell asleep.

*   *   *

No dream disturbed him. There was only an infinitely pleasant warmth spreading soft carpets under his body. After a while he woke out of it. And then he almost screamed. There, sitting on his bed, was Basini! And in the next instant, with crazy speed, Basini had flung off his night-clothes and slid under the blankets and was pressing his naked, trembling body against Törless.

As soon as Törless recovered from the shock, he pushed Basini away from him.

"What do you think you're doing—?"

But Basini pleaded. "Oh, don't start being like that again! Nobody's the way you are! They don't despise me the way you do. They only pretend they do, so as to be different then afterwards. But you—you of all people! You're even younger than me, even if you are stronger. We're both younger than the others. You don't boast and bully the way they do . . . You're gentle . . . I love you . . ."

"Here, I say! I don't know what you're talking about! I don't know what you want! Go away! Oh, go *away!*" And in anguish Törless pushed his arm against Basini's shoulder, holding him off. But the hot proximity of the soft skin, this other person's skin, haunted him, enclosing him, suffocating him. And Basini kept on whispering: "Oh yes . . . oh yes . . . please . . . oh, I should so gladly do whatever you want!"

* * *

Törless could find nothing to say to this. While Basini went on whispering and he himself was lost in doubt and consideration, something had sunk over his senses again like a deep green sea. Only Basini's flickering words shone out on it like the glint of little silvery fishes.

He was still holding Basini off with his arms. But something made them heavy, like a moist, torpid warmth; the muscles in them were slackening . . . he forgot them. . . . Only when another of those darting words touched him did he start awake again, all at once feeling this very instant, as in a dream, his hands had drawn Basini closer.

Then he wanted to shake himself into wakefulness, wanted to shout at himself: Basini's tricking you, he's just trying to drag you down to where he is, so that you can't despise him any more! But the cry was never uttered, nor was there any sound anywhere in the whole huge building; throughout the corridors the dark tides of silence seemed to lie motionless in sleep.

He struggled to get back to himself. But those tides were like black sentinels at all the doors.

Then Törless abandoned his search for words. Lust, which had been slowly seeping into him, emanating from every single moment of desperation, had now grown to its full stature. It lay naked at his side and covered his head with its soft black cloak. And into his ear it whispered sweet words of resignation, while its warm fingers thrust all questionings and obligations aside as futile. And it whispered: In solitude you can do what you will.

Only in the moment when he was swept away he woke fleetingly, frantically clutching at the one thought: This is not myself! It's not me! . . . But tomorrow it will be me again! . . . Tomorrow . . .

On Tuesday evening the first of the other boys returned. The rest were arriving only by the night trains. There was unceasing bustle in the building.

Törless met his friends curtly and sullenly; he had not forgotten. And then, too, they came back bringing from outside such a whiff of vigour and man-of-the-world confidence. It shamed him, who now cared only for the stuffy air between four narrow walls.

He was, indeed, often ashamed now. But it was not actually so much because of what he had let himself be seduced into doing—for that was nothing so very rare at boarding-school—as because he now found he could not quite help having a kind of tenderness for Basini, while on the other hand he felt more intensely than ever how despised and humiliated this creature was.

He quite often had secret meetings with him. He took him to all the hiding-places he had learnt of from Beineberg, and since he himself was not good at such furtive adventurings, Basini soon knew the way everywhere better than he did and became the leader.

But at night he could not rest for jealousy, keeping watch on Beineberg and Reiting.

These two, however, held aloof from Basini. Perhaps they were already bored with him. At any rate, some change seemed to have taken place in them. Beineberg had become gloomy and reserved; when he spoke, it was only to throw out mysterious hints of something that was imminent. Reiting seemed to have diverted his interest to other things; with his usual deftness he was again weaving the web for some plot or other, trying to win over some by doing

them little favours and frightening others by showing them that—
by some obscure cunning of his own—he knew their secrets.

However, when the three of them were at last alone together,
the other two urged that Basini should very soon be given orders
to appear once more in the cubbyhole or the attic.

Törless tried, on all sorts of pretexts, to postpone this, and at
the same time suffered ceaselessly because of this secret sympathy
for Basini.

Even a few weeks earlier such a state of mind would have been
utterly alien to him; for he came of sturdy, sound, and natural
stock.

But it would be entirely wrong to believe that Basini had aroused
in Törless a desire that was—however fleetingly and perplexedly—
a thorough-going and real one. True, something like passion had
been aroused in him, but 'love' was quite certainly only a casual,
haphazard term for it, and the boy Basini himself was no more than
a substitute, a provisional object of this longing. For although Törless did debase himself with him, his desire was never satisfied by
him; on the contrary, it went on growing out beyond Basini, growing out into some new and aimless craving.

*　　*　　*

At first it had been purely and simply the nakedness of the boy's
slim body that dazzled him.

The feeling it had given him was no different from what he would
have felt had he been confronted with the naked body of a little
girl, a body still utterly sexless, merely beautiful. It had been an
overwhelming shock . . . a state of marvel . . . And the inevitable
purity of this feeling was what lent the appearance of affection—
this new and wonderfully uneasy emotion—to his relationship with
Basini. Everything else had little to do with it. All the other feelings—the erotic desire itself—had been there long before; it had
all been there much earlier, indeed even before he had come to
know Božena. It was the secret, aimless, melancholy sensuality of
adolescence, a sensuality attaching itself to no person, and like the
moist, black, sprouting earth in early spring, or like dark, subterranean waters that some chance event will cause to rise, sweeping
the walls away.

The experience that Törless had gone through turned out to be
this event. Surprise, misunderstanding, confusion about his own

feelings, all combined to smash open the hushed hiding-places where all that was secret, taboo, torrid, vague and solitary in his soul was accumulated, and to send the flood of dark stirrings moving out in Basini's direction. And here it was that for the first time they encountered something warm, something that breathed and was fragrant, was flesh, in which these vaguely roving dreams took on form and had their share in the beauty of the flesh, instead of in squalor such as they had been blighted with, in the depths of his loneliness, by his experience with Božena. This now all at once flung open a gate, a way ahead into life, and in the half-light of this condition everything now mingled—wishes and reality, debauched fantasies and instant impressions that still bore the warm traces of life itself, stimuli from without, and flames that came flaring up from within, mantling the sensations in such a glare that they were unrecognisable.

But all this was beyond Törless's own power of discrimination; for him it was all run together in a single, blurred, undifferentiated emotion, which in his first surprise he might well take for love.

*   *   *

It was not long before he learnt to evaluate it more accurately. From then on he was restlessly driven hither and thither by uneasiness. Every object he picked up he laid down again as soon as he had touched it. He could not talk to any of the other boys without falling inexplicably silent or absent-mindedly changing the subject several times. It would also happen sometimes that while he was speaking a wave of shame flooded through him, so that he grew red, began to stammer, and had to turn away. . . .

By day he avoided Basini. When he could not help looking at him, it almost always had a sobering effect. Every movement of Basini's filled him with disgust, the vague shadows of his illusions gave way to a cold, blunt lucidity, and his soul seemed to shrivel up until there was nothing left but the memory of a former desire that now seemed unspeakably senseless and repulsive. He would stamp his foot and double up as if thus he could escape from this anguish of shame.

He wondered what the others would say to him if they knew his secret—what would his parents say?—and the masters?

But this last turn of the knife always put an end to his torments. A cool weariness would then come over him; the hot, slack skin of his body would then grow taut again in a pleasurable cold shiver. At such times he would be still and let everyone pass him by. But there was in him a certain contempt for them all. Secretly he suspected the very worst of everyone he spoke to.

And he imagined, into the bargain, that he could see no trace of shame in them. He did not think that they suffered as he knew he did. The crown of thorns that his tormented conscience set on his own brow seemed to be missing from theirs.

Yet he felt like one who had awakened from the throes of some long agony—like one who had been brushed by the silent and mysterious finger-tips of dissolution—like one who cannot forget the tranquil wisdom of a long illness.

This was a state in which he felt happy, and the moments came again and again when he yearned for it.

They always began with his once more being able to look at Basini with indifference and to face out the loathsome and beastly thing with a smile. Then he knew that he *would* debase himself, but he supplied it all with a new meaning. The uglier and unworthier everything was that Basini had to offer him, the greater was the contrast with that awareness of suffering sensibility which would afterwards set in.

Törless would withdraw into some corner from which he could observe without himself being seen. When he shut his eyes, a vague sense of urgency would rise up in him, and when he opened his eyes he could find nothing that corresponded to it. And then suddenly the thought of Basini would loom up and concentrate everything in itself. Soon it would lose all definite outline. It seemed no longer to belong to him, and seemed no longer to refer to Basini. It was something that was encircled by a whirling throng of emotions, as though by lecherous women in high-necked long robes, with masks over their faces.

Törless knew no name for any of these emotions, nor did he know what any of them portended; but it was precisely in this that the intoxicating fascination lay. He no longer knew himself; and out of this very fact his urge grew into a wild, contemptuous debauchery, as when at some *fête galante* the lights are suddenly put out and nobody knows who it is he pulls down to the ground and covers with kisses.

*   *   *

Later, when he had got over his adolescent experiences, Törless became a young man whose mind was both subtle and sensitive. By that time he was one of those aesthetically inclined intellectuals who find there is something soothing in a regard for law and indeed—to some extent at least—for public morals too, since it frees them from the necessity of ever thinking about anything coarse, anything that is remote from the finer spiritual processes. And yet the magnificent external correctitude of these people, with its slight touch of irony, at once becomes associated with boredom and callousness if they are expected to show any more personal interest in particular instances of the workings of law and morality. For the only real interest they feel is concentrated on the growth of their own soul, or personality, or whatever one may call the thing within us that every now and then increases by the addition of some idea picked up between the lines of a book, or which speaks to us in the silent language of a painting the thing that every now and then awakens when some solitary, wayward tune floats past us and away, away into the distance, whence with alien movements tugs at the thin scarlet thread of our blood—the thing that is never there when we are writing minutes, building machines, going to the circus, or following any of the hundreds of other similar occupations.

And so to such people the things that make demands only on their moral correctitude are of the utmost indifference. This was why in his later life Törless never felt remorse for what had happened at that time. His tastes had become so acutely and one-sidedly focused on matters purely of the mind that, supposing he had been told a very similar story about some rake's debaucheries, it would certainly never have occurred to him to direct his indignation against the acts themselves. He would have despised such a person not for being a debauchee, but for being nothing more than that; not for his licentiousness, but for the psychological condition that made him do those things; for being stupid, or because his intellect lacked any emotional counter-weight—that is to say, despising him always only for the picture he presented of something miserable, deprived, and feeble. And he would have despised him in exactly the same way whether his vice lay in sexual debauchery, or in uncontrolled and excessive cigarette-smoking, or in drinking.

And as is the case with all people who are exclusively concerned with heightening their mental faculties, the mere presence of voluptuous and unbridled urges did not count for much with him. It was a pet notion of his that the capacity for enjoyment, and creative talent, and in fact the whole more highly developed side of the inner life, was a piece of jewellery on which one could easily injure oneself. He regarded it as inevitable that a person with a rich and varied inner life experienced moments of which other people must know nothing, and memories that he kept in secret drawers. And all he himself expected of such a person was the ability to make exquisite use of them afterwards.

And so, when somebody whom he once told the story of his youth asked him whether the memory of that episode did not sometimes make him feel uncomfortable, he answered, with a smile: "Of course I don't deny that it was a degrading affair. And why not? The degradation passed off. And yet it left something behind—that small admixture of a toxic substance which is needed to rid the soul of its over-confident, complacent healthiness, and to give it instead a sort of health that is more acute, and subtler, and wiser.

"And anyway, would you try to count the hours of degradation that leave their brand-marks on the soul after every great passion? You need only think of the hours of deliberate humiliation in love— those rapt hours when lovers bend down as though leaning over a deep well, or one lays his ear on the other's heart, listening for the sound of impatient claws as the restless great cats scratch on their prison walls. And only in order to feel their own trembling! Only in order to feel terrified at their loneliness up there above those dark, corroding depths! Only—in their dread of being alone with those sinister forces—to take refuge wholly in each other!

"Just look young married couples straight in the eyes. What those eyes say is: So that's what you think, is it?—oh, but you've no notion how deep we can sink! What those eyes express is light-hearted mockery of anyone who knows nothing of so much that they know, and the affectionate pride of those who have gone together through all the circles of hell.

"And just as such lovers go that way together, so I at that time went through all those things, but on my own."

*   *   *

Nevertheless, even if that was Törless's view of it later on, at this time, when he was still exposed to the storm of solitary, yearning feelings, he was far from always being confident that everything would turn out all right in the end. The enigmas that had been tormenting him only a short time ago were still having a vague after-effect, which went on vibrating in the background of his experiences, like a deep note resounding from afar. These were the very things he did not want to think of now.

But at times he remembered it all. And then he would be overwhelmed with utter despair, and was at the mercy of a quite different, weary, hopeless sense of shame.

Yet he could not account for this either.

The reason for it lay in the particular conditions of life at this school. Here youthful, upsurging energies were held captive behind grey walls and, having no other outlet, they filled the imagination with random wanton fancies that caused more than one boy to lose his head.

A certain degree of debauchery was even considered manly, dashing, a bold gesture of taking for oneself the pleasures one was still forbidden. And it seemed all the manlier when compared with the wretchedly respectable appearance of most of the masters. For then the admonishing word 'morality' became ludicrously associated with narrow shoulders, a little paunch, thin legs, and eyes roaming as harmlessly behind their spectacles as the silly sheep at pasture, as though life were nothing but a flowery meadow of solemn edification.

And, finally, at school one still had no knowledge of life and no notion of all those degrees of beastliness and corruption, down to the level of the diseased and the grotesque, which are what primarily fills the adult with revulsion when he hears of such things.

All these inhibiting factors, which are far more effective than we can really appreciate, were lacking in him. It was his very naivety that had plunged him into vice.

For the moral force of resistance, that sensitive faculty of the spirit which he was later to rate so high, was not yet developed in him either. However, there were already signs of its growth. True, Törless went astray, seeing as yet only the shadows cast ahead into his consciousness by something still unrecognised, and mistaking them for reality: but he had a task to fulfil where he himself was concerned, a spiritual task—even if he was still not equipped to undertake it.

All he knew was that he had been following something as yet undefined along a road that led deep into his inner being; and in doing so he had grown tired. He had got into the way of hoping for extraordinary, mysterious discoveries, and that habit had brought him into the narrow, winding passages of sensuality. It was all the result not of perversity, but of a psychological situation in which he had lost his sense of direction.

And this disloyalty to something in himself that was serious and worth striving for was the very thing that filled him with a vague sense of guilt. An indefinable hidden disgust never quite left him, and an indistinct dread pursued him like one who in the dark no longer knows whether he is still walking along his chosen road or has lost it, not knowing where.

Then he would endeavour not to think of anything at all. He drifted through life, dumb and bemused and oblivious of all his earlier questionings. The subtle enjoyment that lay in his acts of degradation became ever rarer.

It had not yet left him entirely; but still, at the end of this period Törless did not even try to oppose when further decisions were taken regarding Basini's fate.

This happened some days later, when the three of them were together in the cubby-hole. Beineberg was very grave.

Reiting spoke first: "Beineberg and I think things can't go on as they have been going in the matter of Basini. He's got used to being at our beck and call. It doesn't make him miserable any more. He's become as impudently familiar as a servant. So it's time to go a step further with him. Do you agree?"

"Well, I don't even know yet what you mean to do with him."

"Yes, it isn't so easy to work that out. We must humiliate him still more and make him knuckle under completely. I should like to see how far it can go. The question is only how to do it. Of course I have one or two rather nice ideas about it. For instance, we could give him a flogging and make him sing psalms of thanksgiving at the same time . . . it would be a song well worth hearing, I think—every note covered with gooseflesh, so to speak. We could make him bring us the filthiest things in his mouth, like a dog. Or we could take him along to Božena's and make him read his mother's letters aloud while Božena provided the suitable kind of jokes to go with it. But there's plenty of time to think about all that. We can turn it over in our minds, polish it up, and keep on adding new refinements. Without the appropriate details it's still a bit of a bore, for the present. Perhaps we'll hand him right over to the class to deal with. That would be the most sensible thing to do. If each one of so many contributes even a little, it'll be enough to tear him to pieces. And anyway, I have a liking for these mass movements. Nobody means to contribute anything spectacular, and yet the waves keep rising higher and higher, until they break over everyone's head.

You chaps just wait and see, nobody will lift a finger, but all the same there'll be a terrific upheaval. Instigating a thing like that gives me really quite particular pleasure."

"But what do you mean to do first of all?"

"As I said, I should like to save *that* up for later. For the time being I should be content with softening him up again in every respect, either by threats or by beating him."

"What for?" Törless asked before he could stop himself.

They looked each other straight in the eye.

"Oh, don't go and play the innocent!" Reiting said. "You know perfectly well what I'm talking about."

Törless said nothing. How much had Reiting found out? Or was he only taking a shot in the dark?

"Don't tell me you've forgotten what Beineberg told you that time—about what Basini will lend himself to."

Törless drew a breath of relief.

"Well, there's nothing to look so amazed about. You gaped just the same that time, too, but it's not as if it were anything so very frightful. Incidentally, Beineberg does the same with Basini—he's told me so himself." And Reiting looked across at Beineberg with an ironical grimace. That was very much his way: he had no scruple about giving somebody else away in public.

Beineberg did not respond at all. He remained sitting in his thoughtful attitude, scarcely glancing up.

"Well, aren't you going to come out with your idea?" Reiting said to Beineberg, and then, turning to Törless, he went on: "The fact is he has a crazy notion he wants to try out on Basini, and he's set on doing it before we do anything else. I must say it's quite an amusing one, too."

Beineberg remained grave. He now looked hard at Törless and said: "You remember what we talked about that time behind the coats?"

"Yes."

"I never got talking about it again, because after all there's no point in just talking. But I've often thought about it—I assure you, often. And what Reiting has just been telling you is true too. I've done the same with Basini as he has. In fact, perhaps a bit more. And that was because, as I told you that time, I believe sex may perhaps be the right gateway. It was a sort of experiment. I didn't see any other way to get to what I was looking for. But there's no sense in this random sort of going on. I've been thinking about it—for nights on end—trying to work out how one could put something systematic in the place of it.

"Now I think I've got it, and we shall make the experiment. Now you will see too how wrong you were that time. All our knowledge of the universe is doubtful. Everything really works differently. At that time we discovered this, so to speak, from the reverse side, in looking for points where the perfectly natural explanation falls over its own feet. But now I trust I am able to demonstrate the positive side—the other side!"

Reiting set out the tea-cups. As he did so, he nudged Törless cheerfully. "Now pay attention. It's a pretty smart thing he's thought up!"

But Beineberg made a quick movement and extinguished the lamp. In the darkness there was only the flame of the spirit-stove, casting flickering bluish gleams on their faces.

"I put the lamp out, Törless, because it is better to talk about such things in the dark. And you, Reiting, can go to sleep for all I care, if you're too stupid to understand profounder things."

Reiting laughed as if he were amused.

"Well," Beineberg began, "you remember our conversation. At that time you yourself had discovered that little peculiarity in mathematics, that example of the fact that our thinking has no even, solid, safe basis, but goes along, as it were, over holes in the ground—shutting its eyes, ceasing to exist for a moment, and yet arriving safely at the other side. Really we ought to have despaired long ago, for in all fields our knowledge is streaked with such crevasses—nothing but fragments drifting in a fathomless ocean.

"But we do not despair. We go on feeling as safe as if we were on firm ground. If we didn't have this solid feeling of certainty, we would kill ourselves in desperation about the wretchedness of our intellect. This feeling is with us continually, holding us together, and at every moment protectively taking our intellect into its arms like a small child. As soon as we have become aware of this, we cannot go on denying the existence of the soul. As soon as we analyse our mental life and recognise the inadequacy of the intellect, we feel all this very clearly. We feel it—do you understand? For if it were not for this feeling, we should collapse like empty sacks.

"Only we have forgotten to pay attention to this feeling. But it is one of the oldest feelings there is. Even thousands of years ago peoples living thousands of miles apart from each other knew of it. Once one has begun to take an interest in these things, one can no longer deny them. But I don't want to talk you into believing what I believe. I'm only going to tell you the bare essentials, so that you won't be quite unprepared. The facts themselves will provide the proof.

"Now, assuming that the soul exists, it follows as a matter of course—doesn't it?—that we cannot have any deeper longing than to restore the lost contact with it, become familiar with it again, learn to make better use of its powers again, and gain for ourselves a share in the supernatural forces that are dormant in its depths.

"For all this is possible. It has been done more than once. The miracles, the saints, and the holy men of India—they all bear witness to such events."

"Look here," Törless interjected, "you're rather talking yourself into believing this, aren't you? You had to put the lamp out specially so that you could. But would you talk just the same if we were sitting downstairs among the others, who are doing their geography or history or writing letters home, where the light is bright and the usher may come round between the desks? Wouldn't this talk of yours seem a bit fantastic even to yourself there, a bit presumptuous, as though we were not the same as the others, but were living in another world, say eight hundred years ago?"

"No, my dear Törless, I should maintain the same things. Incidentally, it's one of your faults that you're always looking at what the others are doing. You're not independent enough. Writing letters home! Thinking of your parents where such things are concerned! What reason have you to believe they could at all follow us here? We are young, we are a generation later, and perhaps things are destined for us that they never deamt of in all their lives. At least, I feel that it is so.

"Still, what's the use of going on talking? I shall prove it to you both anyway."

After they had been silent for a while, Törless said: "And how, if it comes to that, do you mean to set about getting hold of your soul?"

"I'm not going to explain that to you now, all the more since I shall have to do it in front of Basini anyway."

"But you could at least give us some sort of idea."

"Well, it's like this. History teaches that there is only one way: entering into one's own being in meditation. Only this is where the difficulty begins. The saints of old, for instance, at the time when the soul still manifested itself in miracles, were able to reach this goal by means of fervent prayer. The fact is at that time the soul was of a different nature. Now that way is not open to us. Today we don't know what to do. The soul has changed, and unfortunately between then and now there lie times when nobody paid proper attention to the subject and the tradition was irrevocably lost. We can only find a new way by means of most careful thought. This is what I have been intensively occupied with recently. The most obvious choice is probably to do it by the aid of hypnosis. Only it has never yet been tried. All they do is keep on performing the same commonplace tricks, which is why the methods haven't yet been tested for their capacity to lead towards higher things. The final thing I want to say now is that I shall not hypnotise Basini by the usual methods but according to one of my own, which, if I am not mistaken, is similar to one that was used in the Middle Ages."

"Isn't Beineberg a treat?" Reiting exclaimed, laughing. "Only he ought to have lived in the age when they went round prophesying the end of the world. Then he would have ended up by really believing it was due to his soul-magic that the world remained intact."

When Törless looked at Beineberg after these mocking words, he saw that his face was quite rigid and distorted as though convulsed with concentration, and in the next moment he felt the touch of ice-cold fingers. He was startled by this high degree of excitement. But then the tension relaxed, the grip on his arm slackened.

"Oh, it was nothing," Beineberg said. "Just an idea. I felt as though something special were just going to occur to me, a clue to how to do it. . . ."

"I say, you really are a bit touched," Reiting said jovially. "You always used to be a tough sort of chap, you only went in for all this stuff as a sort of game. But now you're like an old woman."

"Oh, leave me alone—you've no idea what it means to know

such things are at hand and to be on the point of reaching them today or any day now!"

"Stop quarrelling," Törless said. In the course of the last few weeks he had become a good deal firmer and more energetic. "For all I care each of you can do what he likes. I don't believe in anything at all—neither in your crafty tortures, Reiting, nor in Beineberg's hopes. For my own part, I have nothing to say. I'm simply going to wait and see what you two produce."

"So when shall it be?"

The night after the next was decided on.

Törless made no resistance to its approach. And indeed in this new situation his feeling for Basini had completely died out. This was quite fortunate for him, since at least it freed him all at once from the wavering between shame and desire that he had been unable to get out of by exerting his own strength. Now at least he had a straightforward, plain repugnance for Basini; it was as if the humiliations intended for the latter might be capable of defiling him too.

For the rest he was absent-minded and could not bring himself to think of anything seriously, least of all about the things that had once so intensely preoccupied him.

Only when he went upstairs to the attic together with Reiting—Beineberg and Basini having gone ahead—the memory of what had once gone on in him became more vivid again. He could not rid himself of the sound of the cocksure words he had flung at Beineberg, and he yearned to regain that confidence. He lingered a little on each of the stairs, dragging his feet. But his former certainty would not return. Though he recalled all the thoughts he had had at that time, they seemed to pass him by, remote as though they were no more than the shadowy images of what he had once thought.

Finally, since he found nothing in himself, his curiosity turned again to the events that were to come from outside; and this impelled him forward.

Swiftly he followed Reiting, hurrying up the last of the stairs.

While the iron door was groaning shut behind them, he felt, with a sigh, that though Beineberg's plan might be only laughable hocus-pocus, at least there was something firm and deliberate about it, whereas everything in himself lay in impenetrable confusion and perplexity.

Tense with expectation, they sat down on one of the horizontal beams, as though in a theatre.

Beineberg was already there with Basini.

The situation seemed favourable to his plan. The darkness, the stale air, the foul, brackish smell emanating from the water-tubs, all this generated a feeling of drowsiness, of never being able to wake up again, a weary, sluggish indolence.

Beineberg told Basini to undress. Now in the darkness Basini's naked skin had a bluish, mouldy glimmer; there was nothing in the least provocative about it.

Suddenly Beineberg pulled the revolver out of his pocket and aimed it at Basini.

Even Reiting leaned forward as though preparing to leap between the two of them at any moment.

But Beineberg was smiling—smiling in a strangely distorted way, as though he did not really mean to at all, but rather as if fanatical words welling up in him had twisted his lips into a queer grimace.

Basini had dropped to his knees, as though paralysed, and was staring at the gun, his eyes wide with fear.

"Get up," Beineberg said. "If you do exactly what I tell you, you won't come to any harm. But if you disturb me by making the slightest difficulty, I shall shoot you down like a dog. Take note of that!

"As a matter of fact, I am going to kill you anyway, but you'll come back to life again. Dying is not so alien to us as you think it is. We die every day—in our deep, dreamless sleep."

Once again the wild smile distorted Beineberg's mouth.

"Now kneel down, up there"—he pointed to a wide horizontal beam that ran across the attic at about waist-level—"that's it— quite straight—hold yourself perfectly straight—keep your shoulders back. And now keep looking at this—but no blinking! You must keep your eyes open as wide as you possibly can!"

Beineberg put a little spirit-lamp in front of Basini in such a position that he had to bend his head back slightly in order to look right into the flame.

It was difficult to make anything out exactly in the dimness, but after some time it seemed that Basini's body was beginning to swing to and fro like a pendulum. The bluish gleams were flickering on his skin. Now and then Törless thought he could see Basini's face, contorted with terror.

After a time Beineberg asked: "Are you feeling tired?"

The question was put in the usual way that hypnotists put it.

Then he began explaining, his voice low and husky:

"Dying is only a result of our way of living. We live from one thought to the next, from one feeling to the next. Our thoughts and feelings don't flow along quietly like a stream, they 'occur' to us, which means they 'run against' us, crash into us like stones that have been thrown. If you watch yourself carefully, you'll realise that the soul isn't something that changes its colours in smooth gradations, but that the thoughts jump out of it like numbers out of a black hole. Now you have a thought or a feeling, and all at once there's a different one there, as if it had popped up out of nothingness. If you pay attention, you can even notice the instant between two thoughts when everything's black. For us that instant—once we have grasped it—is simply death.

"For our life is nothing but setting milestones and hopping from one to the next, hopping over thousands of death-seconds every day. We live as it were only in the points of rest. And that is why we have such a ridiculous dread of irrevocable death, for that is the thing that is absolutely without milestones, the fathomless abyss that we fall into. It is in fact the utter negation of this kind of living.

"But it is so only if it is looked at from the point of view of this kind of living, and only for the person who has not learnt to experience himself otherwise than from moment to moment.

"I call this The Hopping Evil, and the secret lies in overcoming it. One must awaken the feeling of one's own life in oneself as of something peacefully gliding along. In the moment when this really happens one is just as near to death as to life. One ceases to live—in our earthly sense of the word—but one cannot die any more either, for with the cancelling out of life one has also cancelled out death. This is the instant of immortality, the instant when the soul steps out of our narrow brain into the wonderful gardens of its own life.

"So now pay close attention to what I say.

"Put all your thoughts to sleep, keep staring into this little flame . . . Don't think from one thing to another . . . Concentrate all your attention in an inward direction . . . Keep staring at the flame . . . Your thoughts are slowing down, like an engine gradually running slower and slower . . . slower . . . and . . . slower . . . Keep staring inward . . . Keep on staring . . . till you find the point where you feel yourself, feeling without any thought or sensation . . .

"Your silence will be all the answer I want. Don't avert your gaze from within!"

Minutes passed.

"Do you feel the point . . . ?"

No answer.

"Do you hear, Basini, have you done it?"

Silence.

Beineberg stood up, and his gaunt shadow rose high beside the beam. Up above, Basini's body could be seen rocking to and fro, drunk with darkness.

"Turn sideways," Beineberg ordered. "What obeys now is only the brain," he murmured, "the brain, which still goes on functioning mechanically for a while, until the last traces of what the soul imprinted on it are consumed. The soul itself is somewhere else— in its next form of existence. It is no longer wearing the fetters of the laws of Nature." He turned to Törless for a moment: "It is no longer condemned to the punishment of making a body heavy and holding it together. Bend forward, Basini—that's right—slowly, slowly. And a bit further. A bit further still. As the last trace is extinguished in the brain, the muscles will relax and the empty body will collapse. Or it will simply float, I don't know which. The soul has left the body of its own accord. This is not the ordinary sort of death. Perhaps the body will float in the air because there's nothing left in possession of it—no force either of life or of death. Bend forward . . . And a bit more."

* * *

At this moment Basini, who had been obeying all these commands out of sheer terror, lost his balance and crashed to the floor at Beineberg's feet.

Basini yelled with pain. Reiting burst out laughing. But Beineberg, who had fallen back a step, uttered a gurgling cry of rage when he realized that he had been tricked. With a swift movement he ripped his leather belt from his waist, seized Basini by the hair, and began lashing him furiously. All the tremendous tension he had been under now found release in these frantic blows. And Basini howled with pain, so that the attic rang with lamentation as if a dog were howling.

* * *

Törless had sat in silence during the whole of the previous scene. He has been secretly hoping that something might happen after all that would carry him back to the emotional realm he had lost. It was a foolish hope, as he had known all along, but it had held him spellbound. Now, however, it seemed to be all over. The scene revolted him. There was no longer any trace of thought in him, only mute, inert repugnance.

He got up quietly and left without saying a word, all quite mechanically.

Beineberg was still lashing away at Basini and would obviously go on doing so to the point of exhaustion.

When Törless was in bed, he felt: This is the end of it. Something is over and done with.

During the next few days he went on quietly with his school work, not bothering about anything else. Reiting and Beineberg were probably now carrying out their programme item by item; but he kept out of their way.

Then on the fourth day, when nobody happened to be there, Basini came up to him. He looked ghastly, his face was wan and thin, and in his eyes there was a feverish flicker of constant dread. Glancing nervously about him, he spoke hurriedly and in gasps: "You've got to help me! You're the only person who can! I can't stand any more of their tormenting me. I've stood everything up to now, but if it goes on like this they'll kill me!"

Törless found it disagreeable to have to say anything in reply to this. At last he said: "I can't help you. It's all your own fault. You're to blame for what's happening to you."

"But only a short time ago you were still so nice and good to me."

"Never."

"But——"

"Shut up! It wasn't me. It was a dream. A mood. It actually suits me quite well that your new disgrace has torn you away from me. For me it's better that way. . . ."

Basini let his head sink. He realized that a sea of grey and sober disappointment lay now between him and Törless. . . . Törless was cold, a different person.

Then he threw himself down on his knees before Törless, beat his head on the floor and cried: "Help me! Help me! For God's sake help me!"

Törless hesitated for a moment. He felt neither any wish to help Basini nor enough indignation to push him away. So he acted on the first thought that occurred to him. "Come to the attic tonight. I'll talk it over with you again." But the next moment he was already regretting it.

'Why stir it all up again?' he wondered, and then said, as though on second thoughts: "But they'd notice. It can't be done."

"Oh no, they were up all last night with me, till dawn. They'll sleep tonight."

"All right then, for all I care. But don't expect me to help you."

*   *   *

It was against his own judgment that Törless had decided to meet Basini. For his real conviction was that inwardly it was all over—there was nothing more to be got out of it. Now only a sort of pedantry, some stubborn conscientiousness, had inspired him with the notion of again meddling with these things, even though he knew from the start that it was hopeless.

He felt the need to get it over quickly.

Basini did not know how he was expected to behave. He had been beaten so much that he scarcely dared to stir. Every trace of personality seemed to have gone out of him; only in his eyes there was still a little residue of it, and it peered out shakily, imploringly, as though clutching at Törless.

He waited to see what Törless would do.

Finally Törless broke the silence. He spoke rapidly, in a bored manner, as though it were merely for the sake of form that he was again going over a matter which had long been settled.

"I'm not going to help you. It's a fact, I did take an interest in you for a time, but that's over now. You're really nothing but a cowardly rotter. Definitely that's all you are. So what should make me take your part? I always used to think there must be some word, some feeling, I could find that would describe you differently. But there's really nothing that describes you better than saying you're a cowardly rotter. That's so simple and meaningless, and still it's all that can be said. Whatever else I wanted from you before, I've forgotten since you got in the way of it with your lecherous desires. I wanted to find a point remote from you, to look at you from there. That was my interest in you. You destroyed it yourself. But that's enough about that, I don't owe you any explanation. Only one more thing—what do you feel like now?"

"What do you expect me to feel like? I can't stand any more of it."

"I suppose they're doing pretty bad things to you now, and it hurts?"

"Yes."

"But just pain—is it as simple as that? You feel that you're suffering and you want to escape from it? Simply that, without any complications?"

Basini had no answer.

"Oh, all right, I was just asking by the way, not really formulating it precisely enough. Still, that doesn't matter. I have no more to do with you. I've already told you that. You don't arouse the slightest feeling in me any more. Do whatever you like."

Törless turned to go.

Then Basini tore his clothes off and thrust himself against Törless. His body was covered with weals. It was a disgusting sight, and his movements were as wretched as those of a clumsy prostitute. Nauseated, Törless shook him off and went.

But he had taken scarcely more than a few paces into the darkness when he collided with Reiting.

"What's all this? So you have secret meetings with Basini, do you?"

Törless followed Reiting's gaze, looking back at Basini. Just at the place where Basini was standing a broad beam of moonlight came in through a skylight, making the bluish-tinged skin with the weals on it look like the skin of a leper. As though he had to find some excuse for this sight, Törless said: "He asked me."

"What does he want?"

"He wants me to protect him."

"Well, he's come to the right person, hasn't he!"

"I might really do it, only the whole thing bores me."

Reiting glanced up, unpleasantly surprised. Then he turned angrily to Basini.

"We'll teach you to start secret plots against us! And your guardian angel Törless will look on in person and enjoy it."

Törless had already turned away, but this piece of spite, so obviously aimed at him, held him back and, without stopping to think, he said:

"Look here, Reiting, I shall not do anything of the kind. I'm not going to have any more to do with it. I'm sick of the whole thing."

"All of a sudden?"

"Yes, all of a sudden. Before, I was searching for something behind it all. . . ." He did not know why he said this or why now again it kept on coming back into his mind.

"Aha, second sight!"

"Yes. But now I can see only one thing—how vulgar and brutal you and Beineberg are."

"But you shall also see how Basini eats mud," Reiting sneered.

"That doesn't interest me any more."

"It certainly used to!"

"I've already told you, only as long as Basini's state of mind was a riddle to me."

"And now?"

"Now I don't know anything about riddles. Things just happen: that's the sum total of wisdom." Törless was surprised to find himself all at once again uttering phrases from that lost realm of feeling. And so, when Reiting mockingly retorted that one did not have to travel far to pick up that sort of wisdom, an angry sense of superiority shot up in him and made him speak harshly. For a moment he despised Reiting so much that he would really have enjoyed trampling him underfoot.

"Gibe away as much as you like. But the things you two are up to are nothing more or less than brainless, senseless, disgusting torture of someone weaker than you are!"

Reiting cast a sidelong glance at Basini, who was pricking up his ears.

"You mind what you say, Törless!"

"Disgusting and filthy! You heard what I said!"

Now Reiting burst out too. "I forbid you to be abusive about us in front of Basini!"

"Oh, to hell with you! Who are you to forbid anything? That time is over. Once I used to respect you and Beineberg, but now I can see what you really are—stupid, revolting, beastly fools!"

"Shut up, or——" and Reiting seemed about to leap at Törless.

Törless retreated slightly, yelling at him: "D'you think I'm going to fight with you? You needn't think Basini's worth that to me! Do what you like with him, but get out of my way!"

Reiting seemed to have changed his mind about hitting Törless; he stepped aside. He did not even touch Basini. But Törless knew him well enough to realize one thing: from now on all that was malicious and dangerous in Reiting would be a perpetual threat to him.

It was in the afternoon, only two days later, that Reiting and Beineberg came up to Törless.

He saw the unpleasant look in their eyes. Obviously Beineberg now bore *him* a grudge for the ridiculous collapse of his prophecies, and Reiting had probably been egging him on, into the bargain.

"I hear you've been abusive about us. And in front of Basini, at that. Why?"

Törless made no answer.

"You realise we are not going to put up with that sort of thing. But because it's you, and we're used to your odd whims, and don't attach overmuch importance to them, we're prepared to let it go at that. There's just one thing you have to do, though." In spite of the amiability of the words, there was something malevolently expectant in Beineberg's eyes.

"Basini's coming to the lair tonight. We're going to discipline him for having set you against us. When you see us leave the dormitory, come after us."

But Törless refused. "You two can do what you like. You'll have to leave me out of it."

"Tonight we're going to have our fun with Basini, for the last time, and tomorrow we're handing him over to the class, because he's beginning to be difficult."

"You can do whatever you like."

"But you're going to be there too."

"No."

"It's in front of you especially that Basini must see nothing can help him against us. Only yesterday he was refusing to carry out our orders. We half thrashed him to death, but he stuck to it. We'll have to resort to moral means again, and humiliate him first in front of you and then in front of the class."

"But I'm not going to be there."

"Why not?"

"I'm not going to be there, that's all."

Beineberg drew a deep breath; it looked as if he were gathering together all the venom he had in him. Then he stepped up very close to Törless.

"Do you really think we don't know why? Do you think we don't know how far you've gone with Basini?"

"No further than you two."

"Indeed? And I suppose that's why he chooses precisely you for his patron saint? Eh? That's why he has this great confidence precisely in you, is it? You needn't think we're stupid enough to believe that!"

Törless grew angry. "I don't care what you know, I don't want to have any more to do with your filthy goings-on!"

"Oh, so you're getting impertinent again!"

"You two make me sick! Your beastliness is utterly senseless! That's what's so revolting about you."

"Now listen to me. You ought to be grateful to us for quite a number of things. If you think that in spite of that you can now set yourself up above us, who have been your instructors, then you're making a grave mistake. Are you coming along tonight, yes or no?"

"No!"

"My dear Törless, if you rebel against us and don't put in an appearance, then you've got coming to you what came to Basini. You know the situation Reiting found you in. That's sufficient. Whether we have done more, or less, won't be of much help to you. We shall use everything against you. You're much too stupid and clumsy in such things to be a match for us.

"So if you don't see reason in good time, we shall expose you to the class as Basini's accomplice. Then it'll be up to him to protect you. Understand?"

A flood of threats, now from Beineberg, now from Reiting, and now uttered by both together, broke over Törless like a storm. And when they had both gone, he rubbed his eyes as if awakening from a dream. But of course it was just like Reiting really; in his anger he was capable of the utmost infamy, and Törless's offensive and mutinous words seemed to have cut him to the quick. And Beineberg? He had looked as if he were shaking with a hatred that he had been concealing for years—and this merely because he had made a fool of himself in front of Törless.

But the more menacingly events hung over Törless's head, the more indifferent he became and the more mechanical it all seemed to him. Their threats frightened him. So much he admitted to himself; but that was all. This danger had drawn him right into the maelstrom of reality.

He went to bed. He saw Beineberg and Reiting leave the dormitory, and then Basini shuffling wearily after them. But he did not follow.

Yet he was tortured by frightful imaginings. For the first time he thought of his parents again with some affection. He could feel that he needed the calm, safe ground of home if he was to consolidate and develop the things in himself that had hitherto only got him into trouble.

But what were these things? He had no time to think about it now and brood over what was going on. All he felt was an impassioned longing to escape from this confused, whirling state of things, a longing for quietness, for books. He felt his soul as black earth in which the seeds were already beginning to sprout, though nobody could yet know what flowers they would bear. He found himself thinking of a gardener, who waters his flower-beds at the break of every day, tending his plants with even, patient kindness. He could not rid himself of the image: that patient certainty seemed now to be the focus of all his longing. This was how it must be! This was the way! Törless now felt it clearly; and, overruling all his fear and all his qualms, there was the conviction in him that he must exert himself to the utmost in order to attain that state of being.

The only thing he was not yet clear about was what had to be done next. For above all else this yearning for tranquil contemplativeness only heightened his loathing for the intrigues he was faced with now. Besides, he was really afraid of the vengeance that he had now to reckon with. If the other two really did set about defaming him to the class, trying to combat that would cost him a tremendous amount of energy; and energy was the very thing he needed for other purposes just now. And the mere thought of this tangle of events, this collision with the intentions and the will-power of others, a collision so utterly lacking in any higher value, made him shudder with disgust.

And then he remembered a letter he had received from home quite a long time before. It was the answer to one he had written to his parents, telling them, as well as he could, about his peculiar states of mind, though this was before he had been drawn into the sexual adventure. Once again it was a thoroughly prosaic answer, full of well-meant, worthy, boring moral reflections, and it contained the advice to get Basini to give himself up and thus put an end to the undignified and dangerous state of subservience he was in.

Later on Törless had read this letter again when Basini was lying naked beside him on the soft blankets in the lair. And it had given him special pleasure to savour these stolid, plain, sober words while reflecting that his parents, living as they did in that excessive brightness of everyday reality, were doubtless blind to the darkness in which his soul was now crouching, like some lithe and cat-like beast of prey.

But today it was with quite different feelings that he remembered that passage.

He felt himself being enfolded by a pleasant sense of relief, as though under the touch of a firm, kindly hand. In this moment the decision was made. A thought had flashed upon him, and he seized hold of it without a qualm, as though under the guidance of his parents.

He lay awake until the three came back. Then he waited until he could tell, by the regularity of their breathing, that they were asleep. Now he hastily tore a page out of his note-book and, by the dim flicker of the night-light, he wrote in large, wavering letters:

"They're going to hand you over to the class tomorrow. You're in for something terrible. The only way out is to go straight to the

Head and confess. He would get to hear about it all anyway, only you'd be beaten half to death first.

"Put it all on R. and B. Say nothing about me.

"You can see I'm trying to save you."

He pushed this piece of paper into the sleeper's hand.

Then, exhausted with excitement, he fell asleep too.

B eineberg and Reiting seemed willing to grant Törless respite for
at least the whole of the next day.

But where Basini was concerned, things really got moving.

Törless saw Beineberg and Reiting going up to this boy and that,
and watched groups forming round them, and eager whisperings
going on.

And still he did not know whether Basini had found his note or
not, for he had no chance to speak to him, feeling as he did that
he was himself under observation.

As a matter of fact, at first he had been afraid they were talking
about him too. But by now, when he was actually confronted with
the danger, he was so paralysed by its repulsiveness that he could
not have brought himself to lift a finger to ward it off.

It was only later that he joined one of the groups, hesitantly
and quite expecting that they would all instantly turn against
him.

But nobody took any notice of him. For the present it was only
Basini against whom the hunt was up.

The excitement grew. Törless could see it growing. Reiting and
Beineberg had doubtless added various lies of their own to the whole
story.

At first there were grins on all faces, then some grew serious,
and here and there hostile glances were cast in Basini's direction.
Finally the class-room grew dense with a silence that was charged
with tension, with dark, hot, sinister urges.

It happened to be a free afternoon.

They all gathered at the back of the room, by the lockers. Then Basini was summoned.

Beineberg and Reiting took up positions one on each side of him, like warders.

The doors having been locked and sentries posted, the customary procedure of stripping was carried out, to the general amusement.

Reiting had in his hand a packet of letters from Basini's mother to her son, and he began to read aloud.

"My dear little lad . . ."

There was a general guffaw.

"As you know, with the meagre financial resources that I, as a widow, have at my disposal . . ."

Ribald laughter and lewd jokes burst from the crowd. Reiting was about to continue his reading, when suddenly somebody gave Basini a push. Another boy, against whom he stumbled, pushed him away again, half jokingly and half in indignation. A third pushed him on a little further. And suddenly Basini, naked as he was, his mouth agape with terror, was being bounced around the room like a ball, to the accompaniment of laughter, cat-calls, and blows—now to this side of the room, now to that—getting bruised and cut on the sharp corners of desks, falling on to his knees, which were beginning to bleed; and finally, streaked with blood and dust, with wildly staring, stupefied, glassy eyes, he collapsed on the floor and lay still, whereupon silence fell and everyone pressed forward to have a good look at him.

Törless shuddered. Now he had seen the terrible reality behind the threat Beineberg and Reiting had made.

And even now he still did not know what Basini was going to do.

Tomorrow night, it was resolved, Basini was to be tied to a bed and whipped with foils.

*   *   *

But to everyone's disconcerted surprise the headmaster came into the classroom early in the morning. He was accompanied by the form-master and two other members of the staff. Basini was removed from the class and taken to a separate room.

Meanwhile the headmaster delivered an angry speech on the

subject of the brutal bullying that had come to light and announced that there was going to be a very strict investigation into the matter.

Basini had given himself up.

Someone must have warned him of what was still in store for him.

Nobody had any suspicions of Törless. He sat there quietly, sunk in his own thoughts, as though the whole thing did not concern him in the least.

Not even Reiting and Beineberg entertained the idea that he might be the traitor. They themselves had not taken their threats against him seriously; they had uttered them merely in order to intimidate him, in order to make him feel their superiority, and to some extent merely in the heat of the moment. Now, when their rage had passed off, they scarcely gave it another thought. What would in any case have prevented their treating Törless in a similar way was the fact of their being acquainted with his parents and having enjoyed their hospitality. This was so much a matter of course that it also prevented them from fearing any hostile act on his part.

Törless felt no remorse for what he had done. The furtive, cowardly quality about it did not count in comparison with the sense of complete liberation he now had. After all the agitation he had been through he now felt that everything within him was wonderfully clear and spacious.

He did not join in the excited conversations all round him about what was going to happen. He went quietly through the day's routine, keeping to himself.

When evening came and the lamps were lit, he sat down in his place, in front of him the copy-book in which he had made those hasty notes some time ago.

But he did not read them for long. He smoothed the pages with his hand, and it seemed to him that there was a faint fragrance rising from them, like the scent of lavender that clings to old letters.

He was overcome by that tenderness mingled with melancholy which we always feel about a part of our life that irrevocably belongs to the past, when a delicate, pale shadow rises up out of that realm as though with withered flowers in its hands, and in its features we discover a forgotten likeness to ourselves.

And this mournful, faint shadow, this wan fragrance, seemed to be dissolving in a broad, full, warm stream—in life itself, which now lay open before him.

One phase of development was at an end; the soul had formed another annual ring, as a young tree does. And this feeling, as yet wordless, but overwhelming, in itself made up for all that had happened.

Now Törless began leafing through his old notes. The sentences in which he had clumsily recorded what was going on—that manifold amazement and bewilderment in the encounter with life—grew vivid again, and seemed to stir, and began to form a picture. It all lay before him like a brightly lit path on which he could see the imprints of his own hesitant footsteps. But something still seemed to be missing. It was not a new idea that he needed. Yet somehow the whole thing would not quite come to life for him.

He still felt unsure of himself. And now there came the fear of having to stand in front of his teachers the next day and justify himself. And how was he to do it? How could he explain to them? How could he make them understand that dark, mysterious way which he had gone? Supposing they asked him why he had maltreated Basini, surely he could not answer: 'Because I was interested in something going on in my own mind, something I don't know much about even now, in spite of everything—something that makes all that I think about the whole thing seem quite unimportant.'

It was only a small matter, a single step between him and the termination of this phase in his mental development, but it appalled him, as though it were a monstrous abyss that lay ahead.

And even before nightfall Törless was in a state of feverish, panic-stricken excitement.

The next day, when the boys were called up one by one for questioning, Törless was not to be found.

He had been last seen in the evening, sitting over a copy-book, apparently reading.

He was searched for throughout the building. Beineberg slipped away up to the lair to make sure that he was not there.

Finally it became evident that he had run away from school, and the police of the whole district were called upon to look out for him and asked to handle him, if he was found, with all possible discretion.

Meanwhile the enquiry began.

Reiting and Beineberg, who believed that Törless had run away out of fear of their threat of implicating him, felt themselves under an obligation to avert all suspicion from him, and they said everything they could in his favour.

They shifted all the blame on to Basini, and one by one the whole class bore witness to the fact that Basini was a thieving, low character who had responded to the most well-meaning attempts at reforming him only by repeating his offences again and again. Reiting solemnly declared that they realised they had acted wrongly, but that it had only been done because they were sorry for Basini and felt that one of their number should not be delivered up to punishment before every means of benevolent guidance had been tried. And once again the whole form asseverated that the ill-treatment of Basini had been nothing but a spontaneous outbreak, since Basini had rewarded the noble sentiments of those who felt mercifully towards him with the most outrageous and vile derision.

In short, it was a well-rehearsed farce, brilliantly stage-managed by Reiting, and the highest possible moral tone was assumed in putting forward excuses that would find favour in the masters' eyes.

Basini preserved a stupefied silence, no matter what was said. He was still paralysed with terror from his experiences of two days earlier, and the solitary confinement in which he was kept, together with the quiet and matter-of-fact course of the investigation, was in itself a tremendous relief to him. All he wished for was that it might be over soon. Besides, Reiting and Beineberg had not failed to threaten him with the most atrocious revenge if he should dare to say anything against them.

Then Törless was brought in. He had been picked up, dead tired and very hungry, in the next town.

His flight now seemed to be the only mysterious element in the whole affair. But the situation was in his favour. Beineberg and Reiting had done their work well, talking about the nervy state he had been in recently and about his moral sensitiveness, which made him feel it was positively a crime that he, who had known about the whole matter all along, had not immediately gone and reported it, and by this omission had become partly responsible for the catastrophe.

As a result there was now a certain measure of sentimental benevolence in the masters' attitude to Törless, and his class-mates did not fail to prepare him for this.

Nevertheless, he was dreadfully agitated, and the fear of not being able to make himself intelligible almost exhausted him.

For reasons of discretion, since there was still a certain anxiety about possible revelations, the enquiry was being conducted in the headmaster's lodgings. Apart from the headmaster himself, those present were the form-master, the chaplain, and the mathematics master, to whom, as the youngest member of the staff, it fell to keep the minutes.

When Törless was asked why he had run away, he remained silent.

There was a general sympathetic wagging of heads.

"Well, yes," the headmaster said, "I think we know all that is necessary about that. But now tell us what induced you to conceal Basini's offence."

It would have been easy for Törless to produce some lies now. But his nervousness had passed off and he was in fact tempted to talk about himself and to try out his ideas on them.

"I don't know exactly, sir. When I heard about it for the first time, it struck me as something quite monstrous—simply unimaginable."

The chaplain looked complacent and gave Törless an encouraging nod.

"I—I couldn't help thinking about Basini's soul. . . ."

The chaplain beamed. The mathematics master polished his spectacles, replaced them, and narrowed his eyes. . . .

"I couldn't imagine what the moment must have been like when such a humiliation descended upon Basini, and this was what kept driving me to seek his company."

"Well, yes—in other words, you mean to say that you had a natural abhorrence of the particular error of your class-mate's ways, and that the sight of vice held you as it were spellbound, just as the gaze of the serpent is said to hold its victims."

The form-master and the mathematics master hastened to express their appreciation of the simile by means of lively gestures.

But Törless said: "No, it wasn't actually abhorrence. It was like this: sometimes I told myself he had done wrong and ought to be reported to those in authority. . . ."

"And that is the way you should have acted."

"But then at other times he struck me as so peculiar that I simply didn't think about his being punished, I looked at him from quite a different point of view. It always gave me a jolt when I thought of him in that way. . . ."

"You must express yourself a little more clearly, my dear Törless."

"There isn't any other way of saying it, sir."

"Oh yes, there is, there is. You are excited. We can see that. You are perplexed and confused. What you said just now was very obscure."

"Well yes, I do feel perplexed. I have had much better ways of putting it. But it all comes to the same thing in the end—there was something quite weird in me. . . ."

"H'm, yes. But after all that is only natural in a matter like this."
Törless reflected for a moment.

"Perhaps one can put it like this: there are certain things that
are destined to affect our lives in, as it were, two different ways.
In my case they have been people, events, dark dusty corners, a
high, cold, silent wall that suddenly came alive . . ."

"Good gracious, Törless, what is all this rambling talk?"

But Törless had suddenly begun to enjoy talking and getting it
all off his chest.

". . . imaginary numbers . . ."

They all glanced now at one another, now at Törless. The mathematics master cleared his throat and said:

"I should like to interpolate, for the elucidation of these obscure
allusions, that Törless here one day came to see me, asking for an
explanation of certain fundamental mathematical concepts—with
particular reference to that of imaginary numbers—things that are
in fact very likely to be a cause of difficulty to the as yet insufficiently
instructed intellect. I must indeed confess that he unquestionably
displayed acuity of mind. On the other hand, he showed a really
morbid insistence on singling out the very things which, so to speak,
seemed—at least to him—to indicate a lacuna in the causality of
thought.

"Do you remember what you said on that occasion, Törless?"

"Yes. I said it seemed to me that at these points we couldn't get
across merely by the aid of thought, and we needed another and
more inward sort of certainty to get us to the other side, as you
might say. We can't manage solely by means of thinking, I felt that
in the case of Basini too."

The headmaster was becoming impatient with this philosophical
deviation from the direct line of the enquiry. But the chaplain was
very satisfied with Törless's answer.

"So what you feel is that you are drawn away from science
towards the religious aspect of things?" he asked, and then, turning
to the others, went on: "Clearly it was really similar where Basini
was concerned. The boy seems to have a receptive sensibility for
the finer aspects, or as I should rather say, for the divine essence
of morality that transcends the limits of our intellect."

Now the headmaster felt he was really obliged to take up the
point.

"Well now, tell me, Törless, is it as the Reverend Father says? Have you an inclination to look behind events or things—as you yourself have put it, in a rather general way—seeking the religious background?"

He himself would have been heartily glad if Törless had at long last given an affirmative answer and thus provided a solid basis on which to judge his case.

But Törless said: "No, it wasn't that either."

"Well, then for heaven's sake, boy, will you please tell us plainly *what* it was!" the headmaster burst out. "After all, we cannot possibly settle down to a philosophical discussion with you!"

But now Törless became stubborn. He himself felt that he had not put his case well, but both the antagonism and the misguided approval he had met with gave him a sense of haughty superiority over these older men who seemed to know so little about the inner life of a human being.

"I can't help its not being all these things you meant. But I myself can't explain properly what I felt each time. Still, if I say what I think about it now, you may understand why it took me so long to tear myself away from it."

He was standing very straight, as proudly as if he were the judge here; and he looked straight ahead, past the men facing him—he could not bear the sight of this ridiculous assembly.

There outside the window was a crow, perching on a branch. Apart from that there was nothing but the vast white plain.

He felt that the moment had come when he would talk clearly, coherently, and triumphantly of the things that had at first been vague and tormenting within him, and later had been lifeless, without force.

It was not that any new idea had come to him, lending him this confidence and lucidity. He simply felt it throughout his being, as he stood there drawn up to his full height and as though standing in the middle of an empty room—felt it with the whole of his being, just like that time when he had let his astonished gaze stray over his class-mates as they sat there writing or memorising, all busily at work.

For it is strange how it is with thoughts. They are often no more than accidentals that fade out again without leaving any trace; and thoughts have their dead and their vital seasons. We sometimes have a flash of understanding that amounts to the insight of genius, and yet it slowly withers, even in our hands—like a flower. The form remains, but the colours and the fragrance are gone. That is to say, we still remember it all, word for word, and the logical value of the proposition, the discovery, remains entirely unimpaired, and nevertheless it merely drifts aimlessly about on the surface of our mind, and we do not feel ourselves any the richer for it. And then, perhaps years later—all at once there is again a moment when we see that in the meantine we have known nothing of it, although in terms of logic we have known it all.

Yes, there are dead and living thoughts. The process of thinking that takes place on the illumined surface, and which can always be checked and tested by means of the thread of causality, is not necessarily the living one. A thought that one encounters in this way remains as much a matter of indifference as any given man in a column of marching soldiers. Although a thought may have entered our brain a long time earlier, it comes to life only in the moment when something that is no longer thought, something that is not merely logical, combines with it and makes us feel its truth beyond the realm of all justification, as though it had dropped an anchor that tore into the blood-warm, living flesh. . . . Any great flash of understanding is only half completed in the illumined circle of the conscious mind; the other half takes place in the dark loam of our innermost being. It is primarily a state of soul, and uppermost, as it were at the extreme tip of it, there the thought is— poised like a flower.

Törless had needed only one great shock to his soul at this time to bring this out in him at last, flowering in the light.

Without paying any attention to the disconcerted faces round about him, and as though soliloquising, he started out from this point and spoke right on without a pause, his eyes fixed on some far distance.

"Perhaps I don't know enough yet to find the right words for it, but I think I can describe it. It happened again just a moment ago. I don't know how to put it except by saying that I see things in two different ways—everything, ideas included. If I make an effort to find any difference in them, each of them is the same today as it was yesterday, but as soon as I shut my eyes they're suddenly transformed, in a different light. Perhaps I went wrong about the imaginary numbers. If I get to them by going straight along inside mathematics, so to speak, they seem quite natural. It's only if I look at them directly, in all their strangeness, that they seem impossible. But of course I may be all wrong about this, I know too little about it. But I wasn't wrong about Basini. I wasn't wrong when I couldn't turn my ear away from the faint trickling sound in the high wall or my eye from the silent, swirling dust going up in the beam of light from a lamp. No, I wasn't wrong when I talked about things having a second, secret life that nobody takes any notice of! I—I don't mean it literally—it's not that things are alive, it's not that Basini seemed to have two faces—it was more as if I had a sort of second sight and saw all this not with the eyes of reason. Just as I can feel an idea coming to life in my mind, in the same way I feel something alive in me when I look at things and stop thinking. There's something dark in me, deep under all my thoughts, something I can't measure out with thoughts, a sort of life that can't be expressed in words and which is my life, all the same. . . .

"That silent life oppressed me, harassed me. Something kept on making me stare at it. I was tormented by the fear that our whole life might be like that and that I was only finding it out here and there, in bits and pieces. . . . Oh, I was dreadfully afraid! I was out of my mind. . . ."

These words and these figures of speech, which were far beyond what was appropriate to Törless's age, flowed easily and naturally from his lips in this state of vast excitement he was in, in this moment of almost poetic inspiration. Then he lowered his voice and, as though moved by his own suffering, he added:

"Now it's all over. I know now I was wrong after all. I'm not afraid of anything any more. I know that things are just things and will probably always be so. And I shall probably go on for ever seeing them sometimes this way and sometimes that, sometimes with the eyes of reason, and sometimes with those other eyes. . . . And I shan't ever try again to compare one with the other. . . ."

He fell silent. He took it quite as a matter or course that now he could go, and nobody tried to stop him.

*   *   *

When he had left the room, the masters looked at each other with baffled expressions.

The headmaster wagged his head irresolutely. It was the form-master who first found something to say.

"Dear me, it strikes me that this little prophet was trying to give us a lecture! It's the very dickens to know what to make of him! Such excitement! And at the same time this bewilderment, this perplexity, about quite simple things!"

"Receptivity and spontaneity of mind," the mathematics master concurred. "Apparently he has been attaching too much importance to the subjective factor in all our experience, and this is what perplexed him and drove him to use those obscure metaphors."

Only the chaplain was silent. In all Törless's talk it was the often recurring word 'soul' that had caught his attention, and he would gladly have taken the boy under his wing.

But then, again, he was not entirely sure what had been meant by it.

However, the headmaster put an end to the situation. "I do not know what is really going on in this boy Törless, but there is no doubt about it that he is in such an extreme state of nervous tension that boarding-school is in all probability no longer what is most suitable for him. What he needs is a more thorough supervision of his intellectual diet than we are in a position to provide. I do not think that we can continue to bear the responsibility. Törless ought to be educated privately. I shall write to his father along these lines."

All hastened to agree to this excellent suggestion on the part of the worthy headmaster.

"He was really so odd that I could almost believe he has some predisposition to hysteria," the mathematics master said to the colleague at his side.

*　　*　　*

At the same time that Törless's parents received the headmaster's letter they also received one from Törless himself, in which he asked them to take him away from the school, since he no longer felt it was the right place for him.

Meanwhile Basini had been expelled, and things at school had resumed their normal course.

It had been decided that Törless was to be fetched away by his mother. It was with indifference that he said good-bye to his classmates. He was almost beginning to forget their names already.

He had never again gone up to the little red room. All that seemed to lie far, far behind him.

Since Basini's expulsion it all seemed dead. It was almost as if that boy, in whom all those relationships had intertwined, had broken the circuit with his departure.

A sort of quietness and scepticism had come over Törless; his desperation had gone. 'I suppose it was just those furtive goings-on with Basini that made everything seem so frantic,' he thought to himself. Otherwise there did not seem to be anything to account for it.

But he was ashamed—just as one is ashamed in the morning after a feverish night during which, from all the corners of the dark room, one has seen dreadful threats looming up and about to overwhelm one.

His behaviour at the interview in the headmaster's room now struck him as unspeakably ridiculous. What a fuss! Hadn't they been quite right? Such a fuss about a little thing like that! But still, there was something in him that robbed this humiliation of its sting. 'I suppose I did behave unreasonably,' he reflected. 'All the same, the whole thing seems altogether to have had very little to do with my reason.' For this was his new feeling about it. He had the memory of a tremendous storm that had raged within him, but all he could muster by way of explanation for it now was entirely inadequate. 'So I suppose it must have been something much more fundamental and inevitable,' he concluded, 'than anything that can be dealt with by means of reasoned argument. . . .'

And the thing that had been there even before passion seized him, the thing that had only been overgrown by that passion—the real thing, the problem itself—was still firmly lodged in him. It was this mental perspective that he had experienced, which alternated according to whether he was considering what was distant or what was near by; it was this incomprehensible relationship that according to our shifts of standpoint gives happenings and objects sudden values that are quite incommensurable with each other, strange to each other. . . .

All this, and the rest besides, he saw remarkably clear and pure—and small. It was as one sees things in the morning, when the first pure rays of sunlight have dried the sweat of terror, when table and cupboard, enemy and fate, all shrink again, once more assuming their natural dimensions.

But just as then there remains a faint, brooding lassitude, so too it was with Törless. He now knew how to distinguish between day and night; actually he had always known it, and it was only that a monstrous dream had flowed like a tide over those frontiers, blotting them out. He was ashamed of the perplexity he had been in. But still there was also the memory that it could be otherwise, that there were fine and easily effaced boundary-lines around each human being, that feverish dreams prowled around the soul, gnawing at the solid walls and tearing open weird alleys—and this memory had sunk deep into him, sending out its wan and shadowy beams.

He could not quite have explained this. But his inability to find words for it, this near-dumbness, was in itself delightful, like the certainty of a teeming body that can already feel in all its veins the faint tugging of new life. Confidence and weariness intermingled in Törless. . . .

So it was that he waited quietly and meditatively for the moment of departure.

His mother, who had expected to find an overwrought and desperately perplexed boy, was struck by his cool composure.

When they drove out to the railway station, they passed, on the right, the little wood with the house in it where Božena lived. It looked utterly insignificant and harmless, merely a dusty thicket of willow and alder.

And Törless remembered how impossible it had been for him then to imagine the life his parents led. He shot a sidelong glance at his mother.

"What is it, my dear boy?"

"Nothing, Mamma. I was just thinking."

And, drawing a deep breath, he considered the faint whiff of scent that rose from his mother's corseted waist.

Translated by Eithne Wilkins and Ernst Kaiser

STORIES

The Perfecting of a Love

"You really can't come?"

"Quite impossible, you know. I must try to get this job finished now as fast as I can."

"But Lilli would be so pleased. . . ."

"I know. Oh, I know. But it simply can't be done."

"And I don't like the idea of travelling without you, not a bit . . ." his wife said as she poured out tea; and she glanced across to where he sat, in the corner of the room, in the bright chintz-covered armchair, smoking a cigarette. It was evening. Outside, looking out upon the street, the dark green shutters were part of a long row of dark green shutters and in no way distinct from the rest. Like a pair of dark eyelids, lowered in indifference, they concealed the glitter of this room, where from a satin-silver teapot the tea now flowed, striking the bottom of each cup with a faint tinkle and then remaining poised in mid-air, straw-coloured, a translucent, twisted column of weightless topaz. . . . In the slightly concave planes of the teapot there lay reflections, green and grey, with here and there a gleam of blue or yellow, a pool of colours that had run together and now lay quite still. But the woman's arm stood out from the teapot, and the gaze with which she looked across at her husband formed an angle with the line of the arm, a rigid pattern in the air.

Yes, there was an angle; that was evident. But there was something else, something almost physical, that only these two people within it could feel, to whom this angle was as taut as a steel strut, holding them fast in their places and yet uniting them, making of them—for all the space between—an almost tangible unity. This invisible support rested on the solar plexus, and there they could feel the pressure of it; yet even while it made them sit stiffly upright in their chairs, with faces immobile and eyes unswerving, there, at the point where it conjoined with them, there was a tender stir of animation, something volatile, as though their hearts were fluttering together and merging like two swarms of tiny butterflies.

On this thin, scarcely real, and yet so perceptible sensation the whole room hung as on a faintly trembling axis, and this in its turn rested on the two people in the room. The objects all around held their breath, the light on the walls froze into golden lace . . . everything was a silence and a waiting and was there because of them. Time, which runs through the world like an endless tinsel thread, seemed to pass through the centre of this room and through the centre of these people and suddenly to pause and petrify, stiff and still and glittering . . . and the objects in the room drew a little closer together. It was that standstill and then that faint settling which occurs when planes all at once assume order and crystal forms: a crystal, forming here round these two people, the centre of it corresponding to their centre—two people gazing at each other through this holding of the breath and this ensphering, this converging upon them, of everything, and gazing at each other as through thousands of mirroring planes, seeing each other as for the first time. . . .

The woman put the teapot down and her hand dropped to the table. As though exhausted by the weight of their happiness, each sank back into the cushions; and while they were still holding each other fast with their eyes, they smiled, as though lost, both feeling the need to speak—and yet not about themselves. So they talked again about the sick man, that mentally sick man, G., in a book they had been reading. Both spoke of a certain passage, and a problem it raised, as if this were what they had just been thinking of; but in fact they were merely resuming a discussion that had strangely fascinated them for days past—as though it were hiding its face and, while seemingly concerned with the book, were actually gazing elsewhere. And indeed after a while their thoughts imperceptibly returned, by way of this unconscious pretext, to a preoccupation with themselves.

"How does a man like that see himself, I wonder?" the woman said. And, sunk in her thoughts, she went on almost to herself: "He corrupts children, he lures young women into debauching themselves, and then he stands smiling and staring in fascination at the little scrap of eroticism that faintly flickers in him like summer lightning. Do you think he realises he's doing wrong?"

"It's hard to say. Perhaps he does—perhaps not," the man answered. "Perhaps one simply can't raise that sort of question about such feelings."

"What *I* think," the woman said—and it was now apparent that she was really speaking not of a random character in a book but of something specific that was beginning to loom up, for her, behind the character—"what I think is that he believes his actions are good."

For a while their thoughts ran on silently side by side, and emerged then in words that were again at a remove; and yet it still was as though they were holding hands in silence and as though everything had been said long ago. ". . . He does his victims harm. He hurts them. He must *know* he's demoralising them, confusing their erotic urge, stirring it up so that it'll never again have a single aim, a point of rest. And yet it's as though one could see him smiling, too—his face quite soft and pale, quite melancholy and yet resolute, and full of tenderness—a smile that hovers tenderly over himself and his victim, as a rainy day hovers over the land—heaven sends it, there's no comprehending why—and in his mournfulness, in the feelings that accompany the destruction he wreaks, there lies all the excuse he needs. . . . Isn't every mind solitary, lonely?"

"Yes, indeed, isn't every mind solitary?"

These two people, now silent again, were joined in thinking of that third person, that unknown, that one out of so many third persons, as if they were walking through a landscape together: trees, meadows, sky, and all at once the impossibility of knowing why here it is all blue and over there the clouds are gathering. They felt all these *third persons* surrounding them, enveloping them like that huge sphere which encloses us and sometimes turns an alien, glassy eye upon us, making us shiver when the flight of a bird cuts an inexplicably lurching streak across it. In this twilit room there was all at once a cold, vast solitude, bright as noon.

Then (and it was like the faintest note drawn from a violin) one of them said: "He's like a house with locked doors. All he has done is within him, like a gentle music perhaps—but who can hear it? It might turn everything into soft melancholy."

And the other replied: "Perhaps he has walked through himself again and again, with outstretched, groping hands, trying to find a door, and in the end he stands still, and all he can do is put his face close to the impenetrable windowpanes, and see the beloved victims from a long way off, and smile. . . ."

That was all they said, but in their blissfully communing silence there was a resonance that rose higher and higher. 'And there's only this smile, overtaking them and floating above them, and binding their last hideous, twitching gestures into a thin-stemmed posy as they bleed to death. . . . And it lingers tenderly, wondering if they can feel what it has done, and lets the posy fall, and then the mystery of its solitude bears it upwards on vibrant wings, it soars resolutely— an alien beast entering into the marvel-crowded emptiness of space.'

It was on this solitude that they felt the mystery of their union rest ed. There was an obscure sense of the world around them, which made them cling to each other; there was a dreamlike sense of chill on all sides except the one where they leaned against each other, disburdening themselves, uniting like two wonderfully well-fitting halves, which, being conjoined, undergoing reduction of their outer limits, in the act of fusion inwardly expand into a larger unity. They were sometimes unhappy because they could not share everything down to the very last and least thing.

"Do you remember," the woman suddenly said, "a few nights ago, when you held me in your arms . . . ? Did you realise there was something between us then? Something had occurred to me at that moment, nothing of the slightest importance, but it was not *you*, and I was suddenly desperate that there could be anything other than you. And I couldn't tell you about it, and then I couldn't help smiling at the thought of how you didn't know and believed yourself very close to me, and later I stopped wanting to tell you and became angry with you for not feeling it yourself, and your caresses could no longer reach me. And I couldn't bring myself to ask you to let me be, for it wasn't anything *real*, I was really close to you, and all the same it was there like a vague shadow, it was as if I could be far from you and could exist without you. Do you know that feeling—how sometimes everything is suddenly there twice over, one sees all the things around one, complete and distinct as one has known them all along, and then once again, pale, twilit, and aghast, as if they were already being regarded, stealthily and with an alien gaze, by someone else? I wanted to take you and wrench you back into myself—and then again to push you away and fling myself on the ground because it could happen at all. . . ."

"Was that the time when . . . ?"

"Yes, that was the time when, in your arms, I suddenly began to weep. You thought it was from excess of longing to enter deeper into your feelings with my own. Don't be angry with me—I simply had to tell you. I don't know why. It was all just fancy, but it hurt so much, and I think that was why I couldn't help thinking of that man G. You do understand . . . ?"

The man in the armchair stubbed out his cigarette and stood up. His gaze interlocked with hers, both of them swaying as with the tension there is in the bodies of two tightrope-acrobats close together on the rope.

Then, instead of speaking, they drew up the shutters and looked out into the street. It seemed to them they were listening to a crackling of tensions within themselves, to something suddenly stirring into life and then becoming dormant again. They knew they could not live without each other, and that only together, like an ingenious structure of supports and counter-supports, could they carry the burden they had chosen. When they thought of each other, it all struck them as almost painfully morbid, so delicate and daring and incomprehensible did their relationship seem in its sensitiveness to the slightest instability within.

After a while, when the sight of the alien world outside had restored their sense of security, they felt tired and wanted only to fall asleep side by side. They felt nothing but each other, and yet there was—though by now quite small, disappearing into darkness—another feeling too: an opening out as to all four quarters of the sky.

*   *   *

The next morning Claudine set out for the little town where her thirteen-year-old daughter Lilli was at boarding-school.

The child had been born in the time of her first marriage, but the father was an American dentist to whom Claudine had gone, being plagued by toothache during a holiday in the country. She had been vainly waiting to be joined by a lover, whose arrival had been delayed beyond the limits of her patience, and in a queer state of intoxication, compounded of frustration, pain, ether, and the dentist's round white face, which she had seen hovering over hers day after day, it had happened. Her conscience never troubled her on account of this episode, nor indeed on account of any other such that had occurred in that first, wasted part of her life. When some weeks later she had to go for more treatment, she went accompanied by her maid, and with that the affair was over; her memory of it was merely of a strange cloud of sensations that had for a while bewildered and agitated her, as if a cloak had been suddenly flung over her head and then had slid swiftly to the floor.

There was something strange about all her actions and experiences at that period. She could not always bring them to such a quick and sober end as on that one occasion: indeed, at times she seemed to be entirely under the domination of one man or the other, for each of whom she was capable of doing everything demanded of her, to the point of complete self-abnegation and lack of any will of her own. Yet she was never left with any sense of having had intense or important experiences. She performed and suffered acts of a passion so violent as to amount to humiliation, but never lost the awareness that whatever she did, fundamentally it did not touch her and essentially had nothing to do with her. These excuses committed by an unhappy, ordinary, promiscuous woman were like a brook rushing along, always away from her, and her only feeling was of sitting quietly on its bank, lost in thought.

It was an awareness of some ultimate integrity deep within her, never clearly defined, yet always present, that brought about this final reserve and assurance that she possessed even in her headlong abandonment of herself to others. Behind all the intricacies of her actual experiences there was a current of something undiscovered, and although she had never yet grasped this hidden quintessence of her life, perhaps even believing that she would never be capable of penetrating to it, nevertheless, whatever happened, it gave her a sense of liberty such as a guest may have in a strange house, knowing he will be there only on that one occasion and therefore resigning himself, nonchalantly and with a trace of boredom, to whatever comes his way while he is there.

And then all she had done and suffered sank into oblivion when she met the man who was now her husband. There and then she entered into a tranquillity and seclusion in which whatever had gone before no longer mattered. All that mattered was what would come of it now, and the past seemed to have existed only so that they might experience each other the more intensely—or else it was simply forgotten. An overpowering sensation of growth rose about

her like drifts of blossom, and only a long way off did there linger
a sense of anguish endured, a background from which everything
detached itself as in the warmth frost-stiffened limbs slowly and
drowsily stir into movement.

There was, perhaps, one feeling that ran, a thin, wan, and scarcely
perceptible thread, from her former into her present life. And her
having to think of that former life again precisely today might have
been chance or might have been because she was travelling to see
her child. Whatever its cause, it had emerged only at the railway
station, when—among all those many people, and oppressed and
disquieted by them—she had suddenly been touched by a sensation
that, even as it drifted by, only half recognised, already vanishing,
conjured up, obscurely and distantly and yet with almost corporeal
verisimilitude, that almost forgotten period of her life.

Claudine's husband had had no time to see her off at the station,
and she was alone, waiting for the train, with the crowd pushing
and jostling and, like a great ponderous wave of slop-water, slowly
shoving her this way and that. Upon the pallid, early morning faces
that were all around her emotions seemed to float through this dark
precinct like spawn on dim pools of stagnant water. It nauseated
her. She felt an urge to brush out of her way, with a negligent
gesture, all that was here drifting and shoving; but—whether what
horrified her was the physical dominance of what surrounded her
or only this murky, monotonous, indifferent light under a gigantic
roof of dirty glass and a tangle of iron girders—while she passed,
with apparent calm and composure, through the crowd, she felt
the compulsion she was under, and she suffered intensely as from
a humiliation. In vain she sought refuge within herself; it was as
though she had slowly and meanderingly lost herself in this throng—
her eyes strayed, she was no longer fully aware of her own existence
and when she strained to remember, a thin soft headache hung like
a cloud before her thoughts, and her thoughts leaned into it, trying
to reach her yesterday. But all that she seized of it was a feeling as
if she were secretly carrying something precious and delicate. And
she knew she must not betray this to others, because they would
not understand and because she was weaker and could not defend
herself and was afraid. Slender, shrinking into herself, she walked
among them, inwardly arrogant but starting and withdrawing
whenever anyone came too near, and hiding behind an unassuming

air. And at the same time, in secret delight, she felt the happiness of her life growing more beautiful as she yielded and abandoned herself to this faint, ravelled anxiety.

And that was how she recognised what it all amounted to. For this was what it had been like at that other period. What she suddenly felt was: *once, long ago* . . . as though for a long time she had been somewhere else, though never really far away. There was something twilit and uncertain in her, like deranged people's frightened concealment of their passions, and her actions tore loose from her in shreds and were borne away in the memories of strangers. Nothing had ever impregnated her with that fruitful germ of experience which softly begins to swell a soul when those who think they have stripped it of its petals turn away, satiated. . . . Yet all she suffered shone as with the pallid glitter of a crown, and the muted whispering anguish that was the background of her life was shot with a tremulous gleam. At times then she felt as if her sorrows were burning like little flames in her, and something impelled her to go on kindling new ones. And, doing so, she seemed to feel the pressure of a diadem cutting into her brow, invisible and unreal as something spun of dream-glass. And sometimes it was only a far-off, circling chant inside her head. . . .

Claudine sat quite still while the train travelled through the landscape, quietly shaking and rocking. The other people in the carriage talked to each other, but she heard it only as a distant buzz. And while she was thinking of her husband, and her thoughts were enclosed in a soft, weary happiness as in snow-filled air, for all the softness there was something that kept her from moving, as when a convalescent, accustomed to being within four walls, is about to take the first steps out of doors—a happiness that keeps one transfixed and is almost agonising. And behind that again there was still that undefined, wavering chant which she could not quite catch, remote, blurred, like a nursery-rhyme, like a pain, like herself. . . . In wide, rippling circles it drew her thoughts after it, and she could not see into its face.

She leaned back and gazed out of the window. It fatigued her to think about that any more. Her senses were alert and achingly perceptive, but there was something behind the senses that wanted to be quiet and expand and let the world glide away over it. . . . Telegraph-poles slid slanting past. The fields with their dark brown furrows standing out of the snow rolled past and away. Bushes stood as though on their heads, with hundreds of straddling little legs from which there hung thousands of tiny bells of water, dripping, trickling, flashing and glittering. . . . There was something gay and light about it all, a dilation as when walls open out— something loosened and unburdened and full of tenderness. And from her own body too the gentle weight was now lifted, leaving in her ears a sensation as of melting snow, gradually passing over into a ceaseless, light, loose tinkling. She felt as if with her husband she were living in the world as in a foaming sphere full of beads and bubbles and little feathery rustling clouds. She closed her eyes and abandoned herself to it.

But after a while she began to think again. The light, regular swaying of the train, the loosening up, the liquescence of nature there outside—it was as if some pressure had lifted; and she suddenly realised that she was on her own. Involuntarily she glanced up. There was still that softly whirling vortex in her senses; but it was like going up to a door that had always been shut and suddenly finding it wide open. Perhaps she had long felt the desire for this; perhaps without her knowing it something had been oscillating in the love between herself and her husband; but all she had known of it was that ever and again it drew them more closely together. And now it had secretly burst open something within her that had long been locked up. Slowly, as out of an almost invisible but very deep wound, in an unceasing stream of little drops, thoughts and feelings welled up, steadily widening the gap.

There are, in the relationship to those one loves, a great many problems that become buried under the edifice of the shared life before they can be fully worked out; and later the sheer weight of things as they have actually turned out leaves one no strength even to imagine it all differently. Then somewhere on the way there will stand some queer sign-post, there will be some face, a hovering fragrance, an untrodden path petering out amid grass and stones, and the traveller knows he should turn and take the other road, but everything urges him forward; and all that impedes his steps is something like cobwebs, dreams, a rustling branch—and he is quietly paralysed by some thought that has never quite taken shape. Recently it had sometimes happened, perhaps increasingly, that there was this looking back, a more intense leaning onto the past. Claudine's constancy revolted against it, for this constancy was not repose but a setting free of forces, a mutual lending of support, an equilibrium arising out of unceasing movement forwards. It was a running hand-in-hand. Then, in the midst of it, there would come this temptation to stand still, to stand there all alone and look around. At such times she would feel her passion as something tyrannical and compulsive, threatening to sweep her away; and even when the temptation was overcome and she felt remorseful and was once again seized with awareness of how beautiful her love was, that awareness was rigid and ponderous as a narcotic state, and she apprehended, with delight and dismay, how each of her movements was laced into it, tall and bulky and stiff as though encased in gold brocade. And yet somewhere there was still a lure, something that lay quiet and pale as March sunlight, the shadows upon earth aching with spring.

Even in her happiness Claudine was occasionally assailed by a sense of how it was all merely a fact, almost accidental; and she sometimes wondered whether there must not be some other kind of life in store for her, different and remote. This was perhaps only the shape of a thought, an outer shell, which had remained with her from earlier times, and not a real thought with any intention behind it—only a sensation such as might once have gone with the real thought, an empty, unresisting motion, all a craning and a peering, which, withdrawing always and never fulfilled, had long lost its content and was like the entrance to a dark tunnel in her dreams.

But perhaps it was some other, solitary happiness, much more wonderful than everything else—something loose, limber, and obscurely sensitive at a point in their relationship where in other people's love there is nothing but a solid substructure, bony and inanimate. There was a faint unrest in her, an almost morbid yearning for extreme tension, the premonition of an ultimate climax. And sometimes it was as though she were destined to suffer some unimaginable sorrow in love.

Now and then when she was listening to music this premonition touched her soul secretly, somewhere a long way out. . . . She would feel a start of terror, suddenly aware of her soul's existence in the realm of the undefined. But every year, as winter passed away, there came a time when she felt nearer to those outermost frontiers than at other times. During those naked, strengthless days, suspended between life and death, she felt a melancholy that could not be that of ordinary craving for love; it was almost a longing to turn away from this great love that she possessed, as though faintly glimmering ahead of her there were the road of an ultimate destiny, leading her no longer to her beloved but away from him, defenceless, out into the soft, dry, withered expanses of some agonising desert. And she realised that this came from a distant place where their love was no longer solely between the two of them, but was something with pallid roots insecurely clutching at the world.

When they walked together, their shadows had only the faintest tinge of colour and dangled loosely at their heels as though incapable of binding their footsteps to the ground they walked on; and the ring of hard earth under their feet was so curt and clipped, and the bare bushes so stared into the sky, that in those hours a-shudder with enormous visibility it was as if all at once all things, the mute and docile objects of the world, had weirdly disengaged themselves from them. And as the light began to fail, they themselves grew tall, towering like adventurers, like strangers, like unreal beings, spellbound by the fading echo of their own existence, knowing themselves to be full of shards of something incomprehensible to which there was nowhere any response and which was rejected by all things, so that only a broken gleam of it fell into the world, forlornly and irrelevantly flickering here and there, now in an object, now in a vanishing thought.

Then she could imagine belonging to another man, and it seemed not like betrayal but like some ultimate marriage, in a realm where they had no real being, where they existed only as music might, a music heard by no one, echoing back from nowhere. For then she felt her own existence merely as a line that she herself incised, gratingly, just to hear herself in the bewildering silence; it was simply something leading from one moment to the next, something in which she became, inexorably and irrelevantly, identical with whatever it was she did—and yet always remained something she could never achieve. And while it suddenly seemed to her as though perhaps they loved each other as yet only with all the loudness of a refusal to hear a faint, frantically intense and anguished call, she had a foreboding of the deeper complications and vast intricacies that came about in the intervals, in the silences, in the moments of awakening out of that uproar into the shoreless world of facts, awakening to stand, with nothing but a feeling, among mindless and mechanical happenings; and it was with the pain of their tall and lonely separateness, standing side by side—something against which all else was no more than an anaesthetising and shutting off and lulling of oneself to sleep with sheer noise—that she loved him when she thought of doing him the final, the mortal injury.

Even weeks after such an experience her love still had this colouring; then that would gradually fade. But often, when she felt the proximity of another man, it would return, though fainter. It sufficed that there should be someone there—a man of no real concern to her, saying something of no real concern to her—and she would feel herself being gazed at as from that other realm, with a look of amazement that held the question: 'Why are you still here?' She never felt any desire for such outsiders; it was painful to her to think of them; indeed it disgusted her. But all at once there would be that intangible wavering of the stillness around her; and then she would not know whether she was rising or sinking. . . .

Claudine looked out of the window. Out there it was all just the same as before. But—whether as a result of her thoughts or for some other reason—now it was overlaid by a stale, unyielding resistance, as if she were looking through a film of something milky and repugnant. That restless, volatile, thousand-legged gaiety had become unendurably tense; it was all a prancing and trickling, all feverishly excited and mocking, with something in it of pygmy footsteps, far too lively and yet, for her, dull and dead. Here, there, it flung itself upwards, an empty clatter, a grinding past of tremendous friction.

It was physically painful to gaze out into all that stir, for which she no longer had any feeling. All that life, which only a short while ago had been one with her emotions, was still there outside, overbearing and rigid; but as soon as she tried to draw it to her, the things crumbled away and fell to pieces under her gaze. What came about was an ugliness that twisted and turned in her eyes, as though her soul were leaning outwards there, leaning far out, taut, stretching after something, groping into emptiness.

And all at once it occurred to her that she too—just like all that was around her—spent her life passively, a captive in her own being, committed to one place, to a particular city, to one house in that city, one habitation and one sense of herself, year after year within that tiny area; and with that it seemed as though, if she were to stop and linger for one single moment, her happiness might rush past her and away, like this rumbling, roaring mass rushing through the countryside, rushing away from everything.

This, it seemed to her, was no mere random thought. On the contrary, there was in it an element of that unbounded, uprearing blankness in which her feelings groped vainly for any support. She was impalpably assailed by something like what comes upon a climber on the rock-face; an utterly cold, still moment when she could hear herself as an unintelligible small sound on that huge surface and then, in the abrupt silence, realised the faintness of her own existence, creeping along, and how great, in contrast, and how full of dreadful forgotten sounds, was the stony brow of the void.

And while she was shrinking from this like a delicate skin, feeling in her very fingertips the voiceless fear of thinking about herself, and while her sensations clung to her like granules and her emotions trickled away like sand, she again heard that peculiar sound: a mere point it seemed, like a bird hovering high in the empty air.

She was overwhelmed by a sense of destiny. It lay in her having set out on this journey, in the way nature was withdrawing before her, in her having been so scared and huddled and timid even at the very beginning of the journey—scared of herself, of others, and of her happiness. And all at once her past seemed the imperfect expression of something that was yet to come.

She continued to gaze anxiously out of the window. But gradually, under the pressure of the huge strangeness out there, her mind began to be ashamed of all its protestation and struggle, and it seemed to pause. And now it was becoming imbued with that very subtle, final, passive strength which lies in weakness, and it grew thinner and slighter than a child, softer than a sheet of faded silk. And it was only now with a mildly looming delight that she experienced this ultimate human ecstasy in being a stranger in the world, in seeming to take leave of it, a sense of being unable to penetrate into the world, of finding, among all her decisions, none that was meant for herself; and, being forced by them to the very edge of life, she felt the moment before the plunge into the blind vastness of empty space.

She began obscurely to yearn for her past, wasted and exploited as it had been by people who were strangers to her—yearning for it as for the pale, weak wakefulness there was in the depths of illness, when in the house the sounds moved from one room to another and she no longer belonged anywhere, but, relieved of the pressure of her own personality, continued to lead another life, floating somewhere else.

Outside, the landscape stormed soundlessly by. In her thoughts people grew very tall and loud and confident, and she huddled into herself, escaping from that, until there was nothing left of her but her nullity, her imponderability, a drifting somewhere towards something. And gradually the train began to travel very quietly, with long, gently rocking movements, through country that still lay under deep snow, and the sky came lower and lower until it seemed only a few paces ahead, trailing along the ground in grey, dark curtains of slowly drifting flakes. Inside the train twilight gathered, yellowish, and the outlines of her fellow-passengers were only vaguely visible: they swayed to and fro slowly and spectrally. She was no longer aware of what she was thinking, and pleasure in being alone with strange experiences now took a quiet hold of her: it was like the play of very faint, scarcely tangible inquietudes and of great shadowy stirrings of the soul, groping for them. She tried to re-member her husband, but all she could find of her almost vanished love was a weird notion as of a room where the windows had long been kept shut. She made an effort to get rid of this, but it yielded only a very little and remained lurking nearby. And the world was as pleasantly cool as a bed in which one stays behind alone. . . .

Then she felt as if she were about to be faced with a decision, and she did not know why she felt this, and she was neither glad nor resentful; all she felt was that she did not want either to act or to prevent action. And her thoughts slowly wandered into the snow outside, without a backward glance, always deeper and deeper into the snow, as when one is too tired to turn back and so walks on and on.

* * *

Towards the end of the journey the man opposite said: "An idyll, an enchanted island, a lovely woman at the centre of a fairy-tale all white *dessous* and lace . . ." and he made a gesture towards the landscape. 'How silly,' Claudine thought, but she could not think of anything to say.

It was like someone knocking at the door and a big dark face floating behind pale window-panes. She did not know who this person was; she did not care who he was. All she felt was that here was someone wanting something. And now something was beginning to take on shape and become real.

As when a faint wind rises among clouds, ordering them in a row, and slowly passes away, so she felt the motion of this materialising reality stirring the still, soft cloudiness of her feelings—insubstantial, passing through her, passing her by. . . . And, as with many sensitive people, what attracted her in the unintelligible passage of events was all there was in it that did not pertain to herself, to the spirit: what she loved was the helplessness and shame and anguish of her spirit—it was like striking something weaker than oneself, a child, a woman, and then wanting to be the garment wrapped about its pain, in the darkness alone.

So they arrived, late in the afternoon, the train almost empty. One by one people had trickled away out of the compartments; station after station had sifted them out from among the other travellers. And now they were swept swiftly together, for there were only three sleighs available for the hour's trip from the station to the township, and these had to be shared. Before Claudine knew where she was, she found herself seated with four other people in one of these small conveyances. From in front there came the unfamiliar smell of the horses steaming in the cold, and ripples of scattered light from the lanterns. But at times, too, darkness came flooding right up to the sledge, and away over it, and then she realised they were travelling between two ranks of tall trees, as though along a dark corridor that grew ever narrower the closer they came to their goal.

Because of the cold she sat with her back to the horses. Opposite her was that man—big, bulky, encased in his fur coat. He blocked the way along which her thoughts strove to travel back home. Suddenly, as though a door had slammed, every glance of hers encountered his dark figure there before her. She was aware of glancing at him several times in order to make sure what he looked like, as though that were all that mattered now and everything else were long settled. She was excited to find that he remained entirely vague: he might have been anyone; he was no more than a sombre bulk of alien being. And sometimes this seemed to be drawing nearer to her, like a moving forest with its mass of tree-trunks. And it was like a weight upon her.

Meanwhile, talk spread like a net among the people in the little sleigh. He joined in, making remarks of the tritely well-turned kind that many people make, with a pinch of that spice which is like a sharp, confident aura enveloping a man in a woman's presence. In these moments of male dominance, so much a matter of course she became uneasy and embarrassed and ashamed at not having effectively rebuffed his earlier insinuating advances to her. And yet when she, in her turn, could not avoid speaking, she felt it came to her all too easily, and she had an awareness of herself as of a feeble, ineffective waving with the stump of an amputated arm.

Then indeed she observed how helplessly she was being flung this way and that, at each curve in the road being touched now on the arms, now at the knees, sometimes with the whole upper part of her body leaning against some other person's body; and remotely, by some analogy, she experienced it as if this small sledge were a darkened room and these people were seated around her, hot and urgent, and she were timidly a prey to shameless acts that she endured, smiling, as if not noticing anything, her eyes focused straight ahead.

All this was like feeling an irksome dream in half-sleep, always remaining slightly conscious of its unreality, always marvelling at feeling it so strongly. Then a moment came when that man leaned out, looked up at the sky, and said: "We're going to be snowed up."

With a start her thoughts leapt into complete wakefulness. She glanced around: the people were exchanging cheerful, harmless pleasantries, as those do who at the end of a long journey through darkness get their first glimpse of light and of tiny figures in the distance. And all at once she had a strangely indifferent, sober sense of reality. But she noticed with astonishment that something nevertheless touched her, moved her intensely. It frightened her a little, for it was a pallid, almost unnatural lucidity, in which nothing could sink into the vagueness of reverie and through which no thought moved and within which nevertheless people now and then became jagged and huge as hills, as if suddenly gliding through an invisible fog where all that was real expanded, taking on a gigantic, shadowy, second outline. Then she felt something that was almost humility and dread of them; yet she never quite lost the awareness that this weakness was only a peculiar faculty: it was as if the frontiers of her being had extended, invisibly and sensitively, and everything came into faint collision with them, setting up tremors. And for the first time she was truly startled by this queer day, the solitariness of which, like a passage leading underground, had gradually sunk with her into the confused whisperings of multitudinous inner twilight and now suddenly, in a distant region, ascended into the midst of inexorably actual events, leaving her alone in a vast, unfamiliar, unwanted reality.

Furtively she looked across at the stranger. He was striking a match: for an instant his beard was lit up, and one eye. And even this trivial act seemed remarkable; she felt the solidity of it, felt how naturally one thing linked with the next and was merely there, insensate and calm and yet like a simple and tremendous power, stone interlocked with stone. She reflected that he was certainly quite an ordinary person. And at that she had again a faint, elusive, intangible sense of her own existence; she felt herself floating in the dark before him, dissolved and tattered, like pale, frothing foam, and felt an odd stimulus in answering him agreeably. And even while speaking she watched herself and what she was doing, helpless, unmoved in spirit, and yet with an enjoyment that was divided between pleasure and torment, which made her feel as though she were crouching in the innermost depths of some great and ever expanding exhaustion.

It struck her that this was the way it had sometimes begun in the past. At the thought of such a recurrence her mind reeled with voluptuous, enervated horror as of some still nameless sin. She wondered whether he had noticed her looking at him, and her body filled with a faint, almost docile sensuality—a dark hiding-place for the stealthy urges of the soul within. But the stranger sat there in the darkness, big and calm, merely smiling sometimes—or perhaps even that only seemed so to her.

So they travelled on into the falling night, at close quarters, facing each other. And gradually her thoughts were again invaded by that softly forward-thrusting unrest. She tried telling herself that all this was nothing but delusions, arising out of the confused inner stillness of this sudden lonely journey amid strangers, and then again she would think it was the wind wrapping her with its stiff, searing cold, petrifying her, robbing her of her will; and then at other times it oddly seemed to her as if her husband were very near to her and all this sensual weakness were some ineffable aspect of their great love. And once—when she had just glanced across at the stranger again and was concious of this shadowy abandonment of her will, all her firmness and inviolability gone—suddenly there was a radiance high and bright over her past, as over an indescribable, strangely ordered panorama. It was a queer premonition, as if all that seemed long past and gone were still alive. But in the next moment it was no more than a fading streak of intuition in the darkness and all that remained was something faintly reverberating within her, rather as if it had been the never-before-glimpsed landscape of her love, filled with colossal forms and a quiet rushing sound, confused and alien, already beyond her grasp. And she felt herself lingeringly and softly enveloped in her own being, which was full of strange, not yet comprehensible resolutions whose origin was in that other realm.

She could not help thinking of the days to come, isolated from the rest of her days, lying ahead of her like an *enfilade* of remote rooms, each one opening into the next. And all this time she heard the beat of the horses' hooves, bearing her—helplessly flung into the meaningless actuality of this situation, these close quarters here in the sleigh—nearer to all that was to come. With hasty, nervous laughter she joined in a commonplace conversation; but within her everything was vast and ramified, and she was helpless before the incomprehensibility of all things as under a huge cloak of silence.

*   *   *

In the night she woke up: it was as though little bells had been jingling. She knew at once it was snowing. She looked towards the window; there it was in the air outside, soft, and heavy as a wall. Barefoot, she tiptoed to the window. It was all a matter of an instant. Darkly she sensed that she put her naked feet to the ground like an animal. Then, with her face close to the glass, she stared numbly out into the dense trellis-work of the snowflakes. She did all this as one may, starting up from sleep, with a consciousness so narrowly confined that it is like a little uninhabited island emerging from the sea. It was as if she were standing a long way off from herself. And all at once she remembered, and remembered even the emphasis with which he had said it: 'We're going to be snowed up.'

She tried to collect herself. Turning round, she saw how small and cramped the room was. And there was something strange in this smallness, as of being caged, of being beaten. She lit a candle and held it high, moving its light over the things. Slowly the sleep began to ebb from them, but they were still as though they had not yet quite found their way back into themselves. Wardrobe, chest of drawers, and bed, there they were, and yet there was somehow either too much or too little, a mere shadowy nothing, a harsh whispering shadow of nothingness. Blank and sunken they stood in the bleak half-light from the flickering candle, and over table and walls there lay an endless feeling of dust, and of walking, walking barefoot through an infinity of dust. Outside the room there was a narrow passage with a wooden floor and whitewashed walls; at the top of the stairs, she knew, there was a dim lamp hanging in a wire ring, casting five pale, swaying circles on the ceiling, and beyond that the light trickled away on the chalky walls, like marks left by the fumbling of greasy hands. Five pale, inanely swaying circles were like five sentries guarding a strangely excited emptiness. . . . All around were people she did not know, all asleep. She felt a wave of sudden unreal heat and she almost began to scream, faintly, the way cats sometimes scream in fear and desire, as she stood there, wide awake in the night, while soundlessly the last shadow of her actions, strange even to herself, slipped back behind the walls of her inner being and these grew smooth again. And suddenly she thought: 'Supposing he came now . . . and just did what I know he wants to. . . . '

She was more startled than she realised. Something rolled away over her like a glowing ball. For minutes there was only this wild panic and behind it the constriction of the room, a soundless strait, tense as a cracked whip. She tried to form a mental image of the man. But she failed; all she could feel was the warily prowling, beast-like tread of her own thoughts. Only now and then she caught a partial glimpse of him as he was in reality—his beard, one eye lit up. . . . And she was sickened. She could never again belong to a stranger. And precisely there, precisely coincident with this abhorrence of all other men that rose in her body, with its mysterious yearning only for the one, she felt—as though on some other, deeper plane—a leaning over, a vertigo, and had a sense of all human insecurity. And with it went something like dread of herself, something that was perhaps also an intangible, irrational, groping desire that the stranger should really come. Fear swept through her like the biting cold that comes as though driven by the current of some destructive lustful urge.

Somewhere a clock began placidly talking to itself. Footsteps passed under her window and faded away. Quiet voices. . . . The room was chilly; the warmth of sleep slipped away from her skin, and vaguely, unresistingly, she swayed to and fro with it in the dark as in a cloud of faintness. The things around her made her feel ashamed, hard and straight as they were—once again disengaged, once again entirely themselves, blankly staring at nothing, while she was confusedly conscious of standing there, waiting for a stranger. And yet she realised obscurely that it was not the stranger who tempted her, but simply this standing and waiting, a fine-toothed, savage, abandoned ecstasy in being herself, in being alive, awake here among these lifeless objects—ecstasy that had opened like a wound. And while she felt her heart beating, like some frenzied wild creature trapped within her breast, her body in its quiet swaying drew itself up, like a great exotic, nodding flower that suddenly shudders with the infinitely expanding rapture of mysterious union as it closes round its captive. And softly, far off, she could hear the beloved's heart wandering unquiet, restless, homeless, chiming through the stillness like the lilt of some wind-blown, remote music, flickering as starlight; and she was moved by the haunting loneliness of those chords that were in quest of her, moved as by some vast diapason resounding far beyond the limits of the human soul.

Now it seemed to her that something was about to reach fulfilment and, standing there, she lost all count of time. Minutes . . . hours . . . time lay motionless around her, fed by invisible springs, a shoreless lake, without beginning or end. Only once, at some moment she was but vaguely aware of, something slid darkly across the outermost reaches of her mind: a thought, a notion. . . . And as it passed, she recognised it as the memory of dreams long lost, of dreams belonging to her former life, in which she thought herself enslaved by enemies and was compelled to perform humiliating acts; but even as she recognised it, it began to diminish and disappear. One last time it rose out of the hazy distance, phantom-clear, sharply outlined against the background like the rigging of a ship, masts and tackle . . . and she remembered how she had always been defenceless, remembered her own shrieks waking her from sleep, and how she had struggled in dull despair until her strength gave out and her senses reeled—all the shapeless, boundless misery of that earlier life. . . . Then it was gone. In the stillness that closed in round her again there was only a radiance, a last receding wave, a lull, as though something unutterable had happened. And then from there beyond—just as once, behind her dreams, this terrible helplessness of hers had lived another, second life, remote, intangible, imaginary—suddenly she was overtaken by a sense of promise, a glimmer of longing, and knew a surrender such as she had never known before, a naked, bare self-awareness that the irrevocability of her fate had stripped of anything personal and which, while driving her towards ever deeper frenzies of exhaustion, yet weirdly bemused her, as though it were, far within her, the stray tender particle of a love in quest of its own perfection—a love for which there are still no words in the language of day, that language with its heavy upright gait on solid ground.

She did not know whether it had been only a short time ago, just before waking, that she dreamt that dream once more. For years she had not dreamt it, had not even thought of it, and now all at once this dream and the time to which it belonged seemed to be quite close, hovering just behind her. It was like turning round and suddenly staring into a face. How strange it was!—as if here in this lonely room her life were turning back upon itself like tangled traces going round and round in an enormous plain.

Behind her back there shone the little light that she had lit; her face was in darkness. Gradually she lost the feeling of her own shape, and her outlines seemed to become the limits of some monstrous cavity in this darkness, in this lingering moment that enveloped her. She began to feel as if she were not really here at all, as if merely something of herself had long ago set out and had been travelling ever since through space and through the years, and were now wakening here, alone and lost, at an infinite remove from that real self which she was, she herself standing still somewhere in the sunken realm of her old dream. Somewhere . . . a place she lived in . . . people . . . a dreadful maze of fear. . . . The blood shot into her face, her lips grew soft, and she realised: it *was* going to happen all over again . . . another of them. . . . And the feeling of her loosened hair, her open arms, was different and as of long ago, as if all she had done then were an act of unfaithfulness here and now.

And as in dismay she clung to the wish to keep herself for her beloved—her raised, imploring hands now slowly tiring—there came the thought:

'We were unfaithful to each other before we knew each other. . . .'

It was the mere gleam of a thought, hardly more than a tremor—an exquisite and lovely bitterness, just as in the wind that rises from the sea there is sometimes a whiff of keener freshness, an intenser presence that lingers fleetingly and then drifts away—almost the thought: 'we loved each other before we knew each other'. And it was as if the infinite tension of their love all at once expanded far beyond the present into that earlier unfaithfulness from which it had first come to them, as though deriving from some older form of its eternal existence between them.

She sank down and for a long time, as though stunned, was aware of nothing except of sitting on a hard chair at a bare table. Her thoughts strayed to the talk they had had before her journey, about the man G., that figure in a novel—the veiled words and the words never uttered. And then she realised that through a chink in the window there came the moist, mild air of the snow-laden night, faintly caressing her bare shoulders. And remotely, mournfully, as a wind blows over rain-darkened fields, she began to think it would be a delight like quiet rain, like a sky over-arching a landscape, to be unfaithful—a mysterious, last, deathly delight.

* * *

With the morning there came a queer atmosphere of the past, pervading everything.

Claudine intended going to the school. She had woken early and it had been like rising out of heavy, clear water. She remembered nothing of all that had stirred her during the night. She moved the looking-glass to the window and began to put her hair up. It was still dark in the room. But while she was doing her hair, straining her eyes to see herself in the small, tarnished glass, she was overcome by a feeling that, somehow, here was a peasant girl beautifying herself for her Sunday outing. She felt quite strongly that it was all for the benefit of the schoolmasters who would see her, or perhaps for the stranger. She could not rid herself of this senseless notion. It did not spring from her inner being, but it clung to everything she did: all her movements took on something of oafishly sensual affectation, at once straddling and mincing, and slowly, disgustingly, irresistibly, it seeped from the surface down into the depths. For a while she paused to rest her arms. All this was really quite silly and could not prevent what was bound to happen. But while the fancy remained—merely swinging to and fro, with an intangible suggestion of things forbidden and things desired and undesired, all part of another chain of events that was mistier and less corporeal than that of real decisions, yet remotely accompanying all she did— and while her fingers slid through her soft hair, the sleeves of her wrap slipping up her bare arms, it seemed to her again that at some point in time—once? always?—it had all been like this before. And it struck her as odd that now when she was awake, here in the emptiness of the morning, her arms were moving up and down as though subject not to her own will but to some other, alien, indifferent power. And then slowly the mood of the past night began to reassert itself, and memories rose almost to the surface of her mind, only to sink away again. A tension lay between her and those half-remembered experiences, like a quivering curtain.

Outside the windows day was breaking, bright and uneasy. Looking out into the monotonous, blank light, Claudine felt a stirring like the voluntary loosening of her fingers' grasp, a slow, alluring sensation of gliding down among silvery shining bubbles and motionless fishes, strange and goggle-eyed. The day began.

She took a sheet of paper and wrote a few words to her husband: 'It's all so odd. It'll only be for a few days, but I feel as if I were somewhere high above myself, involved in something I don't understand. Tell me, what is our love? What is it? I need help, I need to hear you! I know it is like a tower, but what I feel is only the trembling of something rising into the air, slim and tall. . . .'

When she went to the post-office to post the letter, she was told that communications had broken down.

She walked to the edge of the little town. There the plain stretched away into the distance, a wide, white sea all around. Sometimes a crow flew through this whiteness; here and there a bush stood out, black and stiff. Only some small, dark dots strewn along the far skyline were a sign that over there, too, there was human life.

Turning back, she walked through the streets, restlessly, for perhaps an hour. She went through all the side streets, after a while finding herself covering the same ground, only in the other direction, and turned aside again, crossing squares where she had the feeling of how she had walked there just a few minutes earlier. Everywhere there was the same white play of reflections from the empty plain, a feverish flicker sliding through this little town that was cut off from all reality. Before the houses there lay high banks of snow. The air was clear and dry. It was still snowing a little, but the flakes were falling thinly—flat, almost shrivelled, glittering little scales— as if it might stop soon. Here and there, from above the shut doors of the houses, windows looked down into the street with a bright blue glassy gaze, and the ground underfoot rang like glass too. Sometimes a piece of hard, frozen snow crashed down through a gully, tearing a jagged hole in the stillness. And suddenly the wall of a house would glow in rosy light, or in delicate canary-yellow. . . . Then all Claudine did seemed oddly heightened, more intensely alive; and in the hushed silence all things visible seemed to light one another up, as it were echoing one another in a larger visibility. And then it would all withdraw into itself again and in meaningless streets the houses were like little groups of mushrooms in the woods, or like a thicket of wind-bent shrubs on a wide plain, while she still felt a dizziness and an immensity beyond. There was in her some kind of fire, some burning, bitter fluid, and while she walked and mused, she seemed to herself a huge, mysterious vessel that was being carried through the streets—a thin-walled, flaming vessel.

She tore up the letter and went to the school, where she spent the time till midday in discussion with the masters.

The rooms there were quiet. When, from where she sat, she looked through the sombre, heavy vault out into the open, every-thing seemed remote and muted, veiled in grey, snowy light. Then the men with her seemed too corporeal, oppressively ponderous, like great weights pressing down on hard, sharp ground. Her discussions with them were of the most matter-of-fact kind, but at moments even that seemed almost like abandonment. She wondered at this, for she did not like these men at all. There was not one among them who was in the slightest attractive to her; they all repelled her by their manners, which revealed their lowly origins. Yet she sensed the masculinity, the other sex, in them with an acuteness never experienced before, or at least not for many years. She realised that this was caused by the expression of their faces, which the half-light enhanced by the dull commonness in them that was incomprehensibly transformed by their very ugliness, by a whiff of rutting-time, of enormous, clumsy, troglodyte beasts, that hung about them like an aura. She recognised again, here too, that old feeling of defencelessness which had overcome her time and again since she had been alone. A peculiar submissiveness crept into all she did and said, into every detail, every turn of the conversation. It was there in the attentiveness with which she felt compelled to listen, even in the very fact that she was there, sitting in a chair, talking.

Claudine grew restive. She had lingered much too long, and the atmosphere and the half-darkness of the rooms closed in on her, suffocating and bewildering her. For the first time she was struck by the idea that all that had prevented her from sliding back into her former life was the fact that she had never before been away from her husband, on her own.

What she felt now was no longer vague, roving, inscrutable: it was now associated with real people. Yet it was not these men she was afraid of, but her own reactions. While their talk surrounded her, something stirred within her, shook her mysteriously—not one distinct emotion, but the very foundation of all emotions—as it may happen when one walks through other people's homes, places that fill one with distaste, and gradually, insidiously, one begins to think how these other people can live and be happy there, until there comes a moment when it all takes hold of one, as if one were one of those people, and one wants to jump free, but, transfixed, feels on all sides how the world revolves, solidly, quietly, round this centre too.

In the grey gloom here these black, bearded men became giant shapes inside twilit bubbles, alien worlds, and she wondered what it would feel like to be enclosed in such a world. Her thoughts seemed to sink deep into soft, swampy ground; and then there was only a voice, roughened by smoking, and words, muffled in a haze of cigarette-smoke, that constantly brushed against her face, and after that another voice, high and tinny, and she tried to imagine this second voice breaking and deepening in sexual excitement. Then again clumsy gestures caught her attention, drawing her feelings after them in weird convolutions. There was one ludicrous Olympian whom she tried to regard as would a woman who took him seriously. Something strange that had nothing to do with her own life rose up before her, casting its shadow on her, too close, too big, like a shaggy animal that gave off an overpowering smell.

She felt for a moment as if all she wanted were a whip to lash it with, and then, suddenly checked, but without really understanding, she caught the play of expressions intimately known of old in a face that somehow resembled her own.

Then she thought secretly: 'People like us might even be able to live with men like these. . . .' And in this thought there lay a queerly tormenting fascination, an expanding titillation of the brain; and there was something like a thin pane of glass before it, against which her thoughts pressed painfully to stare through it into a vague murkiness. She enjoyed looking into these men's eyes meanwhile with a limpid, innocent gaze. Then she tried to picture her husband, estranged and as though seen from that murky region beyond. She succeeded in thinking of him quite calmly: he remained a wonderful, an incomparable person, but something imponderable, something that reason could not grasp, had left him, and he seemed somehow faded and not so close to her as before. Sometimes, when an illness reaches its last critical stage, one's experiences have that cool, detached lucidity. How odd that once it had been possible really to experience these things with which she was now toying, that there had been a time when, undisturbed by any questionings, she would undoubtedly have felt about him just as she had been trying to feel about him now! All at once everything seemed very strange.

One moves, day in, day out, among the same people: one walks through the same countryside, through the same town, the same house; and his landscape, these people, go along with one, always, every day, at every step, in every thought, unresistantly. Then one day, with a faint jolt, they stop: and there they stand, incomprehensibly stark and still, aloof, in some alien, stubborn atmosphere. And when one turns to look back at oneself, there is a stranger standing there with them. And so one has a past. 'But what is it?' Claudine asked herself. And there was no seeing what could have made the difference.

There was nothing simpler than the answer that it was oneself that had become different. But she began to feel a peculiar resistance to granting that possibility. And perhaps one does experience all that is great and fateful in the pattern of one's life only in some oddly reversed state of mind? While at one moment she could not understand the ease with which she felt a stranger to a past that once had been as close to her as her own body, and at the next moment could not understand how anything could ever have been different from the way it was now, something else occurred to her: now and then it happens that one sees something in the distance, an unfamiliar thing, and walks towards it, and at a certain point it enters into the circle of one's own life; but the place where one was before is now strangely empty. Or one has only to reflect: yesterday I did this, did that. . . . A moment always comes that is like an abyss, and, left behind at its brink, there stands a sick person whom one does not know and who is gradually fading from sight. Only one does not often think of it. And in a flash of illumination she saw her whole life dominated by this inexplicable, unremitting betrayal that one commits in every instant, by cutting loose from oneself without knowing why and nevertheless sensing in it an ultimate, inexhaustible tenderness far removed from conscious thought, a tenderness through which one is more intimately linked with oneself than with any of one's actions. And while this is going on, for everyone else one remains always one and the same person.

And while these feelings were still shining clearly in her, their very depths revealed, it seemed to her as if the certainty that bore her outer life along, making it revolve round her, had all at once ceased to work. Her life began to fan out into a multitude of possibilities, unfolding, one behind the other, like stage-scenery of many different lives; and, in a pallid, empty, unquiet area between, the schoolmasters loomed up, obscure, floating shapes, and sank as though in search of something, gazing at her, until, heavily, they fell into place again. She felt a quaint and melancholy pleasure in being the strange lady, sitting here before them with an unapproachable smile, entrenched behind her physical appearance, while within herself she was merely a haphazard being, separated from them only by a deciduous husk, the fabric of chance and actuality. And while talk issued from her lips, fast and meaningless, soulless, facile, unwinding like thread from a spool, she was slowly becoming bewildered by the thought that if the atmosphere peculiar to any of these men were to close around her, all she would do then would be just as truly herself as if any given 'reality' were something without significance, merely something that comes spouting up through an indifferent crack in the surface of things, while far below, out of one's own reach, one's solitary self floats along in a stream of unborn realities whose otherworldly, gentle music no one else can hear. All her security, all her anxious clinging to the one beloved, now suddenly appeared arbitrary, irrelevant, and merely superficial, compared with her apprehension—almost beyond the grasp of mind—of the utterly other communion of their beings at that depth of solitude, in boundless, final, immutable inwardness.

And there was the lure when now she suddenly remembered the stranger. She realised that, since he desired her, all that was here still a mere toying with possibilities would, with him, become reality.

Something in her shuddered, something warned her. Sodomy, she thought. That is what it would amount to. But behind that there lay her love's ordeal: 'So that in the realm of reality you shall feel it is I . . . I . . . here under this beast! The unimaginable thing! So that, over there, you can never again blieve in me, *me* solidly and simply. So that I shall become a mirage beyond your grasp, a fading glimmer as soon as you let go of me. Only a mirage, which means you will know: I am only something within you and by virtue of your own existence, as long as you hold me fast, and am something different—anything—when you let go of me, my beloved, with whom I am so strangely united. . . .'

She was overtaken by the quiet, fickle sadness of the adventurer, that mournfulness attaching to things one does not for their own sake but for the sake of having done them. She felt that somewhere the stranger was now standing, waiting for her. Her shrunken field of vision was already dense with his breathing, and the air close to her seemed filled with the smell of him. Growing uneasy, she prepared to take her leave. She knew that her way was leading her straight to him, and the thought of the moment when it would have happened was like a cold hand gripping her body. It was as if something had taken hold of her and were dragging her towards a door. And she knew this door would slam behind her, and she struggled, and yet she was already craning forward, all her senses reaching out ahead.

When she encountered the man again he was no longer someone she was just beginning to know: the whole thing had become imminent. She realised that in the meantime he had been thinking about her too and had laid his plans.

She heard him say: "I have reconciled myself to the thought that you reject me. But never again will any man venerate you as unselfishly as I do."

Claudine did not answer. His words had come slowly, emphatically; they did not affect her, but she could imagine what it would be like if they did.

After a while she said: "Did you know?—we *are* snowed up!"

Everything seemed as if she had experienced it once before; her words seemed to drag in the groove of words she had surely spoken once before. She paid no heed to her actions as such; what interested her was simply the distinction between what she was doing now and something identical in the past—the arbitrariness of it, this sense of something very intimate and yet accidental that went with the experience. And she had a vast, immobile awareness of her own existence with past and present rippling over it, ever recurrent, in little waves.

After a while he said abruptly: "I can feel there is something in you that hesitates. I know that hesitation. Every woman is faced with it at some point in her life. You respect your husband, you certainly don't wish to hurt him, and so you put up a barrier. But actually, you know, you ought to shake all that off, for a while at any rate, and let the great storm sweep over you."

Again Claudine remained silent. He was bound to misinterpret her silence, and that gave her an odd sense of relish. And in her silence she realised more profoundly that there was something in her that could not express itself through any action, that could not be harmed by any action, that could not defend itself because it lay below the realm of words: something that, in order to be understood, had to be loved as it loved itself, something that she shared with no one but her husband. That was the inward communion; and what she was about to abandon to this stranger, for him to ravage, was only the surface of her being.

So they strolled along, talking. But her feelings were bending over the brink, and there was dizziness in her, and it made her feel ever more deeply the marvellously incomprehensible nature of belonging to her only beloved. At moments it seemed to her that she was beginning to adapt herself to the man at her side, even though outwardly she might appear unchanged; and then sometimes it was as if repartee, phrases, and gestures from her earlier life were coming back to her, things that she had thought herself grown out of long ago. "The lady has a wit," he said.

When he spoke thus, walking at her side, she observed how his

words went out into an utter void, which they gradually populated—first with the houses they were walking past—only these
houses were a little different now, askew as one sees them mirrored
in window-panes; and then there was the street too, and after a
while herself, also a little changed and distorted, though still recognisable. She felt the force, the elemental vitality, emanating from
this otherwise unremarkable man—causing a scarcely perceptible
displacement of the surrounding world, a shifting and bending of
things, flattening them out. It disconcerted her to see her own image
too within that mirrorlike sliding world; it was as if she had only
to yield a little more and she would be entirely that image.

Then there was a moment when he exclaimed: "Believe me, it's
all a matter of habit. If, let's say, at seventeen or eighteen, you had
met some other man and married him, today you would find it just
as difficult to imagine yourself the wife of the man whom, as it
happens, you *have* married."

They came to where the church was. Tall and solitary they stood
there in the wide square, and, looking at her companion, Claudine
saw his gestures projecting out of him into the emptiness round
about. For a moment she felt as if thousands of crystals bound
together to form her body were bristling and writhing; a scattered,
splintered, restlessly flickering light rose within her, and the man
on whom it fell all at once looked quite different in the glitter of
it: his outlines shifted closer to her, twitching, jerking like her own
heart, and she felt each of his movements inside her, passing through
her body. She wanted to cry out, reminding herself who he was; but
this feeling was only an insubstantial chaotic gleam floating strangely
somewhere within her, as though it had nothing to do with her.

And then everything seemed to disappear in a vortex of misty
light. She glanced about her: there were the houses, as before,
standing straight and silent around the square. In the tower the
clock began to strike. Round and metallic the chimes came bowling
through the dream-holes, scattering as they fell, and skimming away
over the roofs. Claudine imagined them rolling on over the countryside, far away, resounding. . . . And all at once, in awe, she felt:
voices go through the world, many-towered and massive, clangor-
ous as brazen cities—something that is beyond reason, an independent, incomprehensible world of feeling, combining as it were
arbitrarily and at random with the everyday world of reason and

then again vanishing into stillness—something that is like those vast abysmal wings of darkness that sometimes move softly across a blank and rigid sky.

It was as if something were standing all around her and gazing at her. She felt the excitement in the man beside her, a surging and billowing, a lashing out, lonely and sombre, in an expanse of futility. And gradually it began to seem to her that what this man desired of her, this act ostensibly so great and important, was something entirely impersonal; it amounted to no more than being gazed at like this, with a gaze all stupor and vacuity—just as dots in space, combined into a random pattern, gaze at each other inertly. It made her shrink, compressing her until it seemed that she herself was no more than such a dot. And this gave her a peculiar sense of her own existence: it was remote from normal rationality and self-awareness and yet left her intrinsically unchanged. All at once she ceased to feel how repellently commonplace was the way this man's mind worked. And she felt as if she were standing somewhere in open country, and around her the sounds in the air and the clouds in the sky stood quite still, etched into the surface of this fleeting instant. And she herself was no different from them, a vapour merely, an echoing . . . and it seemed to her she could understand the way the animals loved, and the clouds, and the sounds in the air.

She felt the man's eyes searching for hers, and all at once she was frightened and longed for the solid certainty of her own existence. She felt her clothes clinging to her, a husk enclosing the very last of the tenderness she knew to have been her own, and beneath that she felt her blood pulsing, and she could almost smell its quivering pungency. And all she had was this body that she was now to surrender, and this utterly other, spiritual feeling, this yearning beyond all reality—a sense of the soul that was now a sense of the body—ultimate bliss. And she did not know whether now her love was taking the final, most daring step of all, or was already fading and her senses were curiously, inquisitively, opening all their windows. . . .

*　　*　　*

Later, that evening, in the dining-room, she felt lonely.

A woman spoke to her across the table: "I saw your little girl waiting for you this afternoon. What a charming child! She must be a great joy to you."

Claudine had not been to the school again and she had nothing to say to this. She felt as if only some insensitive part of herself were present here among these people—her hair or nails, or a body that was all of horn. Then she did make some noncommittal reply, and even while she spoke it seemed that her words became entangled in something, caught in something that was like a sack or a net. Her own words seemed alien among the alien words of others, like fishes struggling and jerking among the moist, cold bodies of other fishes, in the incoherent mesh of opinions.

She was overcome by disgust. Once again she felt that what mattered was not what she could say about herself, what she could explain in words, but that all justification lay elsewhere—in a smile, in a way of falling silent, in listening to oneself within. Suddenly she felt an ineffable longing for that one and only man who was as solitary as she and whom nobody here would understand either— for him who had nothing but that soft tenderness filled with floating pictures, a tenderness that like the veils of fever absorbed the hard thrust of material things, leaving all outer happenings behind in vast, dim flatness, while within everything remained secure in the eternal, mysterious balance of self-awareness.

But whereas at other times, in similar moods, a room crowded like this would be a solid, heavy, hot mass revolving round her, enveloping her, here and now it was different and there was at times some furtive standstill, a dislocation of the things—a sideboard, a table, that then jumped into place again—an atmosphere of sullen rejection. Discord grew between her and these familiar objects; there was something uncertain, wavering, about them. All of a sudden there was again that ugliness which she had experienced on the journey, not a plain, straightforward ugliness, but something that made her perceptions, when they reached out like a hand for solid things, go right through them and come out the other side. Gaps opened up, as if—since that ultimate certainty within her had dreamily begun to contemplate itself—something in the order of things, at other times impalpably embedded in her, had worked loose, and where there had been a coherent chain of impressions, a world of harmony, now everything was rent and riven, the surrounding world turned into mere unceasing uproar.

Gradually it made her feel as someone might who walks at the edge of the sea. One cannot make any impression on this roaring that tears away every thought and every act down to the bare bones of the very instant. And gradually there comes uneasiness, an increasing sense of overflowing one's limits, of losing one's identity and pouring away: an urge to shout, a yearning for incredible, enormous gestures, a soaring flash of will, action without end— action with the sole purpose of making one's own existence real. There was a ravening, devouring, annihilating force in this sense of dissolution, and every second of it was wild, irresponsible solitude, cut off from everything, staring at the world in oblivious stupor. And it wrenched gestures and words from her, which seemed to rush past her, coming from somewhere else, and which yet were part of herself. And there before her sat that stranger, that man, and could not fail to notice how this was drawing her body closer to him, like a vessel containing all her longing and desire, all the deepest love she knew. Then she no longer saw anything but his beard going up and down as he talked, monotonously, lulling her to sleep, going up and down like the beard of some horrible he-goat that sat there muttering, slowly munching wisps of words.

* * *

She felt very sorry for herself. Everything turned into a rocking sing-song of grief at the thought that all this could really happen.

He said: "I can tell—you are one of those women whose destiny it is to be swept away by a storm. Oh yes, you have your pride— and so you try to deny it. But believe me, a man who understands women is not deceived."

It was as if she were sinking, irresistibly, back into her past. But when she gazed around her, as she sank through aeons of the soul's life, which were like layer upon layer of deep water, what struck her was the random nature of her surroundings: not the fact that everything looked the way it did, but that this appearance persisted, adhering to things as if it were part of them, perversely holding on to them as with claws. It was like an expression that has remained on a face long after the emotion has gone. And oddly—as though a link had snapped in the silently unwinding chain of events and swivelled out of its true position, jutting out of its dimension—all the people and all the things grew rigid in the attitude of that chance moment, combining, squarely and solidly, to form another, abnormal order. Only she herself went sliding on, her swaying senses outspread among these faces and things—sliding downwards—away.

The whole complex pattern of her emotions, interwoven with the years of her life, was momentarily visible in the distance behind all this, isolated, dreary, and almost of no account. She thought: 'One digs a line in the ground, any unbroken line by which to keep one's bearings among the silent, towering things that tilt in all directions. That is our life. It's like talking on and on and deceiving oneself into believing that every word relates to the word before and demands the next, because one dreads to think how, if the thread broke, if words failed, one would sway and stagger and be swallowed up by the silence. But that's only weakness, only fear of the horribly gaping contingency of all one does. . . .'

"It's a matter of destiny," he went on. "There are men whose destiny it is to bring unrest with them wherever they go, and it's no good barricading oneself in—there's no defence against it."

But she scarcely heard what this stranger said. Her thoughts were moving in queer, aloof, contradictory ways. She wanted to free herself with one single phrase, with one wild gesture, to take refuge at her beloved's feet: there was still time. But something restrained her, made her shrink from the mere thought of such screaming, panic-stricken flight. She did not want to turn from the great river's bank for fear of being swept away, to hug her life to herself for fear of losing it, to sing merely for fear of falling into bewildered silence. She rejected that. She groped for hesitant, meditative words. She did not want to shriek, as all the others did for fear of the silence around them. Nor did she want to sing. What she longed for was a whispering, a falling silent . . . nothingness, the void. . . .

And then there came a slow, soundless edging forward, a bending over the brink. "Don't you love the theatre, the illusion of the stage?" she heard him say. "What I value in art is the subtlety of the right ending, which consoles us for the humdrum of everyday life. Life is disappointing, so often depriving us of the effect on which the curtain should fall. If we were to leave it at that, wouldn't it mean accepting the bleak matter-of-factness of things?"

And suddenly she heard it quite distinctly, very close to her. Somewhere there was still that other hand, that faint warmth reaching out for her, a conscious flash: You. . . . And she let go of herself, borne up by an inner certainty that even now for each other they were all that counted, that they belonged together, wordless, incredulous, a fabric light and slight as the sweetness of death, an arabesque belonging to a style not yet evolved, each of them a note resounding meaningfully only in the other's soul and ceasing to exist when that soul no longer listened.

Her companion straightened up and looked at her. And then she realised she was here with him, and how far from her was that other man, her beloved. What was he thinking now? Whatever it was, she would never know. And she herself? Hidden in the darkness of her body there was a swaying, aimless urge. At this moment she felt her body—that sheltering home and hedge around its own feelings—as a vague and formless obstacle. She recognised its independent existence and how its feelings and urges shut her in, closer than anything else—recognised in it the inevitable act of betrayal separating her from her beloved. And in a darkening of her senses such as she had never known before, she felt as if, suddenly, in some uncanny innermost depth, her ultimate fidelity, which she still preserved in her body, were turning into its opposite.

Perhaps all she wished now was to yield this body to her beloved, but the profound spiritual uncertainty with which it trembled somehow turned that impulse into desire for this stranger here with her. She faced the possibility that, even while she was being ravaged in her body, this body might still give her the sense of being herself, and she shuddered, as at a darkness, a void, into which she was being locked, at the body's autonomy and its mysterious power to disregard all decisions of the mind. And a blissful bitterness tempted her to disown, to abandon this body, to feel it in its sensual forlornness dragged down by a stranger and as though slashed open with knives, filled to the brim with the helpless twitchings of horror, violence, and disgust—and yet to feel queerly, and as in ultimate truthfulness and constancy, its presence round this nothingness, this wavering, shapeless omnipresence, this certainty of sickness that was the soul—feeling it in spite of everything as in a dream the edges of a wound are felt, striving in endlessly renewed, agonising endeavour to close, each torn part vainly searching for the other.

As a light rises behind a delicate network of veins, out of the expectant darkness of the years the mortal nostalgia of her love rose up among her thoughts, gradually enveiling her. And then all at once, from a long way off, from some radiant expanse, and as though she had only now understood the implication of the stranger's words, she heard herself say: "I don't know whether he could bear it. . . . "

It was the first time she had spoken of her husband. She was startled: it did not seem part of this reality. But she instantly saw the meaning in the words she had just uttered, and their inevitable consequence.

Seizing upon this, her companion said: "Do you mean to say you love him?"

She did not miss the absurdity of the assurance with which he flung this at her. Trembling but determined, she said: "No, no, I don't love him at all."

When she was upstairs again, in her room, she wondered how she could have uttered such a lie; but she relished the masked, enigmatic fascination of it. She thought of her husband. Now and then in her mind's eye she caught a glimpse of him—it was like standing in the street, looking through a window at someone moving about in a brightly lit room. Only then did she really grasp what she was doing. He seemed beautiful in that light and she wanted to be there with him, for then she too would partake of the radiance about him.

But she shrank back into her lie again, and once more it was like being outside in the street in darkness. She shivered with cold; it was anguish merely to be alive—anguish to look at things, to breathe. The feeling that bound her to her husband was like a globe of warm light into which she could easily slip back. There she was safe; there the things could not thrust at her like the sharp prows of ships looming up out of the night; there everything was softly padded and the things were warded off. And yet she rejected that.

She remembered that she had lied once before. Not in her earlier life, for then the lie had been simply part of herself. But once in this second life of hers she had told a lie, even though what she had actually said was true enough—that she had been out for a walk, in the evening, for two hours. She suddenly realised that that was the first time she had told a lie. Just as she had sat among the people downstairs tonight, so at that time she had walked about in the streets, forlorn, restless as a stray dog, and had gazed into the windows of the houses. And somewhere somebody opened his front door, letting a woman in, smugly satisfied with his own affability, his gestures, the style of his welcome. And somewhere else a man walked arm in arm with his wife, going out for the evening, filled with dignity from head to toe, smug in the security of wedlock. And everywhere, as in a broad river that placidly shelters multifarious life, there were small whirling eddies, each revolving on its own centre, gazing inwards, blind and windowless, closed to the indifferent world. And within, in everyone, there was the same feeling of being held in balance by one's own echo in a narrow space that catches every word and keeps it ringing until the next is uttered, so that one does not hear the insufferable interval, the chasm between the impact of one action and the next, the chasm between two sounds, where one drops away from the sense of one's own identity, plunging into the silence between two words, which might just as well be the silence between the words of somebody utterly different.

And then she had been assailed by the secret thought: 'Somewhere among all these people there is someone—not the right one, someone else—but still, one could have adjusted oneself even to him, and then one would never have known anything of the person that one is today. For every feeling exists only in the long chain of other feelings, each supporting the next; and all that matters is that one instant of life should link up with the next without any lacuna, and there are hundreds of different ways in which it can do so.' And for the first time since the beginning of her love the thought had flashed through her mind: 'It is all chance—by some chance something becomes reality, and then one holds on to it, that's all.'

For the first time she had felt her being, down to its very foundations, as something indeterminate, had apprehended this ultimate faceless experience of herself in love as something that destroyed the very root, the absoluteness, of existence and would always have made her into a person that she called herself and who was nevertheless not different from everyone else. And it was as if she must let go, let herself sink back into the drift of things, into the realm of unfulfilled possibilities, the no-man's-land. And she hurried through the mournful, empty streets, glancing in through windows as she passed, wanting no other company than the clatter of her heels on the cobbles—reduced to that last sign of physical existence, hearing nothing but her own footsteps echoing now in front of her and now behind her.

At that time all she had been able to grasp was the dissolution, the ceaselessly shifting background of shadowy unrealised feelings that frustrated any power by which one might have held on to another human being—that, and the devalued, undemonstrable, and incomprehensible nature of her own life. She had almost wept with confusion and fatigue, entering that realm of utter isolation.

But now, in this moment when it all came back to her, it carried her right to the end of whatever possibilities of real love, real union, there were in this transparently thin, glimmeringly vulnerable world of illusion—of illusions without which life could not be maintained: all the dream-dark straits of existing solely by virtue of another human being, all the island solitude of never daring to wake, this insubstantiality of love that was like a gliding between two mirrors behind which nothingness lay. And here in this room, hidden behind her false confession as behind a mask, and waiting for the adventure that she would experience as though she were someone else, she knew the wonderful, dangerous intensification of feeling that came with lying and cheating in love. She felt herself stealthily slipping out of her own being, out into some territory beyond anyone else's reach, the forbidden territory, the dissolution of absolute solitude— entering, for the sake of greater truthfulness, into the void that sometimes gapes for an instant behind all ideals.

And then suddenly she heard a furtive tread, a creaking first of the stairs and then of the floorboards outside her door, a faint creaking under the weight of someone who had stopped there.

Her eyes turned towards the door. How strange that there out-side, behind those thin panels, there was another human being, standing motionless. . . . And on each side of this indifferent, this accidental door tension rose high as behind a dam.

She had already undressed. Her clothes lay on the chair by the bed, where she had just flung them, and from them the vague scent of what had been next to her body rose and mingled with the air of this room that was let one day to this person, the next day to another. She glanced round the room. She noticed a brass lock hanging loose, on a chest of drawers. Her gaze lingered on a small threadbare rug, worn thin by many footsteps, at the side of her bed. Suddenly she could not help thinking of all the bare feet that had stepped on this rug, permeating it with their smell, and how this smell was given off again and entered into other people's being, a familiar, protective smell, somehow associated with childhood and home. It was an odd, flickering, double impression, now alien and abhorrent, now fascinating, as if the self-love of all those strangers were a current flowing into her and all that was left of her own identity were a passive awareness of it.

And all the while that man was there, standing on the other side of her door, his presence known to her only through the faint, hardly detectable sounds that he could not help making.

Then she was seized by a wild urge to throw herself down on this rug and kiss the repulsive traces of all those feet, exciting herself with their smell like a bitch on heat. But this was no longer sexual desire; it was something crying within her like a small child, howling like a high wind.

Suddenly she knelt down on the rug. The stiff flowers of the pattern loomed larger, spreading and intertwining senselessly before her eyes, and over them she saw her own heavy thighs, a mature woman's thighs, hideously arched and without meaning, yet tense with an incomprehensible gravity. And her hands lay there before her on the floor, two five-limbed animals staring at each other.

All at once she remembered the lamp in the passage there outside and the horribly silent moving circles it cast upon the ceiling, and the walls, the bare walls, remembered the emptiness out there and then again the man who was standing there, faintly creaking sometimes as a tree creaks in its bark, his urgent blood in his head like the thicket of the leaves. And here she was on her hands and knees, only a door between her and him. And still she felt the full sweetness of her ripe body, felt it with that imperishable remnant of the soul that stands quietly, unmoved, beside the ravaged body even when it is broken open and disfigured by the infliction of devastating injuries—that stands beside it, in grave and constant awareness and yet averted from it, as beside the body of a stricken beast.

Then she heard the man outside walking cautiously away. And even through the turmoil in her rapt senses she realised: all this was betrayal itself, greater and weightier than the mere lie.

Slowly she began to rise on her knees, spellbound by the baffling thought that by now it might all have really happened, and she trembled like someone who has escaped from danger by mere chance, not by any effort of his own. She tried to picture it. She saw her body lying underneath that stranger's body, saw it with a lucidity that branches out into every smallest detail, like spilt water seeping into every cranny. She felt her own pallor and heard the shameful words of abandonment and saw above her the man's eyes, holding her down, hovering over her, like the outspread wings of a bird of prey. And all the time she was thinking: '*This* is betrayal!' And now she pictured herself at home again after all this and how he would say: 'I can't feel you from inside. . . . 'And she had no answer but a helpless smile, a smile that tried to say: 'Believe me, it was not meant against us. . . . '

And yet there was one knee still pressed against the floor—a senseless, alien thing—and she felt her very existence in it, inaccessible, with all the forlorn, defenceless frailty there is in the ultimate human potentialities that no word can hold fast and no return can ever weave into the pattern of life as it once has been.

She was empty of thought. She did not know if she was doing wrong. Everything turned into strange and lonely grief—and the grief itself was like another room around her, enclosing a gentle darkness, a diffuse, floating room, softly rising in the air. And then gradually she perceived a strong, clear, indifferent light shining from above. In it she saw everything she did, her own gestures of surrender, and the abandonment of her innermost being, torn out of her in ecstasy, all that in its enormity seemed so real and yet was mere appearance. . . . There it lay, crumpled, small, and cold, all its relevance lost, far, far below her. . . .

And after a long time it seemed to her as if a cautious hand were again trying the door, and she knew he was there outside, listening intently. A whirling dizziness took hold of her, almost forcing her to creep to the door on all fours and draw back the bolt.

But she remained crouching on the floor in the middle of the room. Once again something held her back—a sense of her own sordidness, the atmosphere of the past. Like a single, violent thrust cutting her sinews, there was the thought that perhaps it was all nothing but a relapse into her past. She raised her hands above her head. 'Oh my beloved, help me, help me!' she cried out in her thoughts, and felt the cry was true. And yet it was only a soft, caressing thought: 'We moved towards each other, mysteriously drawn through space, through all the years . . . and now, by sad and hurtful ways, I enter into you.'

And then there was stillness, a great expanse: strength that had been painfully dammed up now pouring in through the breaches in the walls. Like a quiet, mirroring pool of water her life lay there before her, past and future united in the present moment. There are things one can never do—one does not know why. Perhaps those are the most important things? Indeed one knows they are the most important things. And one knows: a deadly languor lies upon life, one feels the stiffness and numbness of it as in frozen fingers. And sometimes again it loosens its hold, dissolves like snow and ice on meadows—one marvels, one is a sombre brightness expanding far, far away. But life, one's own hard and bony life, one's irrevocable life, resumes its callous grip—somewhere the links close—one does nothing at all.

Suddenly she rose to her feet, and the thought that now she *must* do this drove her soundlessly forward. Her hands drew the bolt back. There was no sound. The door did not move. And then she opened the door and looked out into the passage: there was no one there. In the dim light from the lamp the bare walls stared at each other through empty space. He had gone without her hearing it.

She went to bed, her mind full of self-reproaches. And, already on the borders of sleep, she thought: 'I am hurting you.' But at the same time she had the strange feeling: 'It is you who do whatever I am doing.' And sinking towards oblivion she knew: 'We are casting away everything that can be cast away, to hold on to each other all the more tightly, to wrap around us closely what no one can touch.' Then for an instant, thrown up into wakefulness, she thought: 'This man will triumph over us. But what is triumph?'

*　　*　　*

Sinking back into sleep, her thoughts slid down along that question into the depths and her bad conscience accompanied her like a last caress. A vast egoism, deepening and darkening the world, rose over her as over someone dying. Behind closed eyes she saw bushes and clouds and birds, and she became quite small among them, and yet it all seemed to be there only for her sake. And then there was the moment of closing up, of shutting out everything alien; and on the threshold of dream there was perfection, a great and pure love mantling her in a trembling light, dissolution of all apparent contradictions.

The visitor did not return. She slept undisturbed, her door un-latched—quiet as a tree on a meadow.

*　　*　　*

With the next morning a mild, mysterious day began. She woke as though behind bright curtains keeping out all the reality of the light outside. She went for a walk; and he accompanied her. Her mind swayed with an intoxication that came from the blueness of the air and the whiteness of the snow. They walked to the edge of the little town, and there the white plain before them lay radiant and festive.

They stood by a fence and looked at a small path behind it. A peasant woman was throwing corn to her hens. A patch of lichen shone yellow in the wintry light.

"Do you think——?" Claudine asked, gazing back through the street and up into the pale blue air; but she did not finish her sentence. After a while she said: "Look at that wreath—I wonder how long it's been hanging there. Does the air feel it? Is it alive?" That was all she said and she did not even know why she said that. He smiled.

She stood beside him, and it was as if everything were engraved in metal, still trembling from the pressure of the engraver's burin. And while she felt him looking at her, observing her, something within her fell into shape and lay wide and brilliant as fields lie one next to the other under the eyes of a circling bird.

'This life, now bright blue, now dark—somewhere a small bright patch of yellow—what is the meaning of it? This voice calling to the hens, this faint patter of the strewn grains of corn, and then all at once something that strikes across it all like the tolling of a bell on the hour—what does it say, and to whom? This thing without a name, eating its way down into the depths and only sometimes shooting up through the narrow slit of seconds and flashing through some passer-by and at other times lying as though dead—what can it mean?' She looked around with quiet eyes and felt all the things about her without thinking of them, felt them as one feels the touch of hands laid on one's forehead when there is nothing more to say.

And after that she listened merely with a smile. It was obvious that he felt he was carefully drawing his net tighter round her, and she let him have his way. While he talked to her she felt no more than one feels when walking between houses, hearing people talk indoors. The pattern of her thoughts was sometimes invaded by another current, which drew her thoughts along with it, now this way, now that; and she would follow of her own free will—then for a short time, half emerging from shadowy depths, would almost return to herself, and once again would follow the current, would sink. Softly and silently the entangling flow of it took her captive.

And in between she felt this man's love of himself as intensely as if it were a feeling of her own. His tenderness towards himself infected her with a faint sensual excitement. It was like entering a realm where everything was hushed, and silent decisions prevailed, decisions not of one's own making. She knew herself hard pressed and knew herself to be giving way, but it no longer mattered. Something far within her was like a bird upon a branch, singing. . . .

*   *   *

She ate a light supper and went to bed early. There was a deadness in things now; she no longer felt any erotic excitement. Yet after a short sleep she woke, thinking: 'He's downstairs, waiting.' She groped for her clothes and dressed, simply got up and dressed—without feeling, without thought, with only a remote awareness of doing wrong; and then perhaps, at the very last moment, there was a sense of being exposed and defenceless. And so she went downstairs.

The room was deserted. The tables and chairs were tense and still, looming indistinctly in the silence of the night. In one corner, there he sat.

She said something, without quite knowing what—perhaps: "I was feeling so alone there upstairs. . . ." And she knew just how he was bound to misinterpret it. After a while he took her hand. She rose, hesitated, and then ran out of the room. She knew this was behaving like any silly little woman, and there was a thrill in that. On the stairs she heard footsteps behind her. The stairs creaked. Her thoughts were suddenly very remote and abstract, but her body was trembling like an animal hunted down, deep in the forest.

Then, sitting in her room, he said: "You are in love with me, aren't you? I grant you, I'm no artist or philosopher, I'm just human— but a whole man, yes, I think I may say, a whole man."

"What is a *whole man?*" she asked.

"What a queer question!" he exclaimed, chafing.

"No, that's not what I mean," she said. "I'm thinking how odd it is that one can be fond of someone just because one is fond of him—fond of his eyes, his tongue—not his words, but the sound of them. . . ."

He kissed her and said: "So that is how you love me?"

Claudine found the strength to answer: "No, what I love is being with you—the fact, the mere chance, of being with you. One might equally well be among the Eskimos, wearing trousers made of skins, and have drooping breasts. And be delighted with it all. Can't there, after all, be other kinds of *whole* people?"

But he said: "You're mistaken. You are in love with me. Only you can't face it yet. And just that is the sign of true passion."

Involuntarily something in her shrank when she realised how he was assuming possession of her.

But he murmured: "No, don't say anything."

Claudine was silent. But while they were undressing, she began to talk—again out-of-place, aimless, even senseless talk, merely like a disconsolate movement of her hands, an urge to stroke and smooth away, a sort of by-play.... "It's like slipping through a narrow pass—suddenly everything's changed. Animals, people, flowers, oneself—it's all quite different. You wonder: if I'd always lived here, how would I think about this, how would I feel about that? Isn't it odd that there's only a line—only one line one has to cross? I should like to kiss you and then jump back across that line and look from over there. And then jump back to you, time and again. And each time, crossing the frontier, surely I'd feel it more and more distinctly. I should grow paler all the time, people would die—no, not die, shrink, shrivel up.... And so would the trees and animals. And in the end there'd be nothing left but faint, faint smoke ... and then only a tune ... floating through the air ... over a void. ..."

And all at once she said: "Go away. Please. ... It sickens me."

But he only smiled.

"Please go away," she said.

But he sighed with satisfaction. "At last, at last, you sweet little dreamer, you admit you love me!"

And then she felt in horror how, in spite of everything, her body was swelling up with lust. Yet at the back of her mind there was a shadowy memory of something she had once experienced on a day in spring: a state that was like giving herself to everyone and yet belonging only to the one beloved. ...

And from a long way off—as children say of God: He is great—she saw and knew the image of her love.

Translated by Eithne Wilkins and Ernst Kaiser

Grigia

There is a time in life when everything perceptibly slows down, as though one's life were hesitating to go on or trying to change its course. It may be that at this time one is more liable to disaster. Homo had an ailing little son. After this illness had dragged on for a year, without being dangerous, yet also without improving, the doctor prescribed a long stay at a spa; but Homo could not bring himself to accompany his wife and child. It seemed to him it would mean being separated too long from himself, from his books, his plans, and his life. He felt his reluctance to be sheer selfishness, but perhaps it was rather more a sort of self-dissolution, for he had never before been apart from his wife for even as much as a whole day; he had loved her very much and still did love her very much, but through the child's coming this love had become frangible, like a stone that water has seeped into, gradually disintegrating it. Homo was very astonished by this new quality his life had acquired, this frangibility, for to the best of his knowledge and belief nothing of the love itself had ever been lost, and during all the time occupied with preparations for their departure he could not imagine how he was to spend the approaching summer alone. He simply felt intense repugnance at the thought of spas and mountain resorts.

So he remained alone at home, and on the second day he received a letter inviting him to join a company that was about to re-open the old Venetian gold-mines in the Val Fersena. The letter was from a certain Mozart Amadeo Hoffingott, whom he had met while travelling some years previously and with whom he had, during those few days, struck up a friendship.

Yet not the slightest doubt occurred to him whether the project was a sound one. He sent off two telegrams, one to tell his wife that he was, after all, leaving instantly and would send his address, the other accepting the proposal that he should join the company as its geologist and perhaps even invest a fairly large sum in the re-opening of the mines.

In P., a prosperous, compact little Italian town in the midst of mulberry-groves and vineyards, he joined Hoffingott, a tall, hand-some, swarthy man of his own age who was always enormously active. He now learnt that the company was backed by immense American funds, and the project was to be carried out in great style. First of all a reconnaissance party was to go up the valley. It was to consist of the two of them and three other partners. Horses were bought, instruments were due to arrive any day, and workmen were being engaged.

Homo did not stay in the inn, but—he did not quite know why— in the house of an Italian acquaintance of Hoffingott's. There he was struck by three things. The beautiful mahogany beds were indescribably cool and soft. The wallpaper had an indescribably bewildering, maze-like pattern, at once banal and very strange. And there was a cane rocking-chair. Sitting in that chair, rocking and gazing at the wallpaper, one seemed to turn into a mere tangle of rising and falling tendrils that would grow within a couple of sec-onds from nothingness to their full size and then as rapidly dis-appear into themselves again.

In the streets the air was a blend of snow and the South. It was the middle of May. In the evening the place was lit by big arc-lights that hung from wires stretched across from house to house, so high that the streets below were like ravines of deep blue gloom, and there one picked one's way along, while away up in the universe there was a spinning and hissing of white suns. By day one looked out over vineyards and woods. It was still all red, yellow, and green after the winter, and since the trees did not lose their leaves, the fading growth and the new were interlaced as in graveyard wreaths. Little red, blue, and pink villas still stood out very vividly among the trees, like scattered cubes inanimately manifesting to every eye some strange morphological law of which they themselves knew nothing. But higher up the woods were dark, and the mountain was called Selvot. Above the woods there was pasture-land, now still covered with snow, the broad, smooth, wavy lines of it running across the neighbouring mountains and up the steep little side-valley where the expedition was to go. When men came down from these mountains to sell milk and buy polenta, they sometimes brought great lumps of rock-crystal or amethyst, which was said to grow as profusely in many crevices up there as in other places flowers grow in the field, and these uncannily beautiful fairy-tale objects still further intensified his impression that behind the outward appearance of this district, this appearance that had the flickering remoteness and familiarity the stars sometimes have at night, there was hidden something that he yearningly awaited. When they rode into the mountain valley, passing Sant' Orsola at six o'clock, by a little stone bridge across a mountain rivulet overhung with bushes there were, if not a hundred, at least certainly a score of nightingales singing. It was broad daylight.

When they were well in the valley, they came to a fantastic place. It hung on the slope of a hill. The bridle-path that had brought them now began sheerly to leap from one huge flat boulder to the next, and flowing away from it, like streams meandering downhill, were a few short, steep lanes disappearing into the meadows. Standing on the bridle-path, one saw only forlorn and ramshackle cottages; but if one looked upward from the meadows below it was as though one had been transported back into a pre-historic lake-village built on piles, for the front of each house was supported on tall beams, and the privies floated out to one side of them like litters on four slender poles as tall as trees. Nor was the surrounding landscape without its oddities. It was a more than semicircular wall of high, craggy mountains sweeping down steeply into a crater in the centre of which was a smaller wooded cone, and the whole thing was like a gigantic empty pudding-mould with a little piece cut out of it by a deep-running brook, so that there it yawned wide open against the high flank of the slope on which the village hung. Below the snow-line there were corries, where a few deer strayed in the scrub, and in the woods crowning the round hill in the centre the blackcock were already displaying. The meadows on the sunny side were flowered with yellow, blue, and white stars, as big as thalers emptied out of a sack. But if one climbed another hundred feet or so beyond the village, one came to a small plateau covered with ploughed fields, meadows, hay-barns and a sprinkle of houses, with a little church, on a bastion that jutted over the valley, gazing out over the world that on fine days lay far beyond the valley like the sea beyond the mouth of a river: one could scarcely tell what was still the golden-yellow distance of the blessed plain and where the vague cloud-floors of the sky had begun.

It was a fine life they led there. All day one was up in the mountains, working at old blocked mine-shafts, or driving new ones into the mountainside, or down at the mouth of the valley where a wide road was to be built: and always one was in gigantic air that was already soft, pregnant with the imminent melting of the snow. They poured out money among the people and held sway like gods. They had something for them all to do, men and women alike. The men they organised into working parties and sent them up the mountains, where they had to spend the week; the women they used as porters, sending them in columns up the almost impassable mountainside, bringing provisions and spare parts. The stone schoolhouse was turned into a depot where their stores were kept and whence they were distributed. There a commanding male voice rapped out orders, summoning one by one the women who stood waiting and chattering, and the big basket on each woman's back would be loaded until her knees gave and the veins in her neck swelled. When one of those pretty young women had been loaded up, her eyes stared and her lips hung open; then she took her place in the column and, at a sign, these now silent beasts of burden slowly began to set one foot before the other up the long, winding track into the heights. But it was a rare and precious burden that they bore, bread, meat, and wine, and there was no need to be too scrupulous about the tools either, so that besides their wages a good deal that was useful found its way to their own households, and therefore they carried the loads willingly and even thanked the men who had brought these blessings into the mountains. And it was wonderful to feel: here one was not, as everywhere else in the world, scrutinised to see what sort of human being one was—whether one was reliable, powerful and to be feared, or delicate and beautiful—but whatever sort of human being one was, and no matter what one's ideas about life and the world were, here one met with love because one had brought blessings. Love ran ahead like a herald, love was made ready everywhere like a bed freshly made up for the guest, and each living being bore gifts of welcome in their eyes. The women could let that be freely seen, but sometimes as one passed a meadow there might be an old peasant there, waving his scythe like Death in person.

There were, indeed, peculiar people living at the head of this valley. Their forefathers had come here from Germany, to work in the mines, in the times when the bishops of Trent were mighty, and they were still like some ancient weathered German boulder flung down in the Italian landscape. They had partly kept and partly forgotten their old way of life, and what they had kept of it they themselves probably no longer understood. In the spring the mountain torrents wrenched away the earth from under them, so that there were houses that had once stood on a hill and were now on the brink of an abyss; but nobody lifted a finger to contend with the danger, and by a reverse process the new age was drifting into their houses, casting up all sorts of dreadful rubbish. One came across cheap, shiny cupboards, oleographs, and humorous postcards. But sometimes too there would be a saucepan that their forebears might well have used in Luther's time. For they were Protestants; but even though it was doubtless no more than this dogged clinging to their beliefs that had prevented their being Italianised, they were certainly not good Christians. Since they were poor, almost all the men left their wives shortly after marrying and went to America for years on end; when they came back, they brought with them a little money they had saved, the habits learned in urban brothels, and the irreligion, but not the acuity, of civilisation.

Right at the beginning Homo heard a story that interested him extraordinarily. Not long before—it might have been some fifteen years previously—a peasant who had been away for a long time came home from America and bedded with his wife again. For a while they rejoiced because they were reunited, and they lived without a care until the last of his cash had melted away. Then, when the rest of his savings, which had been supposed to come from America, still failed to arrive, the peasant girded himself up and—as all the peasants in this district did—went out to earn a living as a peddler, while his wife continued to look after the unprofitable smallholding. But he did not come back. Instead, a few days later, on a smallholding some distance from the first, the peasant returned from America, reminded his wife how long it had been, exactly to the day, asked to be given a meal exactly the same as that they had

had on the day he left, remembered all about the cow that no longer existed, and got on decently with the children sent him by Heaven during the years when he was away. This peasant too, after a period of relaxation and good living, set off with peddler's wares and did not return. This happened a third and a fourth time in the district, until it was realised that this was a swindler who had worked with the men over there and questioned them thoroughly about their life at home. Somewhere he was arrested and imprisoned, and none of the women saw him again. This, so the story went, they all were sorry about, for each of them would have liked to have him for a few days more and to have compared him with her memories, in order not to have to admit she had been made a fool of; for each of them claimed to have noticed something that did not quite correspond to what she remembered, but none of them was sufficiently sure of it to raise the matter and make difficulties for the husband who had returned to claim his rights.

That was what these women were like. Their legs were concealed by brown woollen skirts with deep borders of red, blue, or orange, and the kerchiefs they wore on their heads and crossed over the breast were cheap printed cotton things with a factory-made pattern, yet somehow, too, something about the colours or the way they wore these kerchiefs suggested bygone centuries. There was something here that was much older than any known peasant costume; perhaps it was only a gaze, one that had come down through the ages and arrived very late, faint now and already dim, and yet one felt it clearly, meeting one's own gaze as one looked at them. They wore shoes that were like primitive dug-out canoes, and because the tracks were so bad they had knife-sharp iron blades fitted into the soles, and in their blue or brown stockings they walked on these as the women walk in Japan. When they had to wait, they sat down, not on the edge of the path, but right on the flat earth of the path itself, pulling up their knees like Africans. And when, as sometimes happened, they rode up the mountains on their donkeys, they did not sit on their skirts, but rode astride like men, their thighs insensitive to the sharp wooden edges of the baggage-saddles, their legs again raised indecorously high and the whole upper part of the body faintly swinging with the animal's movement.

And they had, besides, a bewilderingly frank friendliness and kindliness. "Do you come in," they would say, with all the dignity of great ladies, if one knocked at their rustic doors. Or if one stood chatting with them for a while in the open air, one of them might suddenly ask with extreme courtesy and reserve: "Shall I not hold your coat for you?" Once, when Homo said to a charming fourteen-year-old girl: "Come in the hay"—simply because 'the hay' suddenly seemed as natural to him as fodder is to cattle—the childish face under the pointed, ancestral kerchief showed not the slightest dismay: there was only a mirthful puffing and flashing, a tipping this way and that on the rocking shoe-boats, and almost a collapse on to her little bottom, with her rake still on her shoulder, the whole performance conveying, with winsome clumsiness, comic-opera astonishment at the man's intensity of desire.

Another time he asked a tall, Valkyrie-like peasant woman: "Well, and are you still a virgin?" and chucked her under the chin—this time, too, merely because such jests need a touch of virile emphasis.

But she let her chin rest quietly on his hand and answered solemnly: "Yes, of course. . . ."

Homo was taken aback. "You're still a virgin!" he repeated, and laughed.

She giggled.

"Tell me!" he said, drawing closer and playfully shaking her chin.

Then she blew into his face and laughed. "Was once, of course!"

"If I come to see you, what can I have?" he went on with his cross-examination.

"Whatever you want."

"Everything I want?"

"Everything."

"Really everything?"

"Everything! Everything!" and her passion was so brilliantly and passionately acted, that the theatrical quality of it, up here, nearly five thousand feet above sea-level, left him quite bewildered.

After this he could not rid himself of the feeling that this life, which was brighter and more highly spiced than any life he had led before, was no longer part of reality, but a play floating in the air.

Meanwhile summer had come. When he had received the first letter and recognised his ailing little boy's childish handwriting, the shock of happiness and secret possession had flashed right through him, down to the soles of his feet. Their knowing where he was seemed to give everything tremendous solidity. He was here: oh, now everything was known and he had no more need to explain anything. All white and mauve, green and brown, there were the meadows around him. He was no phantom. A fairy-tale wood of ancient larches, feathery with new green, spread over an emerald slope. Under the moss there might be living crystals, mauve and white. The stream in the midst of the wood somewhere ran over a boulder, falling so that it looked like a big silver comb. He no longer answered his wife's letters. Here, amid the secrets of Nature, their belonging together was only one secret more. There was a tender scarlet flower, one that existed in no other man's world, only in his, and thus God had ordered things, wholly as a wonder. There was a place in the body that was kept hidden away, and no one might see it lest he should die: only one man. At this moment it seemed to him as wonderfully senseless and unpractical as only profound religious feeling can be. And only now did he realise what he had done in cutting himself off for this summer and letting himself drift on his own tide, this tide that had taken control of him. Among the trees with their arsenic-green beards he sank down on one knee and spread out his arms, a thing he had never done before in all his life, and it was as though in this moment someone lifted him out of his own embrace. He felt his beloved's hand in his, her voice sounded in his ear, and it was as though even now his whole body were answering to a touch, as though he were being cast in the mould of some other body. But he had invalidated his life. His heart had grown humble before his beloved, and poor as a mendicant; only a little more, and vows and tears would have poured from his very soul. And yet it was certain that he would not turn back, and strangely there was associated with his agitation an image of the meadows in flower round about these woods, and despite all longing for the future a feeling that here, amid anemones, forget-me-not, orchids, gentian, and the glorious greenish-brown sorrel, he would lie dead. He lay down and stretched out on the moss. "How am I to take you across with me?" he asked himself. And his body felt strangely tired, was like a rigid face relaxing into a smile.

Here he was, having always thought he was living in reality— but was there anything more unreal than that one human being should for him be different from all other human beings?—that among innumerable bodies there was one on which his inmost existence was almost as dependent as on his own body?—whose hunger and fatigue, hearing and seeing, were linked with his own? As the child grew older, this had grown—as the secrets of the soil grow into a sapling—into earthly cares and comforts. He loved his child, but just as the boy would outlive them, so too the boy had earlier killed the other-worldly part of them. And suddenly he flushed hot with a new certainty. He was not a man inclined to religious belief, but at this moment he was illumined within. Thoughts cast as little light as smoky candles in this great radiance of emotion that he experienced; it was all simply one glorious word blazing with the light of youth: Reunion. He was taking her with him for all eternity, and in the moment when he yielded to this thought, the little blemishes that the years had wrought in his beloved were taken from her and all was, eternally, the first day of all. Every worldly consideration vanished, and every possibility of tedium and of unfaithfulness, for no one will sacrifice eternity for the sake of a quarter of an hour's frivolity. And for the first time he experienced love beyond all doubt as a heavenly sacrament. He recognised the Providence that had guided his life into this solitude and felt the ground with its gold and jewels beneath his feet no longer as an earthly treasure, but as an enchanted world ordained for him alone.

From this day onward he was released from a bondage, as though rid of a stiff knee or a heavy rucksack. It was the bondage of wanting to be alive, the horror of dying. It did not happen to him as he had always thought it would, when in the fullness of one's strength one seems to see one's end approaching, so that one drinks more deeply of life, savours it more intensely. It was merely that he felt no longer involved, felt himself buoyed up by a glorious lightness that made him supreme lord of his own existence.

Although the mining operations had not progressed according to plan it was indeed a gold-digger's life they were leading. A lad had stolen wine, and that was a crime against the community, the punishment of which could count on general approval. The lad was brought in with his wrists bound. Mozart Amadeo Hoffingott gave orders that he should constitute a warning to others by being tied upright to a tree for a day and a night. But when the foreman came with the rope, in jest portentously swinging it and then hanging it over a nail, the lad began to tremble all over in the belief that he was about to be hanged. And it was always just the same—although this was hard to explain—when horses arrived, either fresh horses from beyond the valley or some that had been brought down for a few days' rest: they would stand about on the meadow, or lie down, but would always group themselves somehow, apparently at random, in a perspective, so that it looked as if it were done according to some secretly agreed aesthetic principle, just like that memory of the little green, blue, and pink houses at the foot of Mount Selvot. But if they were up above, standing around all night tethered in some high corrie in the mountains, three or four at a time tied to a felled tree, and one had started out in the moonlight at three in the morning and now came past the place at half-past four, they would all look round to see who was passing, and in the insubstantial dawn light one felt oneself to be a thought in some very slow-thinking mind. Since there was some thieving, and various other risks as well, all the dogs in the district had been bought up to serve as guards. The patrols brought them along in whole packs, two or three led on one rope, collarless. By now there were as many dogs as men in the place, and one might well wonder which was actually entitled to feel he was master in his own house on this earth and which was only adopted as a domestic companion. There were pure-bred gun-dogs among them, Venetian setters such as a few people in this district still kept, and snappy mongrels like spiteful little monkeys. They too would stand about in groups that had formed without anyone's knowing why, and which kept firmly together, but from time to time the members of a group would attack each other furiously. Some were half starved, some refused to eat. One little white dog snapped at the cook's hand as he was putting down a plate of meat and soup for it, and bit one finger off.

At half-past four in the morning it was already broad daylight, though the sun was not yet up. When one passed the grazing-land high up on the mountain, the cattle were still half asleep. In big, dim, white, stony shapes they lay with their legs drawn in under them, their hindquarters drooping a little to one side. They did not look at the passer-by, nor after him, but imperturbably kept their faces turned towards the expected light, and their monotonously, slowly moving jaws seemed to be praying. Walking through the circle of them was like traversing some twilit, lofty sphere of existence, and when one looked back at them from above, the line formed by the spine, the hind legs, and the curving tail made them seem like a scattering of treble-signs.

There was plenty of incident. For instance, a man might break his leg, and two others would carry him into camp on their crossed arms. Or suddenly the shout of: "Take co-ver!" would ring out, and everyone would run for cover because a great rock was being dynamited for the building of the road. Once, at such a moment, a shower swept a few flickers of moisture over the grass. In the shelter of a bush on the far side of the stream there was a fire burning, forgotten in the excitement, though only a few minutes earlier it had been very important: standing near it, the only watcher left, was a young birch-tree. And still dangling by one leg from this birch was the black pig. The fire, the birch, and the pig were now alone. The pig had squealed even while one man was merely leading it along on a rope, talking to it, urging it to come on. Then it squealed all the louder as it saw two other men come delightedly running towards it. It was frantic at being seized by the ears and unceremoniously dragged forward. It straddled all four legs in resistance, but the pain in its ears forced it to make little jumps onward. Finally, at the other end of the bridge, someone had grabbed a hatchet and struck it on the forehead with the blade. From that moment on everything went more quietly. Both fore-legs buckled at the same instant, and the little pig did not scream again until the knife was actually in its throat. There was a shrieking, twitching blare, which sank down into a death-rattle that was no more than a pathetic snore. All these were things Homo saw for the first time in his life.

When dusk fell, they all gathered in the little vicarage, where they had rented a room to serve as their mess. Admittedly the meat, which came the long way up the mountain only twice a week, was often going off, and not infrequently one had a touch of food-poisoning. But still all of them came here as soon as it was dark, stumbling along the invisible tracks with their little lanterns. For what caused them more suffering than food-poisoning was melancholy and boredom, even though everything was so beautiful. They swilled it away with wine. After an hour a cloud of sadness and ragtime hung over the room. The gramophone went round and round, like a gilded hurdy-gurdy trundling over a soft meadow spattered with wonderful stars. They no longer talked to each other. They merely talked. What should they have said to each other, a literary man of independent means, a business man, a former inspector of prisons, a mining engineer, and a retired major? They communicated in sign-language —and this even though they used words: words of discomfort, of relative comfort, of homesickness— it was an animal language. Often they would argue with superfluous intensity about some question that concerned none of them, and would reach the point of insulting each other, and the next day seconds would be passing to and fro. Then it would turn out that nobody had meant a word of it. They had only done it to kill time, and even if none of them had ever really known anything of the world, each of them felt he had behaved as uncouthly as a butcher, and this filled them with resentment against each other.

It was that standard psychic unit which is Europe. It was idleness as undefined as at other times their occupation was. It was a longing for wife, child, home comforts. And interspersed with this, ever and again, there was a gramophone. "Rosa, we're going to Lodz, Lodz, Lodz . . ." or: "Whate'er befall I still recall. . . ." It was an astral emanation of powder and gauze, a mist of far-off variety-shows and European sexuality. Indecent jokes exploded into guffaws, each joke, it seemed, beginning: "You know the one about the Jew in the train. . . ." Only once somebody asked: "How far is it to Babylon?" And then everyone fell silent, and the major put on the "Tosca" record and, as it was about to start, said mournfully: "Once I wanted to marry Geraldine Farrar." Then her voice came through the horn, out into the room, and this woman's voice that all these drunken men were marvelling at seemed to step into a lift, and the next instant the lift was flashing away up to the top with her, arriving nowhere, coming down again, bouncing in the air. Her skirts billowed out with the movement, with this up and down, this long lying close to, clinging tightly to, one note, and again there was the rise and fall, and with it all this streaming away as if for ever, and yet again and yet again and again this being seized by yet another spasm, and again a streaming out: a voluptuous ecstasy. Homo felt it was that naked voluptuousness which is distributed throughout all the things there are in cities, a lust no longer distinguishable from manslaughter, or jealousy, or business, or motorcar racing—ah, it was no longer lust, it was a craving for adventure—no, it was not a craving for adventure either, it was a knife slashing down out of the sky, a destroying angel, angelic madness—the war?

From one of the many long fly-papers trailing from the ceiling a fly had dropped in front of him and was lying on its back, poisoned, in the middle of one of those pools that the light of the paraffin-lamps made in the scarcely perceptible wrinkles in the oil-cloth—pools with all that sadness of very early spring, as if a strong wind had swept over them after rain. The fly made a few efforts, each weaker than the last, to turn over, and from time to time a second fly that was feeding on the oilcloth ran to see how it was getting on. Homo also kept a careful watch—the flies were a great nuisance here. But when death came, the dying fly folded its six little legs together, to a point, and kept them straight up like that, and then it died in its pale spot of light on the oilcloth as in a graveyard of stillness that could not be measured in inches or decibels, and which was nevertheless there. Someone was just saying: "They say someone's worked out that all the Rothschilds put together haven't enough money to pay for a third-class ticket to the moon."

Homo murmured to himself: ". . . Kill, and yet feel the presence of God? . . . Feel the presence of God and yet kill?" And with a flick of his forefinger he sent the fly right into the face of the major sitting opposite, which caused another incident and thus kept them occupied until the next evening.

By then he had already known Grigia for some time, and perhaps the major knew her too. Her name was Lene Maria Lenzi. That sounded like Selvot and Gronleit or Malga Mendana, had a ring as of amethyst crystals and of flowers, but he preferred to call her Grigia, pronounced Greeja, after the cow she had, which she called Grigia, Grey One. At such times she would be sitting at the edge of her meadow, in her mauve-brown skirt and dotted kerchief, the toes of her wooden clogs sticking up into the air, her hands clasped over her bright apron, and she would look as naturally lovely as a slender little poisonous mushroom, while now and then she called out to the cow grazing lower down the hillside. There were actually only two things she called: "Come a-here!" and: "Come a-up!" when the cow strayed too far. But if her cries were unavailing, there would follow an indignant: "Hey, you devil, come a-*here!*", and in the last resort she herself would go hurtling down the hillside like a flung stone, the next best piece of stick in her hand, to be aimed at the Grey One as soon as she was within throwing distance. Since, however, the cow Grigia had a distinct taste for straying valley-wards, the whole of this operation would be repeated with the regularity of pendulum-clockwork that is constantly dropping lower and constantly being wound higher again. Because this was so paradisically senseless, he teased her by calling her Grigia herself. He could not conceal from himself that his heart beat faster when from a distance he caught sight of her sitting there; that is the way the heart beats when one suddenly walks into the smell of pine-needles or into the spicy air rising from the floor of woods where a great many mushrooms grow. In this feeling there was always a residual dread of Nature. And one must not believe that Nature is anything but highly unnatural: she is earthy, edgy, poisonous, and inhuman at all points where man does not impose his will upon her. Probably it was just this that fascinated him in this peasant woman, and the other half of it was inexhaustible amazement that she did so much resemble a woman. One would, after all, be equally amazed, going through the woods, to encounter a lady balancing a tea-cup.

"Do you come in," she too had said, the first time he had knocked at her door. She was standing by the hearth, with a pot on the fire, and since she could not leave it, she made a courteous gesture towards the bench. After a while she wiped her hand on her apron, smiling, and held it out to her visitors: it was a well-formed hand, as velvety-rough as the finest sandpaper or as garden soil trickling between the fingers. And the face that went with the hand was a faintly mocking face, with delicate, graceful bones that one saw best in profile, and a mouth that he noticed very particularly. This mouth was curved like a Cupid's bow, yet it was also compressed as happens when one gulps, and this gave it, with its subtlety, a determined roughness, and to this roughness again a little trace of merriment, which was perfectly in keeping with the wooden shoes that the slight figure grew up out of as out of wild roots. . . . They had come to arrange some matter or other, and when they left, the smile was there again, and the hand rested in his perhaps a moment longer than when they had come. These impressions, which would have been so insignificant in town, out there in this solitude amounted to a shock, as though a tree had moved its branches in a way not to be explained by any stirring of the wind or a bird's taking flight.

A short time later he had become a peasant woman's lover. This change that had taken place in him much occupied his mind, for beyond doubt it was not something he had done, but something that had happened to him.

When he came the second time, Grigia at once sat down on the bench beside him, and when—to see how far he could already go— he put his hand on her lap and said: "You are the beauty of them all", she let his hand rest on her thigh and merely laid her own upon it. With that they were pledged to each other. And now he kissed her to set the seal upon it, and after the kiss she smacked her lips with a sound like that smack of satisfaction with which lips sometimes let go of the rim of a glass after greedily drinking from it. He was indeed slightly startled by this indecorum and was not offended when she rejected any further advances; he did not know why, he knew nothing at all of the customs and dangers of this place, and, though curious, let himself be put off for another day. "In the hay," Grigia had said, and when he was already in the doorway, saying goodbye, she said: "Goodbye till soon", and smiled at him.

Even on his way home he realised he was already happy about what had happened: it was like a hot drink suddenly beginning to take effect after an interval. The notion of going to the hay-barn with her—opening a heavy wooden door, pulling it to after one, and the darkness increasing with each degree that it closes, until one is crouching on the floor of a brown, perpendicular darkness— delighted him as though he were a child about to play a trick. He remembered the kisses and felt the smack of them as though a magic band had been laid around his head. Picturing what was to be, he could not help thinking of the way peasants eat: they chew slowly, smacking their lips, relishing every mouthful to the full. And it is the same with the way they dance, step after step. Probably it was the same with everything else. His legs stiffened with excitement at these thoughts, as though his shoes were already sticking in the earth. The women lower their eyelids and keep their faces quite stiff, a defensive mask, so as not to be disturbed by one's curiosity. They let scarcely a moan escape them. Motionless as beetles feigning death, they concentrate all their attention on what is going on within them.

And so too it was. With the rim of her clog Grigia scraped together into a pile the scrap of winter hay that was still there, and smiled for the last time when she bent to the hem of her skirt like a lady adjusting her garter.

It was all just as simple and just as magical as the thing about the horses, the cows, and the dead pig. When they were behind the beam, and heavy boots came thumping along the stony path outside, pounding by and fading into the distance, his blood pulsed in his throat; but Grigia seemed to know even at the third footstep whether the footsteps were coming this way or not. And she talked a magical language. A nose she called a neb, and legs she called shanks. An apron was for her a napron. Once when he threatened not to come again, she laughed and said: "I'll bell thee!" And he did not know whether he was disconcerted or glad of it. She must have noticed that, for she asked: "Does it rue thee? Does it rue thee much?" Such words were like the patterns of the aprons and kerchiefs and the coloured border at the top of the stocking, already somewhat assimilated to the present because of having come so far, but still mysterious visitants. Her mouth was full of them, and when he kissed it he never knew whether he loved this woman or whether a miracle was being worked upon him and Grigia was only part of a mission linking him ever more closely with his beloved in eternity. Once Grigia said outright: "Thou'rt thinking other things, I can tell by thy look", and when he tried to pretend it was not so, she said: "Ah, all that's but glozing." He asked her what that meant, but she would not explain, and he racked his brains over it for a long time before it occurred to him that she meant he was glossing something over. Or did she mean something still more mysterious?

One may feel such things intensely or not. One may have principles, in which case it is all only an aesthetic joke that one accepts in passing. Or one has no principles, or perhaps they have slackened somewhat, as was the case with Homo when he set out on his journey, and then it may happen that these manifestations of an alien life take possession of whatever has become masterless. Yet they did not give him a new self, a self for sheer happiness become ambitious and earth-bound; they merely lodged, in irrelevantly lovely patches, within the airy outlines of his body. Something about it all made Homo sure that he was soon to die, only he did not yet know how or when. His old life had lost all strength; it was like a butterfly growing feebler as autumn draws on.

Sometimes he talked to Grigia about this. She had a way of her own of asking about it: as respectful as if it were something entrusted to her, and quite without self-seeking. She seemed to regard it as quite in order that beyond the mountains there were people he loved more than her, whom he loved with his whole soul. And he did not feel this love growing less; it was growing stronger, being ever renewed. It did not grow dim, but the more deeply coloured it became, the more it lost any power to decide anything for him in reality or to prevent his doing anything. It was weightless and free of all earthly attachment in that strange and wonderful way known only to one who has had to reckon up with his life and who henceforth may wait only for death. However healthy he had been before, at this time something within him rose up and was straight, like a lame man who suddenly throws away his crutches and walks on his own.

This became strongest of all when it came to hay-making time. The hay was already mown and dried and only had to be bound and fetched in, up from the mountain meadows. Homo watched it from the nearest height, which was like being high in a swing, flying free above it all. The girl—quite alone in the meadow, a polka-dotted doll under the enormous glass bell of the sky—was doing all sorts of things in her efforts to make a huge bundle. She knelt down in it, pulling the hay towards her with both arms. Very sensually she lay on her belly across the bale and reached underneath it. She turned over on her side and stretched out one arm as far as she could. She climbed up it on one knee, then on both. There was something of the dor-beetle about her, Homo thought—the scarab, of course. At last she thrust her whole body under the bale, now bound with a rope, and slowly raised it on high. The bundle was much bigger than the bright, slender little human animal that was carrying it—or was that not Grigia?

When, in search of her, Homo walked along the long row of hay-stooks that the peasant women had set up on the level part of the hillside, they were resting. He could scarcely believe his eyes, for they were lying on their hillocks of hay like Michelangelo's statues in the Medici chapel in Florence, one arm raised to support the head, and the body reposing as in flowing water. And when they spoke with him and had to spit, they did so with much art: with three fingers they would twitch out a handful of hay, spit into the hollow, and then stop it up again. One might be tempted to laugh; only if one mixed with them, as Homo did when he was in search of Grigia, one might just as easily start in sudden fright at this crude dignity. But Grigia was seldom among them, and when at last he found her, she would perhaps be crouching in a potato-field, laughing at him. He knew she had nothing on but two pet-ticoats and that the dry earth that was running through her slim, rough fingers was also touching her body. But the thought of it was no longer strange to him. By now his inner being had become curiously familiar with the touch of earth, and perhaps indeed it was not at the time of the hay-harvest at all that he met her in that field: in this life he was leading there was no longer any certainty about time or place.

The hay-barns were filled. Through the chinks between the boards a silvery light poured in. The hay poured out green light. Under the door was a wide gold border.

The hay smelt sour—like the African drinks that are made of fermented fruits and human saliva. One had only to remember that one was living among savages here, and the next instant one was intoxicated by the heat of this confined space filled to the roof with fermenting hay.

Hay bears one up in all positions. One can stand in it up to the knees, at once unsure of one's footing and all too firmly held fast. One can lie in it as in the Hand of God, and would gladly wallow in God's Hand like a little dog or a little pig. One may lie obliquely, or almost upright like a saint ascending to heaven in a green cloud.

Those were bridal days and ascension days.

But one time Grigia declared it could not go on. He could not bring her to say why. The sharpness round the mouth and the little furrow plumb between the eyes, which before had appeared only with the effort of deciding which would be the nicest barn for their next meeting, now boded ill weather somewhere in the offing. Were they being talked about? But the other women, who did perhaps notice something, were always as smiling as over a thing one is glad to see. There was nothing to be got out of Grigia. She made excuses and was more rarely to be found, and she watched her words as carefully as any mistrustful farmer.

Once Homo met with a bad omen. His puttees had come undone and he was standing by a hedge winding them on again, when a peasant woman went by and said in a friendly way: "Let thy stockings be—it won't be long till nightfall." That was near Grigia's cottage. When he told Grigia, she made a scornful face and said: "People will talk, and brooks will run", but she swallowed hard, and her thoughts were elsewhere. Then he suddenly remembered a woman he had seen up here, whose bony face was like an Aztec's and who spent all her time sitting at her door, her black hair loose, hanging down below her shoulders, and with three healthy, round-cheeked children around her. Grigia and he unthinkingly passed by her every day, yet this was the only one of the local women whom he did not know, and oddly enough he had never asked about her either, although he was struck by her appearance: it was almost as though the healthiness of her children and the illness manifest in her face were impressions that always cancelled each other out. In his present mood he suddenly felt quite sure it was from here that the disturbing element must have come. He asked who she was, but Grigia crossly shrugged her shoulders and merely exclaimed: "She doesn't know what she says! With her it's a word here and a word over the mountains!" And she made a swift, energetic gesture, tapping her brow, as though she must instantly devalue anything that woman might have said.

Since Grigia could not be persuaded to come again into any of the hay-barns around the village, Homo proposed going higher up the mountain with her. She was reluctant, and when at last she yielded, she said, in a tone that afterwards struck Homo as equivocal: "Well, then, if go we must."

It was a beautiful morning that once again embraced the whole world; far beyond, there lay the sea of clouds and of mankind. Grigia was anxious to avoid passing any dwelling, and even when they were well away from the village she, who had always been delightfully reckless in all arrangements to do with their love-making, showed concern lest they should be seen by watchful eyes. Then he grew impatient and it occurred to him that they had just passed an old mine-shaft that his own people had soon given up trying to put back into use. There he drove Grigia in.

As he turned to look back for the last time, there was snow on a mountain-peak and below it, golden in the sun, a little field of corn-stooks, with the white and blue sky over it all.

Grigia made another remark that seemed strangely pointed. Noticing his backward glance, she said tenderly "Better leave the blue alone in the sky, so it'll keep fine." But he forgot to ask what she meant by this, for they were already intent on groping their way further into darkness, which seemed to be closing around them.

Grigia went ahead, and when after a while the passage opened out into a small chamber, they stopped there and embraced. The ground underfoot seemed pleasantly dry and they lay down without Homo's feeling any of the civilised man's need to investigate it first by the light of a match. Once again Grigia trickled through him like soft, dry earth, and he felt her tensing in the dark, growing stiff with her pleasure. Then they lay side by side, without any urge to speak, gazing towards the little far-off rectangle beyond which daylight blazed white. And within him then Homo experienced over again his climb to this place, saw himself meeting Grigia beyond the village, then climbing, turning, and climbing, saw her blue stockings up to the orange border under the knee, her loose-hipped gait in those merry clogs, he saw them stopping outside the cavern, saw the landscape with the little golden field, and all at once in the brightness of the entrance beheld the image of her husband.

He had never before thought of this man, who was in the company's employ. Now he saw the sharp poacher's face with the dark, cunning eyes of a hunter, and suddenly remembered too the only time he had heard him speak: it was after creeping into an old mineshaft where nobody else had dared to go, and the man's words were: "I got into one fix after another. It's getting back that's hard."

Swiftly Homo reached for his pistol, but at the same instant Lene Maria Lenzi's husband vanished and the darkness all around was as thick as a wall. He groped his way to the entrance, with Grigia clutching his sleeve. But he realised at once that the rock that had been rolled across the entrance was much heavier than anything he could shift unaided. And now too he knew why her husband had left them so much time: he himself needed time to make his plan and get a tree-trunk for a lever.

Grigia knelt by the rock, pleading and raging. It was repulsive in its futility. She swore that she had never done anything wrong and would never again do anything wrong. She squealed like a pig and rushed at the rock senselessly, like a maddened horse. In the end Homo came to feel that this was only in accordance with Nature, but he himself, a civilized man, at first could not overcome his incredulity, could not face the fact that something irrevocable had really happened. He leaned against the rocky wall, his hands in his pockets, and listened to Grigia.

Later he recognised his destiny. As in a dream he felt it descending upon him once again, through days, through weeks, through months, in the way sleep must begin when it will last a very long time. Gently he put one arm round Grigia and drew her back. He lay down beside her and waited for something. Previously he would perhaps have thought that in such a prison, with no escape, love must be sharp as teeth; but he quite forgot to think about Grigia. She had slipped away from him, or perhaps he from her, even though he could still feel her shoulder touching his. His whole life had slipped away from him, just so far that he could still tell it was there, but without being able to lay his hand upon it.

For hours they did not stir. Days might have passed, and nights. Hunger and thirst lay behind them, like one eventful stage of the journey, and they grew steadily weaker, lighter, and more shut into themselves. Their half-consciousness was wide seas, their waking small islands. Once he started up, with glaring awareness, into one such small waking: Grigia was gone. Some certainty told him that it must have been only a moment earlier. He smiled . . . telling him nothing of the way out . . . meaning to leave him behind, as proof for her husband . . . ! He raised himself up on his elbow and looked about him. So he too discovered a faint, glimmering streak. He crawled a little nearer, deeper into the passage—they had always been looking in the other direction. Then he realised there was a narrow crevice there, which probably led out, obliquely, into the open air. Grigia had slender bones, yet even he, if he made an immense effort, might perhaps be able to worm his way through.

It was a way out. But at this moment he was already too weak to return to life, or he had no wish to, or he had lost consciousness.

At this same hour, all efforts having proved unavailing and the futility of the undertaking having been recognised, Mozart Amadeo Hoffingott, down in the valley, gave orders for work to cease.

Translated by Eithne Wilkins and Ernst Kaiser

The Lady from Portugal

In some old charters they were called the seigniors delle Catene, in others Herren von Ketten, meaning: of the chains. They had come down from the North, stopping at the very threshold of the South. They proclaimed their loyalty now to the Guelph, now to the Ghibelline cause, as it suited them, and at bottom regarded themselves as owing no allegiance to anything or anyone but themselves.

It was to one side of the great highway leading across the Brenner Pass into Italy, somewhere between Brixen and Trent, on an almost sheer, lone crag, that their castle stood, with a wild torrent coursing five hundred feet below it, raging so deafeningly that if a man put his head out of one of the windows, he could not have heard even the pealing of church bells in the room behind him. It was an impenetrable curtain of solid noise, through which no sound of the outer world could pass into the castle of the seigniors delle Catene. Only the gaze was unimpeded and, piercing that protective curtain, plunged headlong into the deep encircling panorama.

All the lords delle Catene or von Ketten had the reputation of being keen and alert, and there was no advantage that escaped them as far as their arm could reach. And they were cruel as knives that always cut deep. They never turned red with anger or rosy with joy: in their anger they darkened, and in their joy they shone like gold—a shining as perfect and as rare. All of them, without exception through the years and the centuries, were said also to resemble each other in this: that white threads early mingled with the brown hair of head and beard, and that every one of them died before his sixtieth year; and in this too, that the enormous strength each sometimes displayed seemed not to have its seat and origin in his body, which was slender and of medium stature, but to emanate from the eyes and forehead. This, however, was merely the legend among their overawed neighbours and their villeins. They took whatever they could get, going about it honestly or accomplishing it by violence or cunning as the case might be, but always imperturbably, inexorably. Each lived out his short life without haste, and for each the end was swift, death cutting him down when he had accomplished his task.

It was the custom among the Kettens not to form ties of marriage with any of the nobility who held the surrounding manors, but to seek their brides far off, and rich brides too, in order not to be hindered in making their alliances and carrying on feuds as they chose. The Herr von Ketten who had brought home a beautiful Portuguese bride twelve years earlier was now in his thirtieth year. The marriage had been celebrated in her country, and the very youthful bride was expecting her confinement by the time the jingling procession of attendants and menials, horses, maid-servants, baggage-mules, and dogs crossed the boundary of the Catene land. The year had passed like one long honeymoon. For all the Catene were brilliant cavaliers, yet they proved it only in the one year of their lives when they went wooing. The brides they chose were beautiful, for they wanted handsome sons, and without courtly graces they could not have won such wives abroad, where they did not count for so much as at home. But they themselves did not know whether it was in that one year that they revealed their true selves, or only in all the other years.

A messenger came to meet the cavalcade, bearing weighty news; and though the bright-coloured garments and pennants still resembled a great butterfly, Herr von Ketten himself was changed. When he had galloped back to rejoin the company, he continued to ride slowly beside his wife as though he would not allow any other concern to press him, but his face had altered and was now forbidding as a bank of storm-clouds. Then suddenly, at a turn in the road, the castle towered up before them, scarcely a quarter of an hour's journey ahead, and with an effort he broke his silence.

He told his wife he wished her to turn back and return to her native country. The cavalcade came to a halt. The Portuguese lady pleaded and insisted that they should ride on, urging that there would still be time to turn back when the reasons had been heard. The Bishops of Trent were mighty lords, and the Imperial courts pronounced in their favour. For generations the Kettens had been at feud with them over a question of territory, and sometimes they had invoked the law against each other, sometimes their demands and counter-demands had led to bloodshed, but always it had been the seigniors von Ketten who had been obliged to yield to their opponents' superior strength. In this one matter the gaze that missed no other chance of advantage waited in vain to glimpse it. And father handed on the task to son, and through the generations their pride continued to wait, and never relented.

It was for this Herr von Ketten now that the luck seemed to have changed. He was dismayed to realise how nearly he had missed his chance. A strong party among the nobility was in rebellion against the Bishop, and it had been decided to make a surprise attack and take him prisoner. Ketten's return home might tip the scales in favour of the rebel party. Having been absent for more than a year, Ketten did not know how strong the Bishop's position was; but he did know this would be a long and fearful struggle that would last for years and that the outcome was uncertain, and he also knew it would be impossible to count on each of their party to the bitter end if they did not succeed in taking Trent at the very beginning. He resented it that his beautiful wife had, by her mere existence, almost caused him to miss the opportunity. True, as he rode at her side, keeping one pace to the rear, he delighted in her as much as ever; and she was still as mysterious to him as the many pearl necklaces that she possessed. A man could have crushed such little things like peas, weighing them in the hollow of his sinewy hand— so it seemed to him, as he rode beside her—and yet there they lay, incomprehensibly invulnerable. It was only that this enchantment had been displaced by the news he had received, had been thrust aside like winter's muffled dreams when all at once the boyishly naked, first, sunlight-solid days are there again. Years in the saddle lay ahead, and in them wife and child turned to strangers, vanished from ken.

But meanwhile the cavalcade had reached the foot of the cliff on which the castle stood, and the lady from Portugal, having listened to all he had to say, once more declared that she would remain with him. How fiercely the castle reared into the height! Here and there on the rock-face a few stunted trees sprouted like sparse hair. The rising and falling of the line of wooded mountains was so violent that no one could have imagined that savagery who knew only the waves of the sea. The air was full of some spicy chill, and it was all like riding into a huge cauldron that had burst, spilling everywhere this alien green that it contained. But in the forest there was the stag, the bear, the wild boar, the wolf, and perhaps the unicorn. Further beyond, there was the realm of chamois and eagle. Unfathomed gorges harboured dragons. Many days' journey wide, many days' journey deep this forest was, where the only tracks were those where wild beasts made their way; and high above, where the crags towered, the realm of spirits began. There demons lurked amid the storm and the clouds. No Christian had ever set foot there, or if ever one had the audacity to try to scale those heights, ill-luck followed—stories that the maids told in hushed voices round the fire in winter, while the serving-men smirked in silence and shrugged their shoulders, because a man's life is full of dangers, and such adventures can easily befall one. But of all the tales the lady from Portugal heard, there was one that seemed strangest. Just as no one had ever yet reached the place where the rainbow ends, so too, they recounted, no one had ever yet succeeded in looking out over these great stone walls: there were always more walls beyond, and between them there were ravines like outspread blankets full of stones, stones as big as a house, and even the finest gravel underfoot was no smaller than a man's head. It was a world that was not really a world at all. Often in her dreams of this country, whence came the man she loved, she had imagined it as being of his own nature, and she had imagined the man's nature according to all that he had told her of his native country. Weary of the peacock-blue sea, she had expected a land tense with the unexpected, like the string of a drawn bow. Then, when she came face to face with the secret, she found it unimaginably hideous and longed to escape. The castle was like an agglomeration of hen-houses: stone piled on rock . . . dizzy walls where mould and lichen grew . . . here rotting beams, there unseasoned, unhewn tree-trunks . . . farming tools and war-gear, stable chains and axle-trees. But now that she was here, it was here that she belonged, and perhaps what she saw was not really hideous, perhaps it had a beauty of its own, like a man's ways, to which one had to become accustomed.

Herr von Ketten watched his wife riding up the mountainside and could not bring himself to stop her. He felt no gratitude. Her action was something that neither bested his will nor yielded to it, but eluded him, luring him on into some other realm, making him ride after her in awkward silence, helpless as a lost soul. Two days later he was again in the saddle.

*   *   *

And eleven years later it was still the same. Too rashly attempted, the attack on Trent had failed, costing the nobles a third of their force at the very start, and with it more than half their boldness. Herr von Ketten, though wounded in the retreat, did not at once return home. For two days he lay hidden in a peasant's hut, and then he rode from castle to castle, trying to reawaken his allies' fighting-spirit. Having come too late to take part in their councils and preparations, after this setback he clung to the plan as a dog will cling to a bull's ear. He expounded to the other knights what lay in store for them if the Bishop's forces made a counter-attack before their own ranks were closed again; he urged on the faint-hearted and the miserly, squeezing money out of them, bringing up reinforcements, providing arms—and finally was chosen to be their captain in the field. At first his wounds still bled so profusely that he had to change the bandages twice a day; and, riding and coun-selling and trying to make up for his earlier absence, he gave no thought to his lively Portuguese bride, who was surely anxious for him.

It was not until five days after he was wounded that he came to her, and then he remained only one day. She looked at him without asking questions, yet keenly, as one may follow the flight of an arrow, wondering if it will strike its mark.

He gathered his men together, down to the meanest lad on whom he could lay hands, manned the castle to withstand a siege, issued commands, and saw to everything. That day was all a shouting of men-at-arms, a neighing of horses, hauling of beams, clang of iron and stone. In the night he rode away. He was kind and tender as to some noble creature that one admires, but his gaze went straight ahead as if from under a helmet, even when he wore none. At their leave-taking the lady from Portugal, suddenly overwhelmed by a woman's feelings, pleaded to be allowed, at least now, to bathe his wounds and bind them up afresh. But he refused and took leave of her more hastily than was necessary, laughing as he did so. And then she also laughed.

The way the enemy fought out this campaign was violent wherever it could be so, as befitted the hard man of noble blood who wore the episcopal robes; but it was perhaps from these long womanish robes that he had also learnt to be supple, deceitful, and stubborn. Wealth and extensive possessions gradually proved what they could do, and ground was yielded only inch by inch, always only at the last moment, when rank and influence no longer sufficed to engage the help of allies. It was a way of fighting that avoided decisive action. As soon as resistance stiffened, there was a withdrawal; wherever it seemed to be slackening, there would be an onslaught. So it happened that sometimes a castle would be overrun and, if it had not been abandoned in time, all the inmates put to the sword. But at other times troops might be encamped in a district for weeks and nothing worse would happen than that some peasants' cow would be stolen or a few hens would have their necks twisted. The weeks lengthened into summer and winter, and the seasons revolved into years. Two powers were contending with each other, the one fierce and aggressive, but lacking in strength, the other resembling an indolent, soft, but dreadfully heavy body, made heavier still by the weight of time.

Herr von Ketten was well aware of all this. He had trouble in preventing the weakened, sullen forces of the knights from squandering the last of their strength in a sudden, hasty attack. He was always on the outlook for the exposed position, the turn of events, the unlikely constellation that only chance could bring about. So too his father had bided his time, and his father before him. And if one waits long enough, even the most unlikely event may come to pass. So he waited for eleven years.

For eleven long years he rode to and fro between the nobles' castles and his fighting-forces, keeping resistance alive. In a hundred skirmishes, again and again, he earned a name for reckless courage, in order that none might reproach him with being timid in leadership; and at times he even manoeuvred both sides into a great bloody encounter, lest his allies' taste for battle should falter. But he too avoided decisive action, just as the Bishop did. More than once he received slight wounds, but he was never at home for more than twelve hours. He was battle-scarred and weather-beaten from his roving life. Doubtless he feared to stay at home longer, just as a tired man dare not sit down.

The restiveness of horses hitched to a tree, men's loud laughter, torchlight, flames of a camp-fire rising like a pillar, like a tree-trunk of golden dust in green-glimmering woodland, the smell of rain, curses, boastful knights, dogs sniffing at the wounded, women's petticoats lifted high, scared peasants—such things were his amusements in these years. In the midst of it all he remained slender and graceful. White began to show among the brown hairs of his head, but his face was ageless. He had to find retorts to coarse jests, and did so like a man; but his eyes would remain quite still. Wherever discipline slackened, he restored order with an iron hand; but he did not raise his voice, he spoke quietly and briefly, and the soldiers feared him, for anger never seemed to take possession of him, it was something that streamed out of him like a light, and his face would grow quite dark. In battle he forgot himself. Then everything followed a single course—a wild slashing and blood-letting, a frenzied dance drunk with blood, he did not know what he was doing and yet he always did the right thing. For this his soldiers idolized him, and a legend arose that in his hatred of the Bishop he had sold his soul to the Devil, who dwelt in his castle in the guise of a beautiful outlandish woman that he visited there in secret.

The first time he heard this Herr von Ketten neither frowned nor laughed: but his face became dark golden with joy. Often, when he sat by the camp-fire or at some peasant's hearth and the hard day behind him would seem to soften in the warmth, as rain-stiffened leather will grow soft again, he would think. He would think, at such times, of the Bishop of Trent, who slept on fresh linen, was surrounded by learned clerks, and had painters in his service, while he himself roamed like a wolf, circling round the enemy. He too could have that. He had installed a chaplain in his castle so that the needs of the spirit might be provided for, and a scrivener to read aloud, and a merry maid-in-waiting; a cook had been brought from a great distance, so that the castle's mistress need not hanker for the dishes she had known at home; wandering scholars and students would be given hospitality so that their conversation might afford some days of distraction; costly stuffs and tapestries came, so that the walls might be covered. Only he stayed away.

For a whole year, in that far country and on the journey, he had practised pretty speeches and flattery. For just as every well-made thing, be it steel or strong wine, horse or fountain, has a spirit of its own, so too the lords delle Catene had, and were not lacking in wit. But during that time he was far from his homeland and his essential being was something that he might ride towards for many weeks without reaching it. And even now he would sometimes unthinkingly make gallant speeches, but only so long as the horses were being rested in the stables. He would arrive late at night and ride away the next morning; or else he would be there from when the bell rang for Matins till the Angelus. He was as familiar to her as a thing long worn on one's person. When you laugh, that familiar thing also laughs—is shaken to and fro; when you walk, it goes with you; when your hand touches your own body, you feel the presence of that thing: but if you raise it up and contemplate it, it remains silent, it avoids your eyes. If he had ever remained longer, he would have had to be truly as he was. But he recalled that he had never said: I am this; or: I wish to be that. He had talked to her of hunting, of adventures and of things that he did. Nor had she ever done what young people so often do and asked him what he thought about this and about that, or said anything about what she would wish to be like when she was older; lively as she had been before, she had simply bloomed, silently, like a rose, and she had stood on the church steps ready to depart, as though on a mounting-block from which she would step into the saddle and ride into that other life.

He scarcely knew the two children she had borne him, but these two sons of his also loved him passionately—that remote father with whose fame their childish ears had rung since they could remember. It was a strange memory, that of the evening to which the second son owed his being. There she was, when he came home, in a soft light-grey robe patterned with dark grey flowers; her black hair was already plaited for the night, and her finely chiselled nose cast a sharp shadow into the smooth yellow of a book on which the lamplight shone, illumining the mysterious pictures it contained. It was like magic. Tranquilly the woman sat there, in her rich gown, the skirt flowing down in countless rippling folds—a figure rising out of itself and falling back into itself, like the water of a fountain. And is the water of a fountain anything that can be ransomed and redeemed, can it be set free by anything but magic or some miracle, and thus issue forth wholly out of its self-borne, swaying existence? Embracing the woman, might he not suddenly be brought up short by the force of some magical resistance? This was not so—but is tenderness not even more uncanny? She looked at him, as he entered, like someone recognising an old cloak that one has not worn for a long time, has not even seen for a long time, and which remains a little strange, and yet one wraps it round oneself.

What intimate, familiar things, by contrast, did the strategies of war, and political cunning and anger and killing seem to him! An act is performed because some other act has preceded it. The Bishop relies on his gold pieces, and the captain on the nobility's powers of endurance. To command is a thing of clarity; such a life is day-bright, solid to the touch, and the thrust of a spear under an iron collar that has slipped is as simple as pointing one's finger at something and being able to say: This is *this*. But the other thing is as alien as the moon.

Secretly Herr von Ketten loved this other thing. He took no delight in ordering his household or increasing his wealth. And although he had for years been fighting about possessions not his own, his desire was not a reaching out for the satisfaction of gain; it was a yearning from his very soul. It was in their brows that the Catene's power lay; but all that their power produced was voiceless actions. Every morning that he climbed into the saddle he again felt the happiness of not yielding, and this was the very soul of his soul. But when he dismounted at evening, often a sullen weariness of all the violence he had been living with would sink upon him, as though that day he had been straining all his resources lest, through no doing of his own, he should suddenly be radiant with some inner beauty for which he had no name. The Bishop, that slippered priest, could pray to God when Ketten pressed him hard. Ketten could only ride through standing corn, feel the horse's stubborn, billowing movement under him, and conjure up good will with blows of his iron gauntlet. But he was thankful that it should be so. He was glad that a man could live and cause others to die without that other thing. Thus one could deny and drive off something that crept towards the fire when one stared into the flames, something that was gone the moment one straightened up, stiff from dreaming, and turned round. Herr von Ketten sometimes became entangled in the long, intertwining threads of his thoughts when he remembered the Bishop to whom he was doing all this, and it seemed to him that only a miracle could straighten it all out.

His wife would summon the old steward and roam through the forest with him when she was not sitting gazing at the pictures in her books. Forest opens up before one, but its soul withdraws. She would press through the undergrowth, clamber over boulders, come upon tracks and spoors, and catch glimpses of animals, but she never came home having had more than such small adventures, difficulties overcome, curiosities satisfied, things from which all the life vanished as soon as one emerged from the forest. And that green *fata morgana* of which she had heard tell before she came to this country—as soon as one was no longer entering into it, it closed again behind one's back.

Rather indolently, meanwhile, she kept some order in the castle. As for her sons, neither of whom had ever seen the sea—were they really her children? At times it seemed to her they were young wolves. Once she was brought a wolf-cub that had been taken in the forest. And she looked after him too. He and the great hounds treated each other with uneasy tolerance, letting each other be without exchanging any sign. When the wolf-cub crossed the castle yard, they would stand up and watch him pass, but they neither barked nor growled. And even if he cast a sidelong glance at them, he would keep straight on, scarcely slackening his pace, only a little more stiff-legged, lest he should show any fear. He followed his mistress everywhere. He gave no sign of affection or of familiarity, merely turning his intense gaze to her often—but his gaze said nothing. She loved this wolf for his sineviness, his brown coat, and the silent ferocity and intensity of his gaze, which reminded her of Herr von Ketten.

* * *

At last the moment came for which a man must wait. The Bishop fell ill and died, and the cathedral chapter was without leadership. Ketten sold his goods and chattels, mortgaged his land, and employed all his means to equip a small army entirely his own. Then he negotiated. Faced with the choice between having to continue the old struggle against newly armed forces and coming to terms, the chapter decided for the latter; and it was inevitable that Ketten, the last captain remaining, strong and menacing, in the field, should make advantageous terms for himself, while the cathedral chapter extorted what compensation it could from weaker and more hesitant foes.

So there was an end to what, by the fourth generation, had become like the wall of a room, a wall one sees facing one every morning at breakfast and does not really see at all. All at once this wall was not there. Hitherto everything had been as in the lives of all foregoing Kettens, and all that remained to be done in this Ketten's life was to round things out and set them in order, an artisan's aim in life, no goal for a great lord. And then, as he was riding home, a fly stung him. His hand at once began to swell, and he became very tired. He dismounted at the tavern in a small, poverty-stricken village, and, sitting at the greasy wooden table, he laid his head down on it, overcome by drowsiness. When he woke, at evening, he was in a fever. He would nevertheless have ridden on if he had been in haste; but he was not in haste now. In the morning, when he tried to mount, he was so dizzy that he slipped and fell. The swelling had already spread up his arm to his shoulder. Having forced his armour on, he had to be unbuckled again, and while he was standing there, letting it be done, he was shaken by such a fit of shivering as he had never known. His muscles twitched and jerked so that his hands would not obey him, and the half-unbuckled pieces of armour clattered like a loose roof-gutter in a gale. He felt this was unworthy of him, and laughed, with grimly set face, at his clattering; but his legs were weak as a child's. He sent a messenger to his wife, another to a surgeon, and yet another to a famous physician.

The surgeon, who was the first to arrive, prescribed hot compresses of healing herbs and asked for permission to use the knife. Ketten, who was now much more impatient to reach home, bade him cut—until he had half as many fresh wounds again as he had old ones. How strange it was to let pain be inflicted on one and not defend oneself! For two days he lay wrapped from head to toe in the healing herbal compresses, and then had himself carried home. The journey took three days, but this kill-or-cure treatment, which might indeed have caused his death by exhausting his remaining strength, seemed to have halted the malady: when they arrived, he lay in a high fever from the poison in his blood, but the infection had not spread further.

This fever was like a plain of burning grass, smouldering on day after day, week after week. Daily the sick man dwindled, being consumed in his own fire, but the evil humours also seemed to be gradually consumed by it. More than this even the famous physician could not say, and only the lady from Portugal knew secret signs that she chalked on his door and the bedposts. When, one day, there was almost nothing left of Herr von Ketten, only something like a shape filled with soft, hot ash, suddenly the fever diminished— remaining a mere faint glimmer under the ashes.

If it was strange to suffer pain against which one did not fight, what followed now was something that the sick man did not experience like someone who was himself in the midst of it. He slept a great deal, and was absent even when his eyes were open. But when his consciousness returned, this body without any will of its own, this body as warm and helpless as an infant's, was not his at all, and neither was this weak soul that the faintest breath of air could agitate. Surely he had already died and was all this time merely waiting somewhere, as though he might have to come back again. He had never known that dying was so peaceful. Part of his being had gone ahead into death, separating and scattering like a cavalcade of travellers. While the bones were still lying in bed, and the bed was there, his wife bending over him, and he, out of curiosity, for the sake of some diversion, was watching the changing expressions in her attentive face, everything he loved had already gone a long way ahead. Herr von Ketten and his moon-lady, his nocturnal enchantress, had issued forth from him and softly withdrawn to a distance: he could still see them, he knew that by taking a few great leaps he could still catch up with them, only he no longer knew whether he was already there with them or still here. Yet all this lay in some immense and kindly hand that was benign as a cradle and which nevertheless weighed all things as in scales, imperturbable, unconcerned as to the outcome. Doubtless that was God. But even though he did not doubt it, it did not stir him either. He was waiting for whatever was to come, not even responding to the smile that hovered above him, and those caressing words.

Then the day came when all at once he knew this would be his last if he did not gather up all his will-power in order to remain alive. And it was on the evening of this day that the fever ceased.

When he felt this first stage of returning health like solid ground beneath him, he began to have himself carried out every day to the little green patch of ground on the rocky bluff that jutted, unwalled, above the precipice. Wrapped in blankets, he would lie there in the sun—now dozing, now waking, never sure whether he was asleep or awake.

Once, when he woke, the wolf was there. Gazing into those bevelled eyes, he could not stir. He did not know how much time passed—and then his wife was there beside him, the wolf at her knee. He closed his eyes again, pretending he had not been awake at all. But when he was carried back to his bed, he asked for his crossbow. He was so weak that he could not draw it, and this amazed him. Beckoning to the servant, he bade him take the crossbow. "The wolf," he said. The man hesitated. But Herr von Ketten raged like a child, and that evening the wolf's pelt hung in the castle yard. When the Portuguese lady saw it and learnt only then, from the serving-men, what had happened, her blood froze. She went to his bedside. There he lay, pale as the wall behind him, and for the first time he looked her straight in the eyes again. She laughed and said: "I shall have a hood made of the pelt, and come by night and suck the blood from your veins."

Then he wanted to send away the chaplain, who once had said: "The Bishop can pray to God, and that is a threat to you"—and who had later, time after time, given him Extreme Unction. But this he could not do at once, for the Portuguese lady exerted herself on his behalf, begging him to have patience with the chaplain a short while longer, until he found another place. Herr von Ketten yielded. He was still weak and still spent much time drowsing in the sun, on the patch of grass.

Once—another time when he woke—there was the friend of her youth. He was standing beside the lady from Portugal, having come from her native country, and here in the North he seemed to resemble her. He saluted Herr von Ketten with a nobleman's courtesy, uttering words that, judging by his look and gestures, must have been all grace and cordiality. And the lord of Ketten lay in the grass like a dog, filled with shame.

Unless, indeed, that was not until the second time—for his mind sometimes wandered even now. It was a long time too before he noticed that his cap had become too big for him. The soft fur cap that had always sat so firmly on his head now, at a light touch, slipped down to where his ears stopped it from going further. The three of them were together, and his wife said: "Dear heaven! Your head has shrunk!"

His first thought was that he must have let his hair be cropped too short, though at the moment he could not remember when. Furtively he passed his hand over his head. But his hair was longer than it should have been, and matted since he had been ill. Then the cap must have stretched, he told himself. But it was still almost new—and how should it have stretched, lying unused in a chest? So he made a jest of the matter, remarking that in all the years when he had been living among men-at-arms, instead of with courtly cavaliers, his head might well have shrunk. He felt how awkwardly the jest came from his lips, and it did not even remove the question— can a skull become smaller? The strength in the veins may grow less, the fat beneath the scalp may melt away in fever: but what does that amount to? Now at times he would make a gesture as of smoothing his hair, or pretend to be wiping away sweat, or he would try to lean back into the shade unobtrusively and then, swiftly, using two fingertips as if they were a mason's compass, would measure his skull, placing his fingers now this way, now that. But no doubt remained: his head had become smaller, and if he fingered it from within, with his thoughts, it was even smaller, like two small thin shells fitted together.

There are, of course, many things that one cannot account for, but one does not carry them on one's own shoulders, feeling them every time one turns one's neck towards two people who are talking while one seems to be asleep. Although he had long forgotten all but a few words of that foreign language, once he caught the sentence: "You do not do what you would, and you do what you would not." The tone seemed to be urgent rather than jesting— what could it mean?

Another time he leaned far out of the window, right into the rushing sound of the torrent; he now did this often, as a sort of game: the noise, as confused as wildly whirling hay, closed the ears, and when he returned out of that deafness, his wife's conversation with the other man suddenly stood out clearly, very small and far away. And it was an eager conversation. Their souls seemed to be in harmony with each other.

The third time it was simply that he followed the other two when they went out into the courtyard again in the evening. When they passed the torch at the top of the outside steps, their shadows must fall across the tops of the trees. He bent forward swiftly when this happened, but among the leaves the shadows all blurred into one.

At any other time he would have tried to drive the poison out of his body by calling for his horse and his men, or would have tried to burn it out in wine. But the chaplain and the scrivener gobbled and drank till the wine and food dribbled out of the corners of their mouths, and the young knight would clink the cannikin with them, laughing like one setting two dogs at each other. Ketten felt a disgust for the wine that was swilled by these two clerks, mere oafs under their veneer of scholasticism. They would argue about the millennium, and about learned doctoral questions, and would talk bawdy, now in German, now in Church Latin. A journeying humanist would translate whatever was needed to complement this gibberish and that of the Portuguese; he had sprained his ankle and had every intention of staying on until it was thoroughly strong again.

"He fell off his horse when a rabbit ran by," the scrivener said banteringly.

"He took it for a dragon," Herr von Ketten said with sullen mockery, standing nearby, unsure of himself.

"But then so did the horse!" the castle chaplain bellowed. "Else it would not have shied. And thus the magister understands better than the lord what comes from the horse's mouth!"

The drunken company guffawed at the lord's expense. Herr von Ketten looked at them hard, took a step towards them, and struck the chaplain in the face. He was a plump young peasant, and he turned very red, then deadly pale, but he remained seated. The young knight rose, smiling, and went in search of his friend, the lady of the castle.

"Why did you not stab him to the heart?" the rabbit-humanist hissed when they were alone.

"He is strong as two bulls," the chaplain answered, "and, moreover, Christian teachings are truly of such a nature as to afford consolation in such circumstances."

But the truth was that Herr von Ketten was still very weak, and his life was returning to him all too slowly. He could not reach the second stage of recovery.

The visitor did not resume his travels, and the mistress of the castle failed to understand her lord's hints. For eleven years she had been waiting for her husband, for eleven years he had been her far-off beloved in an aura of fame and glory, and now he went about castle and courtyard, wasted and worn by illness, looking commonplace enough beside the other's youth and courtly grace. She did not give it much thought, but she was a little weary of this country that had promised things beyond the power of words to tell, and she could not bring herself, just because of a cross face, to send away her childhood friend, who had brought back to her the very fragrance of her homeland and thoughts that one could think with laughter. She had nothing to reproach herself with. She had been a shade more superficial during these last weeks, but that was pleasant, and she could now sometimes feel her face lighting up as it had done years before.

A soothsaying woman, whom he consulted, prophesied to Herr von Ketten: "You will be cured only when you accomplish a task." But when he pressed her to tell him what task, she fell silent, tried to slip away and finally declared that that was hidden from her.

He could easily have put a quick, painless end to this visit, for the sanctity of life and the sacred laws of hospitality are of little account to one who has spent years as an unbidden guest among his enemies. But in his enfeebled convalescent state he was almost proud of being clumsy, and any cunning solution seemed to him as unworthy as the young man's frivolous readiness of tongue. Strange things happened to him. Though the mists of weakness that enveloped him his wife's ways seemed to him tenderer than they need be; it reminded him of earlier days, when sometimes, returning home to her love, he had wondered at finding it more intense than at other times. For his absence alone could not, he thought, be the cause. He could not even have said whether he was glad or sorry. It was just as in the days when he had lain so close to death. He could not make any move. When he gazed into his wife's eyes, they were like new-cut glass, and although what the surface showed him was his own reflection, he could not penetrate further. It seemed to him that only a miracle could change this situation. And one cannot make destiny speak when it chooses to be silent. One must simply harken for whatever is on its way.

*　　*　　*

One day when a company of them came up the mountainside together, they found the little cat at the gate. It was standing outside the gate as though it did not want to jump, cat-fashion, over the wall, but to enter as human beings did. It arched its back in welcome and rubbed itself against the skirts and boots of the towering beings who were strangely surprised by its presence. They let it in, and it was like receiving a guest. The very next day it was apparent that what they had opened the gate to was no mere kitten that had come to stay; it was almost as though they had adopted a small child. The dainty little creature's tastes were not for the delights of cellar and attic. It would not leave the human beings' company for a single moment. And it had a way of making them give up their time to it, which was all the less comprehensible in that there were so many other and grander animals at the castle, and the human beings also had their own affairs to occupy them. The fascination seemed positively to originate in their having to keep their eyes lowered, watching the little creature, for it was very unobtrusive in its ways and just a shade quieter, one might almost have said sadder and more meditative, than seemed appropriate to a kitten. It romped in the way it knew human beings expect a kitten to romp; it climbed on to their laps and was, it seemed, studiously charming to them, and yet one could feel that it was also somehow absent. And precisely this—this absence of whatever would have made it into an ordinary kitten—was like a second presence, a hovering double, perhaps, or a faint halo surrounding it. Not that any of them had the hardihood to put this into words. The lady from Portugal bent tenderly over the little creature lying on its back in her lap, in its childlike way beating its tiny paws at her playful fingers. Her young friend, laughing, bent low too—over the kitten, over her lap. And this casual frolicking reminded Herr von Ketten of his illness, now nearly gone, as though the illness and its deathly gentleness had been transformed into that little animal's body and so were no longer merely within him, but there in the midst of them all. A serving-man said: "That cat is getting the mange."

Herr von Ketten was astonished that he had not noticed this himself. The serving-man spoke again: "It will have to be done away with before long."

Meanwhile, the kitten had been given a name taken from one of the fairy-tale books. It had become gentler and more sweet-natured than ever. Soon everyone began to see that it was ill and growing almost luminously weak. It spent more and more time resting in someone's lap, resting from the affairs of the world, its little claws clutching tight in mingled affection and anxiety. And now too it began to look at them, one after the other; at pale Ketten and at the young Portuguese sitting bent forward, his eyes intent on it or perhaps on the breathing movement of the lap where it lay. It looked at them all as though asking forgiveness for the ugliness of what it was about to suffer—in some mysterious way for all of them. And then its martyrdom began.

One night the vomiting began, and the little animal continued to vomit until the next morning. When daylight returned, it lay languid and dizzy as though it had been beaten over the head. Perhaps it was merely that in their excess of love for it they had given the starving kitten too much to eat. However this might be, after that it could not be kept in the bedroom, but was given to the serving-men to look after. After two days the serving-men complained that it was no better; and indeed it was probable that they had put it outside in the night. And now it not only vomited but could not hold its stool, and nothing was safe from it. And this now was an ordeal, a grim trial of strength between that almost imperceptible halo and the dreadful filth, and it was decided—since it had meanwhile been discovered whence the little creature came— to have it taken back there: a peasant's cottage down by the river, near the foot of the hill. This was a kind of deportation, done in the hope of evading both responsibility for the animal and ridicule for all the attention they paid to it. But it weighed on their conscience, and so they also sent milk and a little meat and even money in order to make sure that the peasants, to whom dirt did not matter so much, would look after the cat properly. Nevertheless, the servants shook their heads over their master and mistress.

The serving-man who had carried the kitten down recounted that it had run after him when he left and that he had had to carry it back again. Two days later it was once more up in the castle. The hounds avoided it, the servants did not dare to drive it away for fear of the master and mistress, and when the latter set eyes on it, it was tacitly agreed that nobody would now refuse to let it die up here.

It was now very thin and lustreless, but the disgusting malady seemed to have passed off; now it was merely growing thinner all the time, losing flesh almost before their very eyes. For two days everything was, to a heightened degree, just as it had been before: there was the slow, affectionate prowling about in the refuge where it was cared for; an absent-minded smiling with the paws while striking at a scrap of paper dangled before it; sometimes a faint swaying out of weakness, in spite of having four legs to support it—and on the second day it sometimes collapsed on its side. In a human being this process of disembodiment would not have seemed so strange, but in the animal it was like a metamorphosis into a human being. They watched it almost in awe. None of these three people, each in his or her peculiar situation, could escape the thought that it was his or her own destiny that was being vicariously accomplished in this little cat already half released from earthly bonds.

But on the third day the vomiting and filthiness began again. The serving-man stood by, and even though he did not dare to say it again aloud, his silence said it clearly enough: it will have to be put away. The Portuguese bowed his head as though struggling with some temptation, and then he said to his friend: "It is the only way." It seemed to him he had accepted his own death-sentence. And suddenly everyone looked at Herr von Ketten. He had grown white as the wall, and rose, and left the room. Then the lady from Portugal said to the serving-man: "Take it away."

The man took the sick animal away to his own place, and the next day it was gone. Nobody asked any questions. They all knew that he had killed it. All of them felt the oppression of unspeakable guilt; something had gone from among them. Only the children felt nothing, finding it quite natural that the serving-man should kill a dirty cat that nobody could play with any more. But now and then the hounds would snuffle at a patch of grass on which the sunlight fell in the courtyard, and their legs stiffened, their hair bristled, and they glanced sidelong. At one such moment Herr von Ketten and the lady from Portugal encountered each other. They stopped side by side, looking across at the dogs and finding nothing to say. The sign had been given—but how was it to be interpreted and what was to be done? A great dome of silence surrounded them both.

If she has not sent him away before nightfall, I must kill him—Herr von Ketten thought to himself. But night fell and still nothing had happened. Supper was over. Ketten sat looking grave, heated by a slight fever. After a while he went out into the courtyard, for the cool evening air, and he remained absent for a long time. He could not make the final decision that he had all his life found it so easy to make. Saddling horses, buckling on armour, drawing a sword—all of that, which had once been the very music of his life, now had a harsh, discordant ring; and fighting seemed a senseless, alien mode of action. Even the short way, the way of the knife, was now like an infinitely long road on which a man might die of thirst. But neither was it his way to suffer; he could feel that he would never be wholly well again if he did not wrench himself free of all this. And gradually another thought associated itself with these. . . .

As a boy he had always wanted to climb the unscaleable cliff on top of which the castle stood. The thought was a mad one, a suicidal one, but now it was gradually gaining in obscure conviction, as though it were a matter of trial by ordeal, or something like an approaching miracle. It was not he but the little cat from the world beyond, it seemed to him, that would return this way. Laughing softly to himself, he shook his head in order to make sure it was still on his shoulders, and at the same time he realised that he had already gone a long distance down the stony path to the bottom of the hill.

At the bottom, down by the torrent, he left the path and clambered over great boulders with the water dashing between them, then through the bushes and up to the cliff. In the moonlight little points of shadow revealed crevices where fingers and toes could find a hold. Suddenly a piece of stone broke loose under one foot: the shock ran through his whole body, right into his heart. He strained his ears. It seemed an eternity before the stone splashed into the water far below. He must already have climbed a third of the height. Then it distinctly seemed to him that he awoke and realised what he was doing. Only a dead man could reach the bottom now, and only the Devil himself could reach the top. He groped above him. With each grip his life hung by the ten thin straps of sinew in his fingers. Sweat poured from his face, waves of heat flashed through his body, his nerves were like stony threads. But it was strange to feel how in this struggle with death strength and health came flowing back into his limbs, as though returning into his body from some place outside him. And then the impossible was indeed accomplished. There was one overhanging ledge that had to be circumvented, and then his arm was thrust in through an open window. Doubtless there was no other place where he could have arrived but at this very window, yet it was only now that he knew where he was. He swung himself in, sat on the sill and let his legs dangle inside the room. With his strength his ferocity had also returned. He waited until he had regained his breath. No, he had not lost the dagger from his side. It seemed to him that the bed was empty. But he went on waiting until his heart and lungs were quite calm again. And more and more distinctly it seemed to him that he was alone in the room. He crept towards the bed: nobody had slept in it this night.

Herr von Ketten tiptoed through rooms, corridors, and doorways that no one else would have found at once without guidance—until he came to his wife's bed-chamber. Listening, he waited. There was no sound of whispering. He glided in. The lady from Portugal was breathing quietly in her sleep. He searched dark corners and fumbled along walls and, when he stealthily left the room again, he could almost have sung for joy, joy that shook the very fabric of his unbelief.

He roved through the castle, but now floorboards and flagstones echoed with his tread, as though he were in search of some joyful surprise. In the yard a serving-man called out to him, demanding to know who he was. He asked for the visitor and learned that he had ridden away at the rising of the moon. Herr von Ketten sat down on a pile of rough-hewn timber, and the watchman marvelled at how long he sat there.

All at once he was seized by the certainty that if he were to return to the Portuguese lady's chamber, she would no longer be there. He thundered on the door and went in. His young wife started up as though in her dreams she had been waiting for this, and she saw him standing before her fully dressed, just as he had gone out that evening. Nothing had been proved, nothing had been disposed of, but she asked no question, and there was nothing that he could ask. He pulled aside the heavy curtain hanging before the window, and beyond it there rose the curtain of torrential thunder behind which all the seigniors delle Catene were born and died.

"If God could become man, then He can also become a kitten," the lady from Portugal said.

And perhaps he should have laid his hand upon her mouth to silence this blasphemy, but they both knew that no sound of it could penetrate beyond the walls.

Translated by Eithne Wilkins and Ernst Kaiser

Tonka

I

At a hedge. A bird was singing. And then the sun was somewhere down behind the bushes. The bird stopped singing. It was evening, and the peasant girls were coming across the fields, singing. What little things! Is it petty if such little things cling to a person? Like burrs? That was Tonka. Infinity sometimes flows in droplets.

And the horse was part of it too, the roan that he had tied to a willow. It was during his year of military service. It was no mere chance that it was in that year, for there is no other time of life when a man is so deprived of himself and his own works, and an alien force strips everything from his bones. One is more vulnerable at this time than at any other.

But had it really been like that at all? No, that was only what he had worked it up into later. That was the fairy-tale, and he could no longer tell the difference. In fact, of course, she had been living with her aunt at the time when he got to know her. And Cousin Julie sometimes came visiting. That was how it had been. He remembered being disconcerted by their sitting down at the same table with Cousin Julie over a cup of coffee, for she was, after all, a disgrace to the family. It was notorious that one could strike up a conversation with Cousin Julie and take her back to one's lodgings that same evening; she would also go to the bawdy-houses whenever she was wanted. She had no other source of income. Still, she was a relative, after all, even if one didn't approve of the life she led; and even if she was a frivolous woman, one couldn't very well refuse to let her sit down at the table with one. Anyway, she didn't come very often. A man might have made a row about it, for a man reads the newspaper or belongs to some association with definite aims and is always throwing his weight about, but Auntie merely made a few cutting remarks after Julie had gone, and let it go at that. So long as she was there, they couldn't help laughing at her jokes, for she had a quick tongue and always knew more about what was going on in town than anyone else. So, even if they disapproved of her, there was no unbridgeable gap between them; they had something in common.

The women from the jail were another example of the same thing. Most of them were prostitutes too, and not long afterwards the jail itself had to be moved to another district because so many of them became pregnant while serving their sentence, carrying mortar on the building sites where male convicts worked as bricklayers. Now, these women were also hired out to do housework. For instance, they were very good at laundering, and they were very much sought after by people in modest circumstances, because they were cheap. Tonka's grandmother also had one in on washing-day; she would be given a cup of coffee and a bun, and since one was sharing the work with her it was all right to share breakfast with her too— there was no harm in that. At midday someone had to see her back to the jail, that was the regulation, and when Tonka was a little girl, she was generally the one who had to do it. She would walk along with the woman, chatting away happily, not in the least ashamed of being seen in that company, although these women wore grey prison uniforms and white kerchiefs that made them easily recognisable. Innocence one might call it: a young life in all its innocence pathetically exposed to influences that were bound to coarsen it. But later on, when the sixteen-year-old Tonka was still unembarrassed, gossiping with Cousin Julie, could one say that this was still all innocence, or was it that her sensibilities were blunted? Even if no blame attached to her, how revealing it was!

The house must also be mentioned. With its five windows looking on to the street, it was a survival between towering new buildings that had shot up around it. It was in the back premises that Tonka lived with her aunt, who was actually her much older cousin, and her aunt's little son, the illegitimate offspring of a relationship that she had regarded as permanent, and a grandmother who was not really the grandmother but the grandmother's sister. In earlier days there had also been a brother of her dead mother's living there, but he too had died young. All of them lived together in one room and a kitchen, while the genteel curtains of the five front windows concealed an establishment of ill repute where lower-middle-class housewives of easy morals, as well as professionals, were brought together with men. This was something that the family tacitly ignored, and since they wanted no trouble with the procuress they even passed the time of day with her. She was a fat woman, very set on respectability. She had a daughter of the same age as Tonka, whom she sent to a good school; she had her taught the piano and French, bought her pretty clothes, and took care to keep her well away from the business. She was a soft-hearted creature, which made it easier for her to follow the trade she did, for she knew it was shameful. In earlier times Tonka had now and then been allowed to play with this daughter, and so had found her way into the front part of the house, at hours when it was empty, and to her the rooms seemed enormous, leaving her with an impression of grandeur and refinement that was only reduced to proper proportions after he came on the scene.

Tonka was not her real name. At her baptism she had been given the German name Antonie, and Tonka was the abbreviated form of the Czech diminutive Toninka. The inhabitants of those back streets talked a queer mixture of the two languages.

But where do such thoughts lead? There it was, she had been standing by a hedge that time, in front of the dark open doorway of a cottage, the first in the village as one came out from town. She was wearing laced boots, red stockings, and a gaily-coloured, stiff, full skirt, and as she talked she seemed to be gazing at the moon, which hung pale over the corn shocks. She was at once pert and shy, and laughed a lot, as though she felt protected by the moon. And the wind blew across the stubble fields as if it were cooling a plate of soup. Riding home, he had said laughingly to his comrade-in-arms, young Baron Mordansky: "You know, I shouldn't at all mind having an affair with a girl like that, only it's too dangerous for my liking. You'd have to promise to make up a threesome, to keep me from going sentimental." And Mordansky, who had done a spell as a trainee in his uncle's sugar-mill, had thereupon told him about how, when the time came round for digging the beets, hundreds of such peasant girls laboured in the fields belonging to the mill, and it was said they were as submissive as black slaves to the supervisors and their assistants. And once, he remembered quite distinctly, he had cut short a similar conversation with Mordansky because it was an affront to his feelings. Yet it had not been at that time, he knew—what was now trying to impose itself on him as a memory was really something else, the tangle of thorns that had later grown inside his head.

In reality it was on the Ring that he had first seen her, in that main street with the stone arcades where the officers and the gentlemen who worked in the government offices stood chatting at corners, the students and young business men strolled up and down, and the girls wandered along in twos and threes, arm in arm, after the shops closed, or the more curious of them even during the lunch-hour. Sometimes a well-known local lawyer would make his way slowly through the crowd, lifting his hat to acquaintances, or a local deputy, or, say, a respected industrialist; and there were even ladies to be seen, on their way home after shopping. There her glance had suddenly crossed with his, a merry glance, lasting only for the briefest moment—like a ball accidentally landing in a passer-by's face. The next instant she had looked away, with a feigned air of innocence. He had turned round quickly, supposing that now the usual giggling would follow, but Tonka was walking on, looking straight ahead of her, rather tensely. She was with two other girls, and taller than either of them. She was not beautiful, but her face had a clear-cut, definite quality. There was nothing in it of that petty, cunningly feminine look which seems to result from the face as a whole; in this face mouth, nose, and eyes were each something clearly in their own right and could stand up to being contemplated separately, delighting the beholder simply by their candour and the freshness irradiating the whole face. It was odd that so gay a glance should stick fast like a barbed arrow, and she herself seemed to have hurt herself with it.

So much was now clear. Well, then, at that time she had been working in the draper's shop. It was a large shop, employing a great many girls to handle the stock. Her job was to look after the rolls of material and get the right one down when it was asked for, and the palms of her hands were always slightly moist because of the irritation from the fine hairs of the cloth. There was nothing dream-like about that, and her face was guileless. But then there were the draper's sons, and one of them had a moustache like a squirrel's, turned up at the ends, and always wore patent-leather shoes. Tonka was full of stories about how smart he was, how many pairs of shoes he had, and how his trousers were every night laid between two boards and weighed down with heavy stones to keep them well pressed.

And now, as he got a clear glimpse of something real through the mist, that other smile emerged, the incredulous smile his mother wore—essentially an onlooker's smile, full of pity and disdain for him. That smile was real. What it said was: 'Heavens, not *that* shop, surely?' And although Tonka had still been a virgin when he came to know her, that smile, treacherously furtive or masked, had also turned up in many a tormenting dream he had. Perhaps it had never existed as a single smile; even now he could not be sure of that. And then too there are nuptial nights when one cannot be entirely sure; there are, so to speak, physiological ambiguities, times when even Nature does not give an unequivocal answer. And in the very moment when he remembered that, he knew that Heaven itself was against Tonka.

II

It had been rash of him to bring Tonka to act as nurse and companion to his grandmother. He was still very young then. He had worked out a little stratagem: Tonka's aunt, who went out doing sewing for 'the gentry', sometimes worked for an aunt of his, and he had contrived that she should be asked if she happened to know of a young girl, who . . . and so on. The idea was to get a girl to look after his grandmother, whose merciful release was to be expected in a couple of years. Apart from her wages, the girl would be remembered in the old lady's will.

But meanwhile there had been a number of little episodes. Once, for instance, he was going on an errand with her; there were some children playing in the street, and suddenly they both found themselves gazing at the face of a little girl who was howling—a face that wriggled and writhed like a worm, in the full blast of sunlight. The pitiless clarity of it there in the light seemed to him a symbol of life, over against the orbit of death that they had both just left.

But Tonka was 'fond of children'. She bent down to the child, cheerfully and consolingly, perhaps even slightly amused by it— and that was all, however much he tried to make her see that behind the appearance there was something else. From however many sides he approached it, in the end he always found himself confronted with the same opacity in her mind. Tonka was not stupid, but something seemed to prevent her from being intelligent; and for the first time he felt this wide expanse of pity for her, this pity that was so difficult to account for.

Another time he said to her: "Tell me, how long is it now you've been with Grandmamma, Fräulein Tonka?" And when she had told him, he said: "Oh, really? It's a long time to have spent with an old woman like that."

"Oh," Tonka exclaimed, "I like being here."

"Well, you needn't be afraid to tell me if you don't. I can't imagine how a young girl can manage to put up with it."

"It's a job," Tonka answered, and blushed.

"All right, it's a job. But that isn't all one wants from life. Isn't that true?"

"Yes."

"And have you got that?"

"No."

"Yes, no. Yes, no." He grew impatient. "What's the sense of talking like that? Can't you even grumble about us?" But he saw that she was struggling to find an answer, that she kept on discarding possible answers just when they were on the tip of her tongue. And suddenly he felt sorry for her. "I dare say you'll hardly know what I mean. It's not that I think badly of my grandmother, poor woman. No, it isn't that. I'm not looking at it from that point of view at the moment. I can't help thinking of it from your point of view, and from your point of view she's a perfect old horror. Now do you see what I mean?"

"Yes," she said in a low voice, blushing more than ever. "I understood all right before. But I can't say it."

At that he laughed. "That's something that's never happened to me, not to be able to say something! But now I'm more curious than ever to know what you really think. I'll help you." He looked at her so intently that she became more embarrassed than ever.

"All right, then. Here goes: do you like just having regular duties, a quiet, steady routine? Is that it?"

"Well, I don't know quite how you mean. I like my work all right."

"You 'like it all right'. But you're not exactly mad about it, I suppose? I mean, there are people who don't want anything but a steady job."

"What are you getting at?"

"Desires, dreams, ambition—that's what I'm getting at. Doesn't a fine day like this start something up in you?"

Between the stone walls of the streets the day was full of a quivering light and the honey of springtime.

Now it was she who laughed. "It isn't that either."

"It isn't that? Well, then, perhaps you have a special liking for darkened rooms, for talking in a whisper, for the smell of medicines, and all that? There are such people too, you know. But I can tell from your face that I haven't hit it this time either."

She shook her head and faintly turned her mouth down at the corners—perhaps in shy mockery, perhaps only out of embarrassment.

But he gave her no peace. "You see how wrong I go, how ridiculous I'm making myself in your eyes by keeping on guessing wrong like this! Doesn't that help you to come out with it? Come on now!"

And now at least she came out with it. Slowly. Hesitantly. As if choosing her words carefully, in order to make intelligible something that was very difficult to understand:

"You see, I have to earn my living."

Ah, how simple it all was!

What a fool he had been, and what a stony eternity lay in that so ordinary answer!

And another such time was once when he had secretly gone for a walk with Tonka. They used to go for long walks in the country whenever she had her day off, which was twice a month. It was summer. When evening came, the warmth of the air was exactly the same as that of one's face and hands, and, walking for a moment with closed eyes, one felt as though one were dissolving, expanding, floating. . . . He described this to Tonka and, when she laughed, asked her if she knew what he meant.

Oh, yes!

But he was still not sure that she did and so he tried to get her to describe it to him in her own words. And this she could not do.

So then, he said, she *didn't* know what he meant.

Oh, but she did! And suddenly she said: it made you want to sing.

For heaven's sake!

But yes—that *was* it, she protested.

They went on wrangling like this for a while. And then after all they both began to sing, rather in the spirit of someone firmly placing the *corpus delicti* on the table or inspecting the scene of the crime. They sang pretty badly, and something from a musical comedy, at that, but fortunately Tonka sang softly, and he was glad of that little sign of consideration for his feelings. He was positive she had not been to the theatre more than once in her life and that ever since then these trashy tunes summed up her notions of culture and elegance. However, it turned out that she had merely picked them up from the other girls at the shop where she had worked.

He asked her if she really liked these tunes. It always annoyed him to come across anything still linking her with that shop.

She did not know what it was, whether this music was beautiful or silly, merely that it made her want to be on the stage herself and put her whole heart into making the people in the audience happy or sorrowful. This was perfectly ridiculous, of course, in the light of what poor dear Tonka looked like while she was singing. It depressed him, and his own singing faded out on a sort of growl. Then Tonka suddenly broke off too, as if she felt the same thing, and for a while the two of them walked along in silence.

Then Tonka stopped and said: "That's not what I meant at all, about singing."

And since she saw in his eyes a little glint of responsive kindness, she began to sing again, still softly, but this time folk-songs from her own part of the country. So they walked along, with these simple tunes making everything vaguely sad, like the fluttering of cabbage-whites in the sunshine. And so now all at once it turned out, of course, that Tonka was right.

Now it was he who could not express what was going on in him. Because Tonka did not talk the ordinary language that other people used, but some language of the totality of things, she had had to suffer being thought stupid and insensitive. He realised now what it meant if one said: Songs just come into her head. It seemed to him that she was very lonely. If it were not for him, who would understand her? So they both sang. Tonka recited the Slavic words and translated them into German for him, and then they joined hands and sang together like children. Whenever they had to leave off to regain their breath, there would be a little moment of silence ahead of them too, where the twilight was creeping across the road—and even if the whole thing was foolishness, the dusk itself was at one with their feelings.

And yet another time they were sitting at the edge of a wood, and he was simply gazing into space through half-shut eyelids, not talking, letting his thoughts roam. Tonka began to be afraid she had offended him again. Several times she took a deep breath, as if about to speak, but then syhness held her back. So for a long time there was no sound but the woodland murmur that is so tormenting, rising and sinking away in a different place at every instant. Once a brown butterfly fluttered past them and settled on a long-stemmed flower, which quivered under the touch, swaying to and fro and then quite suddenly being quite still again, like a conversation broken off. Tonka pressed her fingers hard into the moss on which they were sitting, but after a while the tiny blades stood up again, one after the other, row on row, until there was finally no more trace of the hand that had lain there. It was enough to make one weep, without knowing why. If she had been trained to think, like her companion, at that moment Tonka would have realised that Nature consists of nothing but ugly little things that one hardly notices and which live as sadly far apart from each other as the stars in the night-sky. The beauties of Nature. . . . A wasp was crawling over his shoe. Its head was like a lantern. He watched it, contemplating his shoe, which was sticking up broad and black, oblique against the brown of the earth.

Tonka had often thought with dread of the moment when a man would stand before her and she would have no way of escape. The stories that the older girls in the shop had told her with such delight gave her a feeling only of a crude, boring frivolity, something that was not love at all, and she was indignant at the way men were always making amorous advances to her after scarcely exchanging more than a few words with her. As she looked at her companion now, she felt a sudden pang. It was the first time since she had been with him that she realised he was a man; for this was something completely different. He was lying back, resting on his elbows, his chin on his chest. Timidly, she tried to see into his eyes.

What she saw was a peculiar smile. He had one eye shut, and with the other he was gazing along the length of his body, as though aiming at something. Doubtless he knew how ugly his shoe looked at that angle, and perhaps too how little it amounted to that he was lying at the edge of a wood with Tonka. But he did nothing to change anything about it. Each detail was ugly, but the whole thing was happiness.

Quietly, Tonka got up. She suddenly felt a burning inside her head, and her heart was thudding. She could not make out what he was thinking, but she read it all in his eye; and all at once she caught herself wanting to take his head in her arms and cover up his eyes.

"It's time to go," she said. "It'll be getting dark soon."

As they were walking along the road, he said: "I'm afraid you must have been bored. But you will have to get used to me." He took her arm, because it was becoming difficult to see the road distinctly, and he tried to excuse himself for his silence and then, almost against his will, for his thoughts too. She did not really know what he was talking about, but in her own way she sensed the meaning of his words, which came so gravely through the rising mist. And when now he went further, even apologising for talking in such a solemn way, she did not know what to do. Even her silent prayer to the Blessed Virgin was of no avail, and so she linked her arm more closely with his, although she felt dreadfully shy at doing so.

He stroked her hand. "I think we get on well together, Tonka. But do you really understand me?"

After a while Tonka answered: "It doesn't matter if I know what you mean, or not. I couldn't say anything anyway. But I like you to be so serious."

These were all very slight experiences, of course, but the remarkable thing was that they happened all over again, exactly the same. Actually they were always there. And, even more remarkably, later they meant the very opposite of what they had meant in the beginning. Tonka always remained so simply and transparently the same that it was almost like having an hallucination, seeing the most incredible things.

III

Then came an event: his grandmother died before the expected time. Events are, after all, only things that happen untimely and out of place; one is, as it were, mislaid or forgotten, and one is as helpless as an object that nobody bothers to pick up. And even the events that took place much later were only the things that happen thousands of times, all over the world, and the only incomprehensible thing about it was that it should have happened with Tonka.

Well, and so the doctor came, the undertaker's men came, the death certificate was signed, and Grandmamma was buried. One thing followed on the other quite smoothly, as is proper in a respectable family. The will was read. He was glad not to be in any way involved. There was only one item among the bequests that demanded attention: the provision made for Fräulein Tonka with that dreamlike surname, one of those Czech surnames that mean things like 'He sang', or 'He came across the meadow'. There was a contract. Under the terms of the will the Fräulein was to receive—apart from her wages, which were low—a certain fixed sum for every completed year of service, and since it had been assumed that Grandmamma would linger on for quite a while, and since the sum had been fixed in gradually increasing amounts in accordance with the expected increase in the strain of nursing her, it turned out to be a sum that was bound to seem outrageously small to a young man who weighed out in minutes the months of her youth that Tonka had sacrificed.

He was present when Hyacinth reckoned up with her. He was pretending to read—the book was Novalis' *Fragments*—but in reality he was attentively following what was going on. He was ashamed when his 'uncle' named the sum. Even his 'uncle' seemed to feel something similar, for he began to explain to the Fräulein, in detail, the terms of the contract that had been made when she entered their service. Tonka listened intently, her lips tightly closed. The solemnity with which she followed the calculations gave her young face a very appealing look.

"So then that's correct, isn't it?" his uncle said, laying the money on the table.

It was obvious that she had absolutely no idea what it was all about. She pulled out her little purse, folded the notes, and squashed them in; but though they were few, folding them so much made a thick wad of them, and when the little purse had been replaced under her skirt, it made a bulge on her thigh, like a swelling.

She had only one question to ask. "When do I have to leave?"

"Well," his uncle said, "I suppose it will be a few days before the house is shut up. You can certainly stay till then. But you can also go before that, if you like, as you won't be needed any more."

"Thank you," she said and went off to her little room.

Meanwhile the others had begun sharing out the old woman's things among themselves. They were like wolves devouring a dead member of the pack, and they were already in a state of general irritation when he asked whether the Fräulein, who had got so little money out of it all, should not at least be given something of some value in memory of Grandmamma.

"We've decided to give her Grandmamma's big prayer book."

"Well, yes, but I'm sure something useful would please her more. What about this, for instance?" He picked up a brown fur tippet that was lying on the table.

"That's for Emmi"—a cousin of his—"and anyway you must be mad, it's *mink!*"

He laughed. "Is there any law that poor girls can only be given something for the good of their souls? You don't want to make a miserly impression, do you?"

"I'd thank you to leave that to us," his mother said, and because she did not think he was entirely wrong, she added: "These are things you know nothing about. She won't be treated unfairly." And, with a gesture at once lavish and irritable, she put aside for Tonka some of the old woman's handkerchiefs, chemises, and drawers, and then added a black woollen dress that had scarcely been worn. "There, I think that'll do. It's not as though the Fräulein had been such a treasure, and she can't exactly be called sentimental, either. She never shed so much as a single tear, either when Granny died or at the funeral. So please don't let us hear any more about it."

"Some people don't cry easily. I mean, that doesn't prove anything," he said, not because it seemed important to say it, but because he felt the urge to argue for the sake of arguing. "That will do!" his mother said. "Don't you realise that your remarks are out of place?"

At this rebuke he fell silent, not because he was in awe of his mother, but because suddenly he felt vastly pleased at the thought that Tonka had shed no tears. His relatives were all talking eagerly, all at once, and he noticed how skilfully each of them turned the situation to his or her own advantage. They expressed themselves, if not clearly, at least to some purpose and with the courage of their convictions. In the end each of them got what he or she wanted. For them the ability to talk was not a medium of thought, but a sort of capital, something they wore like jewellery to impress others. As he stood by the table with the heaps of things to be given away on it, he found himself recalling a line of verse. 'To him Apollo gave the gift of song, and music sweet to hear', and for the first time he realised that it really was a gift. How inarticulate Tonka was! She could neither talk nor weep. But how is one to define something that neither can speak nor is spoken of, something that dumbly merges with the anonymous mass of mankind, something that is like a little line scratched on the tablets of history? What is one to make of such a life, such a being, which is like a snowflake falling all alone in the midst of a summer's day? Is it real or imaginary? Is it good, or evil, or indifferent? One senses the fact that here the categories have reached a frontier beyond which they cease to be valid.

Without another word he left the room and went to tell Tonka that he would provide for her.

He found her packing up her things. There was a big cardboard box on a chair, and there were two others on the floor. One of them was already tied up with string. The two others were not big enough for the amount of stuff still scattered about the room, and she was trying to solve the problem by taking things out again and putting them in differently—stockings and handkerchiefs, laced boots and sewing things—laying them first this way and then that. However scanty her possessions were, she would never get everything stowed away, for her luggage was still scantier.

Since the door of her little room was ajar, he was able to watch her for some time without her knowing. When she did notice him, she blushed and quickly stepped in front of the open boxes.

"So you're leaving us?" he said, charmed with her embarrassment. "What are you going to do now?"

"I'm going home to Auntie."

"Do you mean to stay there?"

She shrugged her shoulders. "I shall look around for something."

"Won't your aunt be vexed?"

"I've got enough for my keep for a few months. In that time I'll find a situation."

"But that means using up your savings."

"Can't be helped, can it?"

"And what if you don't find it so easy to get a new job?"

"Then I shall just get it served up to me again at every meal."

"Get what served up? How do you mean?"

"Not bringing anything in. That's how it was when I was working at the shop. I wasn't bringing much home, but I couldn't help that, and she never said anything. Only if she was angry. Then she always did."

"And so then you took the job with us."

"Yes."

"Look," he said abruptly, "you mustn't go back to your aunt. You'll find something else. I'll—I'll see to that."

She did not say yes or no. She did not thank him. But as soon as he had gone she began slowly taking one thing after another out of the boxes and putting them back in their places. She had blushed deeply. Now she could not collect her thoughts, and every now and then stood still with something in her hand, gazing blankly ahead of her, simply realising: So this was love.

But when he had gone back to the room where Novalis' *Fragments* was still lying on the table, he was suddenly aghast at the responsibility he had taken on. Quite unexpectedly something had happened that would determine the course of his life, and it was something that did not really concern him intimately enough. At this moment he perhaps even felt slightly suspicious of Tonka because she had accepted his offer without more ado.

Then he began to wonder: What on earth made me propose such a thing? And he did not know the answer to that question any more than why she had accepted. Her face had revealed just the same helplessness and bewilderment that he had been feeling. The situation was painfully comical: he had gone rushing up somewhere as in a dream and now he did not know how to get down again. He had another talk with Tonka. He did not want to be anything but completely honest with her. He talked of personal independence, of intellectual values, of having a purpose in life, ambition, his distaste for the proverbial idyllic love-nest, his expectation that he would later have affairs with women of higher social standing— talked, in fact, like a very young man who wants a great deal and has experienced very little. When he saw something flicker in Tonka's eyes, he was sorry, and, all at once overcome by quite a different feeling, the fear of hurting her, he pleaded: "Don't misunderstand what I've been saying!"

"I understand all right," was all the answer Tonka gave.

IV

"But she's only a common little thing who used to work in that draper's shop!" they had said. What was the point of that? There were plenty of other girls who were quite ignorant, who had never been educated. Talking like that was like pinning a label on to the back of the girl's dress, where she couldn't get at it and take it off. What they meant was that people had to have learned something, had to have principles, had to be conventional and have the right manners. Simply being a human being wouldn't do. And what of all of them, who had all that and who did 'do'? It seemed to him that his mother was afraid of seeing the emptiness of her own life repeating itself in his. Her own choice was not one that she was proud of: her husband, his father, had formerly been an infantry officer—an undistinguished, jolly man. She was bent on seeing her son have a better life. She fought for that. Fundamentally he approved of her pride. So, then, why did the thought of his mother leave him unmoved?

Duty was her nature, and her marriage had taken on meaning only when his father fell ill. Henceforth she assumed a soldierly aspect, standing on guard, defending her position against overwhelming odds, at the side of this man who was steadily declining into imbecility. Up to then she had not been able either to go ahead or to withdraw in her relations with Uncle Hyacinth. He was not a relative at all, but a friend of both parents, one of those 'uncles' whom children have to put up with from the age when they begin to notice things. He was a senior civil servant and, besides, a popular writer whose books sold very well indeed. He brought Mother the breath of culture and worldly sophistication that consoled her in the intellectual desert she lived in. He was well read in history, with ideas that seemed all the more grandiose the emptier they were, extending, as they did, over the sweep of the centuries and the great problems of man's fate. For reasons that had never become clear to the boy, his mother had for many years been the object of this man's steadfast, admiring, selfless love. Perhaps it was because as an officer's daughter she had high standards of honour and duty, which were the source of the moral integrity that lent her glamour in his eyes and made her the model for the heroines in his novels. Perhaps too he was obscurely aware that both the fluency of his talk and his narrative gift derived from his own lack of such integrity. But since he naturally did not care to acknowledge this as a deficiency, he had to magnify it and transform it into something universal, full of weltschmerz seeing the need to be thus complemented by another's strength of spirit as the inevitable destiny of one so rich in intellectual resources as himself. Thus the situation had no lack of agonising exaltation for the woman either. Even in their own eyes they were at pains to disguise their liaison as a spiritual friendship, but in this they were not always successful. At times they were quite dismayed by Hyacinth's weakness of character, which would land them in dangerous situations, and then they would not know whether to let themselves fall or strong-mindedly climb back up again to their wonted heights. It was only when her husband became ill that their souls were provided with the support they needed and, reaching out for it, they gained that inch in spiritual stature which they had sometimes felt lacking. From that time on she was armoured in her duty as a wife and was able to make up by redoubled dutifulness for whatever sins she still committed in spirit. And, by a simple rule that settled everything for them, they were now safe from that particularly distressful wavering between the obligation to be greatly passionate and that to be greatly loyal.

So that was what respectable people turned out to be like, manifesting their respectability in terms of mind and character. And however much love at first sight there might be in Hyacinth's novels, anyone who without more ado simply went after another being— like an animal that knows where it can drink and where not— would to them have seemed like a wild primeval creature devoid of morality. The son, who felt pity for that good-natured animal, his father, in all the little matters of family life fought Hyacinth and his mother as though they were a spiritual plague. Thus he had let these two drive him into the diametrically opposite corner of the field of contemporary attitudes.

This brilliant and versatile young man was studying chemistry, and turned a deaf ear to all questions that had no clear-cut answers. He was, indeed, an embittered opponent of all such considerations and a fanatical disciple of the cool, soberly fantastical, world-encompassing spirit of modern technology. He was in favour of doing away with the emotions. He was the antagonist of poetry, kindness, virtue, simplicity. Song birds need a branch to perch on, and the branch a tree, and the tree the dumb brown earth to grow in; but he flew, he was between the ages, he was somewhere in mid-air. After this age, that destroys just as much as it constructs, there will come one that will inherit the new premises we are so ascetically creating, and only then will it be possible to say what we ought to have felt. Such was more or less his train of thought. For the time being the thing was to be as tough and austere as on an expedition.

With such a strong intellectual drive he could not fail to attract his teachers' attention, even as a schoolboy. He had conceived ideas for new inventions and, after taking his degree, was to spend one or two years devoting himself to working them out—after which he hoped to rise, surely and steadily, above that radiant horizon which is a young man's image of his glamorous unknown future.

He loved Tonka because he did not love her, because she did not stir his soul, but rinsed it clean and smooth, like fresh water. He loved her more than he himself believed. And the occasional tentative, needling enquiries made by his mother, who sensed a danger that she could not come to grips with because she had no certainty of it, impelled him to make all speed. He took his examinations and left home.

V

His work took him to one of the big cities in Germany. He had brought Tonka with him, for he felt he would have been leaving her at the mercy of her enemies if he had left her behind in the same town as her aunt and his mother. Tonka bundled up her things and left home as callously, as inevitably, as the wind goes away with the sun or the rain with the wind.

In the city to which they had moved she got herself a job in a shop. She was quick to pick up the new work and earned much praise. But why then was she so badly paid? And why did she never ask for a raise, which she only did not get because she did not ask for it? Whenever she needed money, she had no qualms about accepting it from him. Not because he minded this, but simply because he was sometimes irritated by her humble ways and lack of worldliness, he would occasionally lecture her on the subject.

"Why don't you tell him he must pay you more?"

"I can't."

"You *can't*. But you keep on telling me you're always the one they call for when they want something special?"

"Yes."

"Well, then, why don't you speak up for yourself?"

Such talk always made Tonka's face take on a stubborn look. She did not argue, but she was impervious to his reasoning.

"Look," he would say, "that's a contradiction." Or: "Look, why don't you tell me——?" It was all no good. Then he would say: "Tonka, I shall be cross with you if you go on like this."

It was only when he cracked that whip that the little donkey-cart of humility and stubbornness would slowly get under way, and then she would come out with some such thing as, for instance, that she was not good at writing and was afraid, too, of making spelling mistakes, things that she had hitherto kept from him out of vanity. Then there would be a quiver of anxiety round her dear kind mouth, and it would curve into a rainbow of a smile only when she realised that she was not going to be found fault with for such blemishes.

On the contrary, he loved these defects as he loved her deformed finger-nail, the result of an injury at work. He sent her to evening classes and was amused by the absurd commercial copperplate that she learnt to write there. Even the wrong-headed notions that she came home with were something he found endearing. She would bring them home, as it were, in her mouth, without eating them. There was something nobly natural in her helplessness, her inability to reject whatever was vulgar and worthless, even while with an obscure sense of rightness she did not adopt it as her own. It was astonishing with what sureness she rejected everything crude, coarse, and uncivilised in whatever guise it came her way, although she could not have explained why she rejected it. And yet she lacked any urge to rise beyond her own orbit into a higher sphere. She remained pure and unspoilt, like Nature herself. But loving this simple creature was by no means so simple.

And at times she would startle him by knowing about things that must be almost outside her ken, such as chemistry. When, preoccupied with his work, he would talk of it, more to himself than to her, he would suddenly find that this or that was something she had heard of before. The first time this happened he had been amazed and had asked her about it. She told him that her mother's brother, who had lived with them in the little house where the brothel was, had been a student.

"And what's he doing now?"

"He died. Right after the exam."

"And how did you pick it up from him?"

"Well, I was quite small, of course," Tonka recounted, "but when he was studying he used to get me to hear his lessons for him. I didn't understand a word of it, but he used to write the questions out for me, on a piece of paper."

That was all. And for ten years all that had been hidden, like pretty stones whose names one does not know, kept in a box! That was the way it was now, too. Sitting quietly in the same room with him while he worked was all she needed to make her happy. She was Nature adjusting itself to Mind, not wanting to become Mind, but loving it and inscrutably attaching itself to it. She was like one of those animals that actually seek man's company.

His relationship to her was at that time in a queer state of tension, equally remote from infatuation and from any wish for a casual affair. Actually they had got on for a remarkably long time at home without the temptations of sex entering into their relationship. They had been in the way of seeing each other in the evenings, going for walks together, telling each other of the day's little happenings and little annoyances, and it had all been as pleasant as eating bread and salt. True, after a time he had rented a room, but only because that was part of the whole thing and, anyway, one can't go walking about the streets for hours on end in the winter. There they had kissed for the first time—rather stiffly, more as though to set the seal on something than for the pleasure of it, and Tonka was very agitated and her lips were rough and hard. Even at that time they had talked of 'entirely belonging to each other'. That is to say, he had talked and Tonka had listened in silence. With that painful clarity in which one's bygone follies insist on recurring to one's memory, he recalled his very juvenile and didactic exposition of why it would have to come to that. It was only then, he had explained, that two people really opened up to each other. And so they had remained suspended between emotion and theory. Tonka merely begged a few times that it might be postponed for some days. Finally, he was rather affronted and asked if she thought it too great a sacrifice. So then a day was fixed.

And Tonka had come: in her little moss-green jacket, in the blue hat with the black pompoms, her cheeks pink from the brisk walk through the evening air. She laid the table, she made the tea. The only difference was that she bustled a little more than usual and kept her eyes fixed on the things she was handling. And he himself, although he had been waiting impatiently all day long, now sat on the sofa, watching her, immobilised by the icy stiffness of his youth. He realised that Tonka was trying not to think of the inevitable, and he was sorry he had insisted on fixing a day for it—it made him feel like a bailiff. But it only now occurred to him that he ought to have taken her by surprise, that he ought to have enticed her into it.

How remote he felt from any joy! On the contrary, he shrank from taking the bloom off that freshness which was wafted to him like a cool breeze every evening they spent together. But it had to be, sooner or later. He clutched at the neccessity of it, and while he watched Tonka rather mechanically bustling about, it seemed to him that his intention was like a rope tied round her ankle, shortening at every turn.

After the meal, which they ate almost without speaking, they sat down side by side. He attempted a joke, and Tonka attempted a laugh. But her mouth twisted, her lips were tight, and the next instant she was grave again.

All at once he asked her: "Tonka, are you sure it's all right? Have we really made up our minds?"

Tonka lowered her head, and it seemed to him that her eyes were veiled for a moment. But she did not say yes, and she did not say that she loved him.

He bent down to her, speaking softly, trying to encourage her, though he himself was embarrassed. "You know, at first it's rather strange, perhaps even rather unromantic. After all, you know, we have to be careful. I mean, it isn't just. . . . So you'd better shut your eyes. And so——?"

The bed was already turned down, and Tonka went over to it. But suddenly irresolute again, she sat down on the chair beside it.

"Tonka!" he called out to her.

She stood up again and, with averted face, began to unfasten her clothes.

An ungrateful thought remained associated with this sweet moment.

Was Tonka giving herself of her own free will? He had not promised her any love. Why did she not rebel against a situation that excluded the highest hopes? She acted in silence, as though she were subdued by the authority of 'the master'. Perhaps she would also obey another who was equally determined?

There she stood in all the awkwardness of her maiden nakedness. It was moving to see how the skin enclosed her body like too tight a garment.

His flesh was wiser and more humane than his youthfully pseudo-sophisticated thoughts, and he made a move towards her.

As though she were trying to escape from him, Tonka slipped into bed, with a movement that was oddly clumsy and unlike her.

All he remembered of what happened after that was that in passing the chair he had felt the thing he was most intimate and familiar with had been left behind on that chair, with the clothes he knew so well. When he came by, there rose from them the dear fresh smell that he was always first aware of whenever they met. What awaited him in the bed was something unknown and strange. He hesitated a moment longer.

Tonka lay there, with her eyes shut and her face turned to the wall, for an endless age, in terrible lonely fear. When at last she felt him beside her, her eyes were wet with warm tears. Then came a new wave of fear, dismay at her ingratitude, a senseless word uttered as though in search of help, as though stumbling out of some infinitely long, lonely corridor, to transform itself into his name—and then she was his. He hardly grasped how magically, and with how much childlike courage, she stole into his being, what simple-minded strategy she had worked out in order to take possession of all she admired in him: it was only necessary to belong to him entirely and then she would be part of it all.

Later, he could not in the least remember how it had all happened.

VI

And then in a single day, in a single morning, it was all transformed into a tangle of thorns.

They had been living together for some years when Tonka one day realised that she was pregnant. It was not just any ordinary day. Heaven had so ordained it that if one counted back from that day it appeared that the conception must have taken place during a period when he was away on a journey. Tonka, however, claimed to have noticed her condition only when it was no longer quite possible to establish the beginning of it with certainty.

In such a situation there are certain obvious ideas that will occur to anyone. On the other hand, there was no man far and wide whom one could reasonably suspect.

Some weeks later destiny manifested itself still more plainly: Tonka fell ill. It was a disease that the mother's blood had been infected with, either by the child she had conceived or directly by the child's father. It was a horrible, dangerous, insidious disease. But whatever way she had been infected, the curious thing was that in either case there was a discrepancy between the various dates. Apart from this, as far as could be medically established with certainty he was not suffering from the disease himself. So there was either some mystical bond linking him with Tonka or she was guilty on an ordinary human level. There were, of course, also other possible explanations—at least theoretically, ideally speaking—but practically speaking their probability was as good as nil. On the other hand, from the practical point of view the probability that he was neither the father of Tonka's child nor the cause of her illness amounted to a certainty.

If one considers the situation for a moment, one can see how difficult it was for him to grasp this. 'From the practical point of view. . . .' If you go to a business man, not with a commercial proposition that will appeal to his profit-making instincts, but to harangue him about the spirit of the times and the moral obligations of the rich, he will know you have come to get money out of him. On that point he will never be mistaken, although there is of course always the possibility that you might have come quite unselfishly, just to give him some good advice. Similarly, a judge will not have a moment's doubt when the accused tells him that the incriminating article found on his person was given to him by 'a man he had never seen before'. And yet there is no reason why this should not really happen once in a while. But the management of human affairs rests on the fact that there is no need to reckon with all the possibilities, because the most extreme cases practically never do occur. But theoretically? The old doctor to whom he had first taken Tonka, and whom he had seen alone afterwards, had shrugged his shoulders. Was it possible? Well, of course one couldn't say that it was entirely impossible. . . . There was a kindly, mournful look in his eyes, and what he evidently meant was: Don't let us waste time talking about that—it's much too improbable to be worthy of serious consideration. A doctor is, after all, a human being, and rather than assume that he is dealing with something that is medically quite improbable, he will assume the cause to be a human lapse. For freaks of Nature are rare.

So the next phase was that of a kind of medical litigiousness. He went to doctor after doctor. The second doctor came to the same conclusion as the first, and the third to the same conclusion as the second. He argued with them. He tried to play off against each other the views of various medical schools of thought. The physicians listened to him in silence, sometimes with a tolerant smile, as though he were a lunatic or a blockhead past praying for. And of course he himself knew, even while he was arguing, that he might just as well have asked: 'Is there such a thing as immaculate conception?' And they would only have been able to tell him: 'We have no medical evidence of it.' They would not even have been able to produce a law excluding the possibility. All they knew was: There was no evidence. And yet if he were to accept this, he would be a cuckold past praying for!

Perhaps, indeed, one of the doctors whom he had gone to see had told him so to his face. Or perhaps he himself had thought of it; after all, there was no reason why he should not have thought of it. But it was as if one were to exert oneself thinking out all the possible combinations and permutations of relevant finger-movements just because one could not fix a collar-stud—for all this time, while he was producing theory after theory, he was confronted by the irrefutable experience of Tonka's face. It was all a walking through cornfields, a sense of the air, the swallows dipping and darting, and in the distance the spires of the town, girls singing . . . remote from all truth, in a world that does not know the concept 'truth'. Tonka was now living in the deep world of fairy-tale. It was the world of the Anointed, of the Virgin, and of Pontius Pilate, and the doctors said that Tonka would need to be nursed and cared for if she was to survive.

VII

Still, he went on trying, of course, every now and again to wring a confession out of Tonka. After all, he was a man, and he was no fool. At this time she was working in a big, trashy shop in a working-class district. She had to be there at seven in the morning and could not leave before half-past nine in the evening—kept there often merely for the sake of some belated customer's few pennies. She never saw the sun. She did not sleep at his place, and there was no time to thrash out their emotional problems. They could not count on even this scanty source of income for any length of time, for sooner or later her pregnancy would be noticed. And they were already in financial difficulties. He had used up the money provided for his studies, and he was not capable of earning anything; this is always particularly difficult at the beginning of a scientific career, and besides, he had come so near to solving the problem he had set himself—though the solution still just escaped him—that he felt he had to concentrate all his energies on this work.

Living like this, never seeing the daylight and perpetually in anxiety, Tonka began to fade. Poor Tonka, of course she did not fade beautifully, as some women do, radiating an intoxicating splendour in decay; she wilted like some dim little herb in a kitchen garden that turns an ugly yellow and shrivels away as soon as it loses the freshness of its green. Her cheeks grew pale and hollow, and this made her nose look too big and prominent; her mouth seemed too wide, and even her ears seemed to stick out. Her body grew gaunt, and the full, curving flesh wasted away, letting the peasant skeleton peer through the skin.

He, whose well-bred face wore better under hardship and whose store of good clothes lasted longer, noticed, whenever he went out with her, that passers-by would sometimes cast an astonished glance at them. And because he was not without vanity, he bore Tonka a grudge for not having the pretty clothes that he could not buy her. He was angry with her for being so shabby, although it was his own fault. But actually, if he could have afforded it, he would have bought her pretty, floating maternity-clothes and would only then have charged her with infidelity.

Every time he tried to extract a confession from her, Tonka would utter the same denial. She said she did not know how it had happened. When he implored her, in the name of their old affection, not to lie to him, an anguished look would come over her face. And when he stormed at her, she merely said she was not lying. And what was anyone to do then? Should he have beaten her and sworn at her? Should he have abandoned her in her dreadful plight? He no longer slept with her. But even on the rack she would not have confessed, if only because she could not talk to him since she had realised that he mistrusted her. And this dumb obstinacy was all the more frustrating for him because his loneliness was no longer alleviated by any element of grace. He had to be tenacious, to watch and wait.

He had made up his mind to ask his mother for financial help. But his father had for a long time been hovering on the brink of death, and this meant there was no money to spare. He had no means of checking this, though he did know his mother was frightened of the possibility that he might intend marrying Tonka some day. Indeed, she was worried by the thought that any other marriage would be made impossible because Tonka was in the way. And when it all dragged on for so long, his studies still unfinished, success not yet achieved, his father still lingering on his death-bed, and all the domestic cares she had to cope with into the bargain, it seemed in some way or another to be all Tonka's fault. Tonka seemed to be not merely the cause of all that was going wrong now, but positively something like an ill omen, a herald of misfortune, in that it was she who had first disturbed the normal tenor of their life. This obscure conviction of his mother's had become apparent to him, both from her letters and during his visits home. What it came to fundamentally was that she felt it was a blot on the family honour for her son to be more attached to a girl 'of that sort' than was generally the case with young men. Hyacinth was made to give him a talking to on the subject. And when the young man, taken aback by the implicit superstitiousness of this attitude, which reminded him of his own painful, irrational experiences, put up vehement opposition Tonka was referred to as 'an ungrateful creature' who had had no consideration for a family's peace of mind. Awkward allusions were then made to 'amorous arts' by means of which she kept 'a hold on him'. In short, what came to light was every respectable mother's entire ignorance of real life. The same thing was manifest in the answer that he got now, as though every single coin that helped to keep him with Tonka could only contribute to his undoing.

At this point he decided to write again and acknowledge himself to be the father of Tonka's child.

By way of answer his mother came in person, 'to straighten the whole thing out'.

She did not come to his lodgings, as though she were afraid of encountering something intolerable there. She summoned him to her hotel. By taking refuge in her sense of duty she had rid herself of a certain amount of embarrassment, and she spoke of the great concern he was causing them all, of the added danger to his ailing father's life, and bonds that would last a lifetime. With clumsy cunning she pulled out all the stops of proper feeling. Yet a note of indulgence pervading all she said kept her listener, bored though he was by the maternal tactics he could so easily see through, in a state of mistrustful curiosity.

"You see," she said, "this misfortune might make everything turn out for the best, even now, and that would be a lucky escape for all concerned. The main thing is to prevent any recurrence of such incidents in future."

To this end she had managed to persuade Father to provide a certain sum of money. So—she explained, as though it were a great benefaction—all the girl's claims could be settled and the child provided for.

To her surprise her son, having calmly asked how much was being offered and having heard the answer, shook his head and merely said, in the same calm tone: "It can't be done."

Clinging to her hopes, she retorted: "It must be done! Don't go on deluding yourself. Many young men commit similar follies, but they let it be a lesson to them. This is really your chance to free yourself. Don't miss it out of a misguided sense of honour. You owe it to yourself and to us."

"How do you mean, it's my chance?"

"It's quite obvious. The girl will show more good sense than you are doing. She knows very well that such relationships always come to an end when a child arrives."

He asked for time to think about it—until the next day. Something had flashed upon him.

His mother, the doctors with all their smiling reasonableness, the smooth running of the underground train by which he made his way back to Tonka, the steady movements of the policeman's arms regulating the traffic, the city's roar like the thundering of a waterfall: it was all one and the same thing. He stood in the lonely hollow space under the cascade of it—untouched by even a splash, but utterly cut off.

He asked Tonka if she would agree.

Tonka said: "Yes." How terribly ambiguous this Yes of hers was! In it there lay all the good sense his mother had predicted, but round the mouth that uttered it there was the twitching of bewilderment.

The next day he told his mother point-blank, before she could ask him any questions, that he was perhaps not the father of Tonka's child, that Tonka was ill, and that for all this he would rather consider himself ill and himself the father of the child than abandon Tonka.

His mother smiled in defeat, confronted with such wilful self-deception, bestowed a last, fond glance on him, and left. He realised she would dedicate herself to saving her flesh and blood from shame, and he now had a powerful enemy in league with him.

VIII

Finally, Tonka lost her job. He had been growing almost uneasy over the fact that this misfortune was so long delayed. The shop-keeper for whom Tonka worked was a small, ugly man, but in their distress he had seemed to them like some superhuman power. For weeks they had been guessing: "He must know by now. . . . Well, obviously he's a decent sort and doesn't hit someone who's down. . . ." and then again: "He hasn't noticed, thank heaven he hasn't noticed anything yet!" And then one day Tonka was called into the office and asked, point-blank, about her condition. She could not get any answer out, her eyes merely filled with tears. And this practical man was quite unmoved by the fact that she was too upset to speak. He gave her a month's wages and dismissed her on the spot. He was so furious that he shouted at her, complaining that it was all her fault if he was now shorthanded and that it had been dishonest of her to conceal her condition when she took the job. He did not even send the typist out of the room before saying such things to her.

Afterwards, Tonka felt very wicked, and even he secretly admired that sordid nameless little tradesman, who had not hesitated for a minute but had sacrificed Tonka to his business sense, and with her tears, a child, and heaven alone knew what inventions, what souls, what human destinies—things of which the man had no notion, things in which he had no interest.

Now they had to have their meals in small, working-class places, amid dirt and incivility, where for a few pennies they got a kind of food that did not agree with him. He would call for Tonka punctually and fulfil his duty by taking her to have these meals. He cut a strange figure, in his well-made clothes, among the labourers and market-porters; grave, taciturn, and constant at the side of his pregnant companion. Many sneering glances were cast at him, and many respectful ones, which were no less painful. It was a strange life he was leading, with his invention in his head, and with his conviction of Tonka's infidelity, amid the flotsam and jetsam of the great city. He had never before felt the common beastliness of mankind so intensely: wherever he walked through the streets, there it went, yapping and growling like a pack of hounds, each person alone in his greed, but all of them together one pack—and only he had no one to whom he could turn for help or to whom he could even have told his story.

He had never had time for friends, doubtless indeed had taken little interest in them, nor had he himself been attractive to others. He went through life burdened with his ideas, and that is a burden dangerous to the very life of him who bears it, so long as people have not realised there is something in it that they can turn to their own advantage. He did not even know in what direction he might have searched for help. He was a stranger in the world. And what was Tonka? Spirit of his spirit? No—perhaps a symbol, some cryptic correspondence to himself, an alien creature who had attached herself to him, with her secret locked within her.

There was a little chink, a far-off gleam towards which his thoughts were beginning to move. The invention he was working at would in the end turn out to be of great importance for others as well as himself, and it was clear that something else was involved besides the intellectual processes—a courage, a confidence, an intuitive sense of the future, that never deceived him, a healthy urge to live, like a star that he followed. And in all this he too was only pursuing the greater probabilities, and always in one of them he would find what he wanted. What he relied on was that everything would turn out to be the way it always was, so that he could hit upon the one thing in which he could discover the desired otherness. If he had set out to test every possible doubt, as he was doing with Tonka, he would never have come to the end of it. Thinking means not thinking too much, and no invention can be made without sacrificing something of the boundlessness of the inventive talent. This half of his life seemed to be under the influence of the star of a happiness or a mystery beyond proving. And the other half lay in darkness.

Now he and Tonka bought sweepstake tickets. On the day of the draw he met Tonka and they went and bought the list of results. It was a miserable little sweepstake with a first prize of only a few thousand marks; but that did not matter, it would have tided them over the immediate future. Even if it had been only a few hundred marks, he could have bought Tonka what she most needed in the way of clothes and underclothes, or have moved her out of the unhealthy garret where she lived. And if it had been only twenty marks, it would have been some encouragement, and he would have bought more sweepstake tickets. Indeed, even if they had won no more than five marks, it would have been a sign that the attempt to restore contact with life was regarded with favour in unknown regions.

But with all their three tickets they drew blanks. Then, of course, he had to pretend he had only bought them for fun. Even while he had been waiting for Tonka there had been an emptiness in him that heralded failure. The truth probably was that he had been wavering between hope and despair all the time. In his circumstances even a few pennies wasted on a newspaper meant a real loss. He suddenly felt there was an invisible power that wished him ill, and he felt himself to be surrounded by hostility.

After that he became downright superstitious. The man who became so was the one who called for Tonka in the evenings, while the other man he was went on working like a scientist.

He had two rings, which he wore alternately. Both were valuable, but one was a piece of fine old workmanship, and the other was only a present from his parents, which he had never particularly cherished. Then he noticed that on days he was wearing the newer one—which was only an ordinary expensive ring—he seemed to be spared further deterioration of his situation rather more than on days when he was wearing the good, old one; and from that time on he could not bring himself to put it on again, but wore the other, like a yoke laid upon him.

Again, one day when he happened not to have shaved, he had good luck. The next day, when he did shave in spite of having observed the omen, he was punished for his transgression by another of those trivial sordid misfortunes that would not have amounted to anything more than absurdity in a situation less desperate than his. From then on he could not bring himself to shave any more. He grew a beard, doing no more than carefully trimming it to a point, and he continued to wear it through all the sad weeks that followed.

This beard disfigured him, but it was like Tonka: the uglier it looked, the more anxiously it was tended. Perhaps his feeling for her became all the more affectionate the more profoundly it was disappointed; for like the beard it was inwardly so good because of the outward ugliness. Tonka did not like the beard and did not know what it meant to him. And without her he would never have known how ugly this beard was, for one knows little of oneself unless one has someone else in whom one is reflected. And since what one knows is really nothing, might it not be that at times he wished Tonka dead so that this intolerable existence might be over and done with? And perhaps he liked the beard simply because it was like a mask, concealing everything.

IX

There were still times when he would, as it were, try to ambush her: he would ask what seemed to be a perfectly harmless question, hoping that the smooth sound of the words would take her off her guard. But more often it was he who was taken unawares and defeated.

"Look, it's absolutely senseless going on denying it," he would say coaxingly. "Come on now, tell me. Then everything'll be just the way it used to be. How on earth did it happen?"

But her answer was always the same: "Send me away if you won't believe me."

That was, of course, her way of making the most of her own helplessness, but it was also the most genuine answer she could give. For she had no medical or philosophical arguments to defend herself with: all she could do was to vouch for the truth of her words with the truth of her whole being.

Then he would go with her whenever she went out, because he did not dare to leave her alone. There was nothing definite that he feared, but it made him uneasy to think of her alone in the great alien streets of the city. And when he would meet her somewhere in the evenings, and they walked along, and in the dusk they would pass some man who gave no sign of knowing them, he would sometimes have the feeling that the man's face was familiar, and it seemed to him that Tonka blushed; and all at once he would re-member that there had been an occasion when they had been to-

gether with this man. Instantly, then, and with a certainty equal to
the certainty he felt when gazing into Tonka's innocent face, he
would have the conviction: This is the one! Once it seemed to be
a well-to-do young man who was learning the business in an export
firm and whom they had met a few times. Once it was a tenor who
had worked in a *café chantant* until he lost his voice and who had
a room in the same lodging-house as Tonka. They were always
such ludicrously marginal figures; they were like dirty parcels thrown
into his memory, tied up with string, each parcel containing the
truth—but at the first attempt to undo it, the package would dis-
integrate, leaving him with nothing but an agonising sense of helplessness and a heap of dust.

These certainties of Tonka's infidelity had, indeed, something of
the quality of dreams. Tonka endured them with all that touching,
dumbly affectionate humility of hers. But how many different meanings that could have! And then, going through his memories, he
began to see how ambiguous they all were. For instance, the very
simplicity of the way she attached herself to him could equally well
mean that she did not care one way or the other or that she was
following her heart. The way she served him could indicate either
apathy or a delight in doing it. Might that dog-like devotion of hers
not mean that she would follow any master like a dog? This was
something he had, after all, sensed in that first night. Had it in fact
been her first night? He had only paid attention to her emotional
reactions, and certainly there had been no very perceptible physical
signs. Now it was too late. Her silence was now a blanket over
everything, and might equally well indicate innocence or obduracy,
it could equally well mean cunning or sorrow, remorse, or fear; but
then too it might mean that she was ashamed on his behalf. Yet it
would not have helped him even if he could have lived all of it all
over again. Once a human being is mistrusted, the plainest signs of
faithfulness will positively turn into signs of unfaithfulness. On the
other hand, where there is trust, the most glaring evidence of unfaithfulness will seem to be signs of misunderstood faithfulness,
crying like a child that the grown-ups have locked out. Nothing
could be interpreted on its own merits alone, one thing depended
on the other, one had to trust or mistrust the whole of it, love it
or take it for deceit and delusion. If one was to understand Tonka,
one had to respond to her in one definite way; one had, as it were,

to call out to her, telling her who she was. What she was, depended almost entirely on him. And so Tonka would become a blur, mildly dazzling as a fairy-tale.

And he wrote to his mother: 'Her legs are as long from the foot to the knee as from the knee to the hip, long legs that walk like a pair of twins, without tiring. Her skin is not delicate, but it is white and without blemish. Her breasts are almost a little too heavy, and the hair in her armpits is dark and matted, which looks charmingly shameful on that slender white body. Her hair hangs down in loose strands over her ears, and at times she thinks she has to take the curling-tongs to it and do it up high, which makes her look like a servant-girl. And that, surely, is the only harm she has ever done in her life. . . .'

Or he would write in answer to his mother: 'Between Ancona and Fiume, or perhaps it is between Middelkerke and some town whose name I don't remember, there is a lighthouse, the light of it flashing out over the sea at night like the flick of a fan. One flick, and then there is nothing. And then another flick. And edelweiss grows in the meadows of the Venna valley.

'Is that geography or botany or nautical science? It is a face, it is something that is there, solitary, quite alone, eternally—and so in a way, too, it isn't there at all. Or what is it?'

Naturally he never posted these senseless answers to his mother's letters.

There was something impalpable missing, something that was needed to make his certainty complete.

Once he had been travelling by night with his mother and Hyacinth, and in the small hours, out of the depths of that inexorable fatigue which makes the bodies in a train sway to and fro in search of some support, it seemed to him that his mother was leaning against Hyacinth, and that she knew she was, and that Hyacinth was holding her hand. His eyes had widened with anger at the time, for he was sorry for his father. But when he leaned forward, Hyacinth was sitting at some distance and his mother's head was inclined to the other side, away from him. Then after a while, when he had settled back in his seat, the whole thing happened all over again. That seeing and not seeing something was torment, and the torment itself was a darkness through which it was hard to see. Finally he told himself that now he was really sure, and he resolved to challenge his mother about it in the morning. But in broad daylight the whole thing had vanished like the darkness itself.

And another time, again when they were on a journey, his mother fell ill. Hyacinth, who had to write to Father on her behalf, said irritably: "But I don't know what to say." This from Hyacinth, who wrote reams to Mother whenever he was away! Then there was a quarrel, for again the boy had grown angry, and his mother began to feel worse: she seemed to be seriously ill. Something had to be done for her, and Hyacinth's hands kept on getting in the way of his, and he kept on pushing them aside. At last Hyacinth asked rather mournfully: "Why do you keep on pushing me away?" The note of unhappiness in that voice quite shocked him. How little one knows what one knows, or wants what one wants.

That is not difficult to understand. Yet he was capable of sitting in his room, tortured by jealousy and telling himself that he was not jealous at all, that it was something quite different, something out of the ordinary, something oddly invented; and yet this was himself and his own feelings. When he raised his head and looked about him, everything seemed to be the same as usual. The wall-paper was green and grey. The doors were reddish brown, with faint gleams of light reflected on them. The hinges were dark, made of copper. There was a chair in the room, brown mahogany and wine-red plush. But all these things seemed to be somehow tilted, leaning to one side. There was a suggestion, in their very upright-ness, that they were about to topple over. They seemed endless and meaningless.

He rubbed his eyes and then looked round again. But it was not his eyes. It was the things. The fact was that belief in them had to be there before they themselves could be there; if one did not look at the world with the world's eyes, the world already in one's own gaze, it fell apart into meaningless details that live as sadly far apart from each other as the stars in the night sky. He only needed to look out of the window to see how the world of, say, a cab-driver waiting in the street below was suddenly intersected by the world of a clerk walking past. The result was something slashed open, a disgusting jumble, an inside-out and side-by-side of things in the street, a turmoil of focal points moving along their tracks, and around each of them there extended a radius of complacency and self-confidence, all aids to walking upright through a world in which there was no such thing as above and below. Volition, cognition, and perception were like a tangled skein. One noticed this only when one tried to find the end of the thread. But perhaps there was some other way of going through the world, other than following the thread of truth? At such moments, when a veneer of coldness separated him from everything, Tonka was more than a fairy-tale: she was almost a visitation.

'Either I must make Tonka my wife,' he told himself, 'or I must give her up and give up these thoughts.'

But no one will blame him for doing neither one nor the other, despite these reasonings of his. For although all such thoughts and feelings may well be justified, nobody nowadays doubts that they are very largely figments of the imagination. And so he went on reasoning, without taking his reasoning seriously. Sometimes it seemed to him that he was being sorely tried, but when he came to himself again and spoke to himself again, as it were, man to man, he had to tell himself that this ordeal consisted, after all, only of the question whether he would force himself to believe in Tonka against the ninety-nine per cent probability that she had been unfaithful to him and that he was simply a fool. Admittedly this humiliating possibility had by now lost much of its importance.

X

It was, oddly enough, a period in which his scientific work went remarkably well. He had solved the main problems involved in his project, and it could not be long now before he got results. There were already people coming to see him, and even if it was chemistry that they talked about, they brought him some emotional reassurance. They all believed that he was going to succeed. The probability of it already amounted to ninety-nine per cent! And he drugged himself with work.

But even though his social existence was now taking on firmer outlines and entering, so to speak, the state of worldly maturity, the moment he stopped working his thoughts no longer ran along in definite grooves. The faintest reminder of Tonka's existence would start a drama going in his mind: figures in a play, one taking over from the other, none of them revealing its meaning, all of them like strangers daily encountering each other in the same street. There was that commercial traveller of a tenor whom he had once suspected of being the man with whom Tonka had betrayed him. And there were all the others to whom he had ever pinned his certainty. It was not that they did anything. They were merely there. Or even if they did do that frightful thing, it no longer meant much. And since they were sometimes two or even more persons rolled into one, it was no straightforward matter being jealous of them. The whole situation became as transparent as the clearest air, and yet clearer still, until it reached that state of freedom and emptiness which was void of all egoism, and under this immovable dome the accidents of terrestrial life pursued their microscopic course.

And sometimes all this turned into dreams. Or perhaps it had all begun in dreams, in a pallid shadowy realm from which he emerged the instant he shed the weight of his working hours, as though it were all meant as a warning to him that this work was not his true life.

These real dreams were on a deeper level than his waking existence; they were warm as low-ceilinged, bright-coloured rooms. In these dream-rooms Tonka would be harshly scolded by her aunt for not having shed any tears at Grandmamma's funeral; or an ugly man acknowledged himself to be the father of Tonka's child, and she, when he looked at her queryingly, for the first time did not deny it, but stood there, motionless, with an infinite smile. This had happened in a room with green plants in it, with red rugs on the floor and blue stars on the walls. But when he turned his eyes away from that infinity the rugs were green, the plants had big ruby-red leaves, the walls had a yellow glimmer as of soft human skin, and Tonka, still standing there, was transparently blue, like moonlight.

He almost fled into these dreams as into some simple-hearted happiness. Perhaps it was all mere cowardice. Perhaps all they meant was that if only Tonka would confess, all would be well. He was much confused by their frequency, and yet they had not the intolerable tension of the half-waking state, which was gradually bearing him higher and higher, away out of it all.

In these dreams Tonka was always as great as love itself, and no longer the care-worn little shop-girl she was in real life. And she looked different every time. Sometimes she was her own younger sister (not that she had ever had a sister) and often she was merely the rustling of skirts, the ring and cadence of another voice, the most unfamiliar and surprising of movements, all the intoxicating charm of unknown adventures, which came to him, the way such things come only in dreams, out of the warm familiarity of her name—and they gave him the floating sense of joy that lies in anticipation, even though still tense with unfulfilment. These ambiguous images made him feel a seemingly undefined, disembodied affection and more than human intensity of emotion, and it was hard to say whether these feelings were gradually detaching themselves from Tonka or only now really beginning to be associated with her. When he reflected on this he guessed that this enigmatic capacity for transference and independence that love had must also manifest itself in waking life. It is not that the woman loved is the origin of the emotions apparently aroused by her; they are merely set behind her like a light. But whereas in dreams there is still a hair's-breadth margin, a crack, separating the love from the beloved, in waking life this split is not apparent; one is merely the victim of *doppelgänger*-trickery and cannot help seeing a human being as wonderful who is not so at all. He could not bring himself to set the light behind Tonka.

The fact that he so often thought of horses at this time must have been somehow connected with this, and obviously was a sign of something significant. Perhaps it was Tonka and the sweepstake in which they drew blanks. Or perhaps it was his childhood—those beautiful brown and dappled horses, their heavy harness decorated with brass and fur. And then sometimes there would be a sudden glowing of the child's heart in him, the heart for which magnanimity, kindness, and faith were not yet obligations that one disregarded, but knights in an enchanted garden of adventures and liberations. Yet perhaps too this was merely the last flaring up of a flame about to die, the itching of a scar that was beginning to form. For it was like this. The horses were always hauling timber, and the bridge was always echoing under their hooves, a muffled wooden sound, and the timbermen wore their short, checkered jackets, purple and brown. They all doffed their hats as they passed the tall cross, with the tin Christ on it, halfway across the bridge. Only a little boy who stood there by the bridge, looking on, in the winter, refused to doff his hat, for he was a clever little boy and didn't believe in such things any more. And then he suddenly couldn't button up his coat. He couldn't do it. The frost had numbed his little fingers, they grasped a button and tugged at it, hard, but just as they were pushing it into the button-hole, it jumped out again, and his fingers were left helpless and amazed. However hard they tried, they always ended up in paralysed bewilderment.

And it was this memory that came back to him so often.

XI

Amid all these uncertainties Tonka's pregnancy took its course, revealing the harshness of reality.

There was the shambling gait, with Tonka seeming in need of a supporting arm, the heavy body that was mysteriously warm, the manner of sitting down, with legs apart, unwieldy and touchingly ugly: all the changing aspects of the miraculous process, steadily transforming the girlish body into a seed-pod, altering all its proportions, broadening the hips and pressing them down, taking the sharpness from the knees, thickening the neck, making the breasts into udders, streaking the skin of the belly with fine red and blue veins, so that it was startling to see how close to the outer world the blood circulated—as though that were a sign of death. All this unshapeliness was in fact a new shape, moulded as much by passivity as by main force; and the same distortion of human normality was reflected in her eyes: they now had a blank look, and her gaze would linger on things for a long time, shifting only with an effort. It would often rest for a long time on him. She was now keeping house for him again, waiting on him laboriously, as though she wanted to prove to him in these last days that she lived only for him. She showed no trace of shame for her ugliness and deformation, only the desire to do as much as she could for him in spite of her awkwardness.

They were now spending nearly as much time together as in earlier days. They did not talk much, but they liked to be near each other, for her pregnancy was advancing like the hand of a clock, and they were helpless in the face of it. They ought to have talked the whole thing out together, but they did nothing about it, and time moved on. The shadowy being, the unreal element in him, sometimes struggled for words, and the realisation that everything

ought to be measured by quite different standards almost broke
surface—but, like all understanding, even this was ambiguous and
without certainty. And time was running on, time was running
away, time was running out. The clock on the wall had more to
do with reality than their thoughts had.

It was a suburban room where nothing of importance could
happen. There they sat, and the clock on the wall was a round
kitchen clock, telling kitchen time. And his mother bombarded him
with letters proving everything up to the hilt. Instead of sending
money to him, she spent it on getting opinions from doctors, in the
hope of making him see reason. He quite understood this and no
longer resented it. Once she sent him a medical statement that made
it really clear to him that Tonka *must* have been unfaithful to him
at that time. But far from upsetting him, it was almost a pleasant
surprise. As though it had nothing to do with him, he wondered
how it had happened, and all he felt was: Poor Tonka, she has had
to pay so dearly for a single passing aberration! Yes, sometimes he
had to pull himself up short, on the point of saying quite cheerfully:
'Listen, Tonka—I've only just realised what we've been forgetting
about—who it was you were unfaithful to me with, that time!' So
everything petered out. Nothing new happened. There was only the
clock. And the old familiar bond between them.

And even though they had not talked about it, this brought back
the moments when their bodies desired each other. They came like
old friends who, returning after long absence, will simply walk into
the room. The windows on the far side of the narrow courtyard
were eyeless in the shadow, the people were all out at work; down
below the yard was dark as a well; and the sun shone into the room
as though through frosted glass, making each object stand out sharply,
in a dead gleam. And there, for instance, lay a little old calendar,
open as though Tonka had just been going through it, and on the
wide expanse of one leaf, like a memorial erected to that one day,
there was a small red exclamation-mark. All the other leaves were
covered with everyday domestic entries, shopping-lists, sums, and
the like, and only this one was empty except for the one sign. Not
for an instant did he doubt that this betokened the memory of the
incident that Tonka denied. The time just about fitted. His certainty
was like a rush of blood to the head. Yet certainty itself merely lay
in this vehemence, and in the next instant it had again dwindled

into nothingness. If one was going to believe in what this exclamation-mark might signify, then one might just as well believe in
the miraculous. What was so appalling was, after all, the very fact
of believing in neither.

There was a startled glance exchanged between them. Tonka had
obviously seen him looking at that page in the calendar.

In the queer indoor light all the things in the room now looked
like mummies of their former selves. The bodies grew cold, the
fingertips became icy, the intestines were hot coils of tubing in which
all vital warmth was contained.

True, the doctor had said that Tonka must be spared any sort
of stress if complications were to be avoided. But at this moment
doctors were the very people whom he must not trust. And yet all
his efforts to trust in something else were also futile. Perhaps Tonka
was not strong enough? She remained a half-born myth.

"Come here," Tonka said gently.

And they shared their anguish and their warmth, in mournful
resignation.

XII

Tonka had gone into hospital. The turn for the worse had come.
He was allowed to see her at visiting-hours. So the time had slipped
away, irrevocably.

On the day she left the house he had his beard shaved off. Now
he was more like himself again.

Later on he discovered that that very day she had lost patience,
lost her head, in fact, and had gone and done something she had
been putting off all this time for the sake of saving money: as though
making a last gesture of independence before going into hospital,
she went and had a decayed molar extracted. Her cheek must now
be sadly sunken, and all because she would never let herself be
properly looked after.

Now his dreams began to intensify again.

One dream recurred in many forms. A fair, plain girl with a pale
complexion was telling him that his new girl—some invented figure
in the dream—had left him, at which he became curious to hear

more and exclaimed: "And do you think Tonka was any better?" He shook his head, with an expression of doubt on his face, to provoke the girl into making some equally vehement protestation of Tonka's virtues, and he already had a foretaste of the relief he would get from her decisive answer. But then he saw a frightful slow smirk gradually spreading over the girl's face. And she said: "Oh, her! But she was a dreadful liar! She was quite nice, of course, but you couldn't believe a word she said. She always wanted to be a smart woman of the world." What caused him most anguish in this dream was not that dreadful smile, which was like a knife cutting into his flesh, but the fact that he could never ward off the eager platitudes at the end of it: powerless in his sleep, he heard them being uttered as though out of the depths of his own mind.

And so when he went to visit Tonka, he would often sit at her bedside with nothing to say. He would gladly have been as magnanimous as in certain dreams he had had earlier, and he might actually have brought himself to be so if he had devoted to Tonka some of the energy with which he was working on his invention.

Although the doctors had never been able to find any trace of the disease in him, he was linked with Tonka by the possibility of some mysterious connection: he only had to believe her, and instantly he would be diseased. And perhaps (he told himself) that would have been possible in some other age. He was beginning to enjoy letting his imagination rove back into the past, telling himself such things as that in some other age Tonka's fame might have spread far and wide and that princes would not have disdained to woo her. But nowadays? This was something he really ought to think about at length some day.

So he would sit at her bedside, being kind and affectionate to her, but never uttering the words: 'I believe you.' And this although he had long believed in her. For he believed her only in such a way that he was no longer able to be unbelieving and angry, and not in such a way that he could face the rational consequences of it. This not believing kept him immune and safely anchored to the earth.

The things that went on in the hospital tormented his imagination: it was all doctors, examinations, routine. The world had snatched Tonka away and strapped her to the table. Yet he was almost beginning to regard this as her own fault; if she was indeed something of deeper significance, under the surface of what the world was doing to her, then everything in the world ought to be different too, so that one would want to fight for it. And he was already beginning to surrender. Only a few days after their separation she was already a little remote from him, for he was no longer able to make daily amends for the strangeness of her all too simple life, that strangeness which he had always felt, in however slight degree.

And because he usually had so little to say when he visited Tonka in the hospital, he wrote letters to her, saying a great deal that he otherwise kept to himself. He wrote to her almost as seriously as to some great love. Yet even these letters stopped short of ever declaring: 'I believe in you.' He was quite disconcerted to receive no answers from Tonka, until he realised that he had never posted these letters. The fact was, he could not be sure that he meant what he wrote; it was simply a state of mind that he could do nothing about except write it out of his system. That made him realise how lucky he was, despite everything—he could express himself. Tonka could not do that. And the moment he saw that, he saw Tonka for just what she was; a snowflake falling all alone in the midst of a summer's day. But the very next moment this no longer explained anything. Perhaps it all amounted to no more than that she was a dear, good girl. And time was passing too quickly. One day he was horribly overtaken by the news that she would not last much longer. He reproached himself bitterly for having been so careless, for not having looked after her properly, and he did not attempt to hide this from her.

Then she told him of a dream she had had a few nights earlier. For Tonka also had dreams.

"In my dream I knew I was going to die soon," she said. "And it's a funny thing, you know, but I was very glad. I had a bag of cherries, and I said to myself: 'Never mind, just gobble them up quick before you go.' "

The next day they would not let him in to see her.

XIII

Then he said to himself: 'Perhaps Tonka wasn't really so good as I imagined.' But that again only went to prove how mysterious her goodness was. It was the kind of goodness that a dog might have had.

He was overwhelmed by a dry, raging grief that swept through him like a storm. It went howling round the solid walls of his existence, crying: 'I can't write to you any more, I can't see you any more.' 'But I shall be with you like God Himself,' he consoled himself, without even knowing what this was supposed to mean. And sometimes he could simply have cried out: 'Help me, help me! Here I am kneeling before you!' Sadly he said to himself: 'Think of it, a man walking all alone with a dog in the mountains of the stars, in the sea of the stars!' And he was agonised with tears that became as big as the globe of the sky and would not come out of his eyes.

Wide awake, he now dreamt Tonka's dreams for her.

Once, he dreamed to himself, when all Tonka's hope had gone he would suddenly come into the room again and be there with her. He would be wearing his large-checked, brown tweed travelling-coat. And when he opened it, underneath it he would be quite naked, nothing on his slender white body but a thin gold chain, with tinkling pendants on it. And everything would be like one single day, she would be quite sure of that.

This was how he longed for Tonka, as she had longed for him. Oh, she was never a loose woman! No man tempted her. If someone pays court to her, she will rather give him to understand, with slightly awkward mournfulness, that such affairs are likely to come to a bad end. And when she leaves the shop in the evening, she is quite full of all the noisy, jolly, annoying events of her day, her ears are full of it all, inwardly she goes on talking of it all, and there is no scrap of room for any stranger. But she knows too that there is a part of her that remains untouched by all this: there is a realm where she is grand, noble, and good, where she is not a little shop-girl, but his equal, deserving of a great destiny. And this was why, in spite of all the difference between them, she always believed she had a right to him. What he was concerned with achieving was something of which she understood nothing at all; it did not affect her. But he belonged to her because at bottom he was good; for she too was good, and somewhere, after all, there must be the palace of goodness where they would live united and never part again.

What then was this goodness? It did not lie in action, nor yet in being. It was a gleam when the travelling-coat opened. And time was moving much too fast. He was still clinging to the earth, he had not yet uttered the thought 'I believe in you!' with conviction, he was still saying: 'And even supposing everything were like that, who could be sure of it?' He was still saying that when Tonka died.

XIV

He gave one of the nurses a tip, and she told him of Tonka's last hours and that she had sent her love to him.

Then it crossed his mind, casually, as one remembers a poem and wags one's head to the rhythm of it, that it was not really Tonka at all he had been living with: it was something that had called to him.

He said these words to himself over and over again; he stood in the street with these words in his mind. The world lay around him. He realised, indeed, that he had been changed in some way and that in time he would be yet again another man, but this was, after all, his own doing and not really any merit of Tonka's. The strain of these last weeks—the strain, that is, of course, of working on his invention—was over. He had finished. He stood in the light and she lay under the ground, but all in all what he felt was the cheer and comfort of the light.

Only, as he stood there looking about him, suddenly he found himself gazing into the face of one of the many children round about—a child that happened to be crying. There in the full blast of sunlight the face wriggled and writhed like a ghastly worm. Then memory cried out in him: 'Tonka! Tonka!' He felt her, from the ground under his feet to the crown of his head, and the whole of her life. All that he had never understood was there before him in this instant, the bandage that had blindfolded him seemed to have dropped from his eyes—yet only for an instant, and the next instant it was merely as though something had flashed through his mind.

From that time on much came to his mind that made him a little better than other people, because there was a small warm shadow that had fallen across his brilliant life. That was no help to Tonka now. But it was a help to him. And this even though human life flows too fast for anyone to hear each of its voices clearly and find the answer to each of them.

Translated by Eithne Wilkins and Ernst Kaiser

PRE-POSTHUMOUS
PAPERS
and Other Prose

The Flypaper

T he flypaper Tanglefoot is approximately fourteen inches long and eight wide. It is coated with a yellow, poisoned glue and comes from Canada. When a fly settles on it—not with any particular eagerness, more from convention, because so many others are there already—he at first sticks fast only with the outermost, upwards-turned parts of all his little legs. A very slight feeling of estrangement, as if we were to walk around in the dark and with naked soles step on something which is only a soft, warm, indeterminate resistance and yet something into which by degrees the horribly human floods, recognized as a hand which is somehow lying there and holds us fast, with its five fingers becoming more and more distinct.

Then they all force themselves to stand upright, like sufferers from spinal tuberculosis or like shaky old soldiers (and a little bowlegged, as when one stands on a sharp edge). They give themselves poise and gather strength and think. After a few seconds they have made up their minds and begin, as best they can, to buzz and lift themselves off. They carry on with this raging action until exhaustion forces them to stop. A pause for breath follows, and a new attempt. But the intervals get longer and longer. They stand there, and I feel how much at a loss they are. Confusing vapors rise up from below. Their tongue gropes out like a small hammer. Their head is brown and hairy, as if made from a coconut: like African idols which resemble people. They bend forwards and backwards on their firmly tangled little legs, go down on their knees and push themselves up the way people do who are making every attempt to lift a burden which is too heavy; more tragically than laborers, more truthful in athletic expression than Laokoon. And then comes the moment, peculiar always in the same way, when the necessity of the present moment prevails over all the powerful drives of existence to endure. It is the moment in which a climber voluntarily relaxes the grip of his hand on account of the pain in his fingers, when someone lost in the snow lies down like a child, when someone pursued stops with his sides burning. They no longer hold themselves up from below with all their strength; they sink in a little, and are at this moment very human. They are immediately grabbed in a new place, higher up on the leg or at the back of the body or the end of a wing.

When they have overcome their mental exhaustion and after a short while resume their struggle for life they are already fixed in an unfavorable position, and their movements become unnatural. They lie propped up on their elbows with their back legs stretched out and try to raise themselves. Or they sit on the earth, rearing up with outstretched arms like women vainly trying to free their hands from the grip of a man's fists. Or they lie on their belly with head and arms in front, as if they had fallen running, and raise only their face. But the enemy is always merely passive, and only gains from their desperate, confused movements. A nothing, and it draws them in. So slowly one can barely follow, and mostly with a sudden speeding up at the end when the final inner collapse comes over them. Then they suddenly let themselves fall forward on their faces, over their legs; or sideways, all their legs stretched away from them; often too on their sides, with their legs rowing backwards. Thus they lie there. Like crashed airplanes with one wing towering into the air. Or like dead horses. Or with endless gestures of despair. Or like sleepers. Sometimes even on the next day one will wake up and grope for a while with a leg or buzz with a wing. Sometimes such a movement passes over the whole field; then they will sink a little deeper into their death. And only on the side of the body, in the area where the legs join it, do they have some kind of very small flickering organ which still goes on living for a long while. It opens and shuts; one cannot make it out without a magnifying glass. It looks like a tiny human eye, incessantly opening and closing.

Translated by Burton Pike

Can a Horse Laugh?

A highly-regarded psychologist has written the sentence: ". . . for the animal knows no laughing or smiling."

This encourages me to say that I once saw a horse laugh. I thought heretofore that one could claim something like that any day, and did not trust myself to make a fuss about it; but since it is so delightful I'll tell all about it.

It was before the war; it may be that since then horses don't laugh any more. The horse was tied to a reed fence which surrounded a small farmyard. The sun shone. The sky was dark blue, the air extremely mild, although it was February. And in contrast to this divine comfort, all human comfort was lacking. In a word, I was in the vicinity of Rome, on a country road in front of the gates, on the boundary between the last modest suburbs of the city and the beginning of the rural Campagna.

The horse too was a Campagna horse: young and graceful, of that well-formed small kind which has nothing pony-like about it, but on which a large rider looks like a grownup on a doll's chair. It was being curried by a merry fellow; the sun shone on its coat, and it was ticklish around the shoulders. Now a horse has, so to speak, four shoulders, and is therefore perhaps twice as ticklish as a person. Besides that, this horse seemed also to have a sensitive spot on the inside of each thigh, and whenever it was touched there it could not keep from laughing.

Already when the comb approached from a distance the horse laid back its ears, became restless, reached for it with its mouth, and when it couldn't get to it bared its teeth. But the comb marched merrily on, stroke for stroke, and the lips exposed more and more of the teeth while the ears lay further and further back and the horse stepped from one leg to the other.

And suddenly it began to laugh. It bared its teeth. With its muzzle it tried to push away the fellow tickling it as hard as it could, in the same way a farm girl would have with her hand, and without its having tried to bite him. It also tried to turn around and push him away with its whole body. But the farmhand kept the advantage. And when the curry-comb came to the vicinity of the shoulders the horse couldn't stand it any more: it turned around on its legs, its whole body trembled, and it pulled back the flesh from its teeth as far as it possibly could. For some seconds it acted exactly like a person who is being tickled so hard he can't laugh any more.

The scholarly doubter will object that this shows that it could not really laugh. One can respond that this is insofar correct as of the two it was the stable-boy who every time whinnied with laughter. To be able to whinny with laughter seems in fact to be an ability possessed only by humans. But nevertheless the two of them played in obvious agreement, and as soon as they began again from the beginning there could be no doubt at all that the horse too wanted to laugh and was already waiting for what was coming.

So the scholarly doubt about the ability of animals limits itself to this, that an animal cannot laugh at jokes.

But that can't always be held against the horse.

Translated by Burton Pike

Hare Catastrophe

The lady had most certainly stepped out of the glass window of a large shop only yesterday; her little doll's face was cute; one would have liked to stir around in it with a little spoon to see it in motion. But one was oneself displaying shoes with honey-smooth, honeycomb-thick soles, and trousers that looked as if they had been sketched with a ruler and white chalk. One was most enchanted by the wind. It pressed the dress onto the lady and made of her a pitiable small skeleton, a stupid little face with a tiny mouth. He, of course, presented a bold face to the observer.

Little hares live unsuspecting beside the white creases and the teacup-thin skirts. The heroism of the island stretches round about them black-green like laurel. Crowds of seagulls nest in the hollows of the heath like beds full of white snowblossoms moved by the wind. The small, white, longhaired terrier belonging to the small white lady adorned with a fur collar hunted through the brush, its nose a finger's-breadth above the ground. No other dog is to be scented far and wide on this island; nothing is there but the incredible romanticism of many small, unknown scents criss-crossing the island. In this wilderness the dog becomes large as a giant, a hero.

Excited, sharp as a knife, he makes noises, his teeth gleaming like those of a sea monster. In vain the lady purses her little mouth to whistle: the wind tears from her lips the little sound she would like to produce.

I have hiked on glaciers with such a wiry terrier; we humans smoothly on skis, he bloody, falling in up to his stomach, cut by the ice, but nevertheless filled with a wild, inexhaustile bliss. This one is now on the track of something: his legs gallop like little sticks, the sound becomes a sobbing. It is remarkable at this moment how much such flat islands floating on the sea remind one of the great cirques and slabs of the high mountains. The skull-yellow dunes smoothed by the wind are perched like rock wreaths. Between them and the sky is the emptiness of the unfinished creation. Light does not illuminate this or that, but splashes over everything as if from a bucket overturned by mistake. One is always astonished that animals live in this loneliness. They take on a mysterious quality; their small soft-wool and feathery breasts hide the spark of life. Over there is a small hare which the terrier is driving on before it. I think: a small, weather-hardened mountain type, the terrier will never get him. A memory from geography class comes to life: Island: are we really standing on the peak of a high seamount? We, ten or fifteen vacationers in colorful madhouse jackets, as prescribed by fashion, standing around idly looking on. I change my thought once again and tell myself that what we have in common is only the inhuman abandonment of the place: where man is in the minority earth is everywhere disturbed like a horse which has thrown its rider. Nature in the high mountains or on small islands is not only not healthy but truly insane. But to our astonishment the distance between the dog and the hare has diminished; the terrier is catching up to it, one has never seen such a thing, a dog that catches a hare! This will be the first great triumph of the dog world! Enthusiasm gives the pursuer wings, his breath exults in spurts, there is no longer any question that within a few seconds he will have overtaken his prey. Then the hare darts to the side. And I recognize by something soft, because this darting lacks abruptness, that it is no hare, it is only a small hare, a baby hare.

I feel my heart. The dog has paused; he has lost no more than fifteen paces; the hare catastrophe is only a few seconds away. The baby hears the pursuer behind his little tail. He is tired. I want to intervene, but it takes such a long time for the will behind the pants creases to get down to the smooth soles; or the resistance was perhaps already in my head. Twenty paces before me—I must have been fantasizing if the little hare did not stop, disheartened, and hold his neck out to his pursuer. The dog sank his teeth into it, swung him back and forth a few times and then threw him on his side and buried its muzzle two or three times into his breast and belly.

I looked up. Laughing, flushed faces were standing around. It had suddenly become like four o'clock in the morning after an all-night dance. The first among us to awaken from the blood lust was the little terrier. He let go, squinted mistrustfully to one side, withdrew; after a few steps he fell into a short, withdrawn gallop, as if expecting a stone to fly after him. The rest of us were immobile and embarrassed. A tepid atmosphere of cannibalistic expressions surrounded us, like "struggle for existence", or "cruelty of nature". Such thoughts are like the shallows of a sea floor, risen from monstrous depths and flat. What I most wanted to do was go back and hit the thoughtless little lady. That was an honest feeling but not a good one, and so I was silent and thus joined the general, uncertain silence now forming around everyone. Finally a tall, relaxed man took the hare in both hands, showed its wounds to those who came up, and carried the rescued corpse like a small coffin into the kitchen of the nearby hotel. This man was the first to rise out of the unfathomable and have the firm ground of Europe under his feet.

Translated by Burton Pike

Monuments

Monuments possess all sorts of qualities. The most important is somewhat contradictory: what strikes one most about monuments is that one doesn't notice them. There is nothing in the world as invisible as monuments. There is no doubt they are erected in order to be seen, indeed to arouse attention, but at the same time they are somehow impregnated against attention: it runs down them like water on oilcloth, without stopping for an instant. You can walk down a street for months: you will know every house number, every store sign, every policeman, and you won't miss a coin lying on the sidewalk; but you will certainly be surprised if you should one day happen to look up at a pretty chambermaid in a second-floor window and discover a metal tablet, by no means small, on which is engraved in indelible letters that on this spot from eighteen-hundred-such-and-such to eighteen-hundred-such-and-more the unforgettable thus-or-not lived and worked here.

A lot of people react the same way to larger-than-life-size statues. One must walk around them every day or use their pedestals for protection; one uses them as a compass or rangefinder if one is heading toward their well-known square. One experiences them as a tree, as part of the scenery, and would stop in momentary confusion should they be missing some morning. But one never looks at them and usually does not have the slightest idea whom they represent, except that one perhaps knows whether it is a man or a woman.

It would be false to let oneself be deceived by a few exceptions, such as those few statues like the Gattamelata or the Colleone which the tourist goes looking for with guidebook in hand, which is a very special attitude; or memorial towers, which block whole landscapes; or monuments which form nationwide clubs, like the Bismarck monuments scattered all over Germany.

Such energetic monuments do exist, and then there are also those which are the expression of a living thought and living feeling; but the profession of most monuments is to call forth a remembrance, or rivet the attention and give the feelings a pious direction because one assumes they somehow need it; and in this, their major profession, monuments always fail. They scare away precisely what they should be attracting. One cannot say that we don't notice them; one would have to say they un-notice us, they withdraw themselves from our senses. This is a thoroughly positive quality they have, tending toward real forcefulness!

Well, doubtless this can be explained. Everything permanent loses its ability to impress. Everything that forms the walls of our lives, so to speak the stage set of our consciousness, loses the ability to play a role in this consciousness. After a few hours we no longer hear a constant, bothersome noise. Pictures we hang on the wall are sucked up by the wall within a few days; it happens very seldom

322 · *Robert Musil*

that one places oneself in front of them and looks at them. Half-read books which one has shelved in the magnificent rows of books in one's library will never be read to the end. For sensitive people it is sufficient to buy a book whose beginning they like, but they will never thereafter pick it up again. In this case the process is aggressive, but one can also pursue its inevitable course in the higher feelings, and there it is *always* aggressive, for example in family life. The firm possession of marriage is distinguished countless times from inconstant desire by the sentence: Must I tell you every fifteen minutes that I love you? How much greater must be those psychological disadvantages to which the permanent is exposed in phenomena of brass and marble!

If one is well-disposed toward monuments, one must inexorably draw the conclusion that they make claims on us which run against our nature, and satisfying them calls for special arrangements. If one were to make warning signs for trucks as inconspicuous in color as monuments it would be a crime. Locomotives, after all, whistle shrilly and not timidly, and even mailboxes are painted in attractive colors. In a word, monuments today should do what we all have to do, make more of an effort! Anybody can stand quietly by the side of the road and allow glances to be bestowed on him; these days we can demand more of monuments. Once one has grasped this thought—which thanks to certain cultural currents is slowly making headway—one can realize how backward the art of monuments is compared with the contemporary development of advertising.

Why, at least, does not the hero cast in bronze try the gesture, long outdated in other circles, of knocking on a windowpane with his finger? Why don't the figures of a marble group rotate around each other, like the better figures in store windows, or at least open and close their eyes? The least one could demand in order to attract attention would be well-tried inscriptions like "Goethe's Faust is best!", or "The dramatic ideas of the famous poet X are cheapest!"

Unfortunately sculptors don't want that. They do not, it appears, understand our age of noise and motion. Whenever they represent a man in civilian clothes he sits motionless on a chair, or he stands there, one hand between the second and third buttons of his coat; he even, sometimes, holds a roll in his hand, but not a muscle twitches in his face. He usually looks like depressed melancholics in nerve clinics. If people were not mentally blind to monuments and would observe what was happening up there as they pass by, their flesh would creep as if they were passing by the walls of an insane asylum. It is creepier still if the sculptor represents a general or a prince. The banner flutters in his hand, but there is no wind. His sword is drawn, but no one is afraid of it. His arm points commandingly forward, but no one thinks of following him. Even the horse which has risen to jump with flaring nostrils remains on his hind hooves, transfixed with astonishment that the people below calmly stick a sausage in their mouths or buy a paper instead of stepping to the side. By God, the figures on monuments never take a step, but they continually make faux pas! It is a desperate situation.

I believe that with these observations I have contributed to the understanding of monuments, commemorative tablets, and the like. Perhaps one person or another will, from now on, look at those he comes across. But what becomes harder and harder to understand the longer one thinks about it is why, if this is the way it is, are monuments erected to great men? It seems to be a neat bit of malice. Since one can no longer harm them in life, one pushes them into the sea of oblivion with, so to speak, a commemorative stone around their necks.

Translated by Burton Pike

Oedipus Endangered

> Although malicious and one-sided, this criticism makes no claim to scientific objectivity.

If classical man had his Scylla and Charybdis, modern man has the Wassermann Test and the Oedipus Complex, for if he succeeds in avoiding the first and setting a posterity on its feet, he can the more surely reckon with being carried off by the second. One might indeed say that today just about nothing is possible without Oedipus, neither family life nor architecture.

Since I myself still grew up without Oedipus, I can of course only express myself with considerable caution on these questions, but I have to admire the methods of psychoanalysis. From my childhood I remember the following: If one of us boys was so overwhelmed by another with bad names that try as he might he could not think of returning the attack with the same force, he simply used the word "yourself!" which, inserted in the other's pauses for breath, turned every insult neatly around and sent it back. And I have been very happy to discover in studying the psychoanalytic literature that all those individuals who claim not to believe in the infallibility of psychoanalysis are immediately shown to have their reasons for disbelieving it, which reasons again, of course, are of a psychoanalytic nature. This is a fine demonstration of the fact that even the methods of science are acquired before puberty.

But if medical science, through the use of this "return coach" principle, reminds us of the glorious old days of travel by postcoach, she does so unconsciously, but by no means without a deep psychological connection. For it is one of her greatest accomplishments that in the midst of the present day's lack of time she educates us in a relaxed application of time, a gentle squandering, so to speak, of this fleeting natural product. As soon as one has placed oneself in the hands of an improver of souls one realizes that the treatment will surely come to an end at some point, but contents oneself entirely with the progress made along the way. Impatient patients do allow themselves to be quickly freed of their neurosis, only to begin immediately with a new one; but whoever has come to the proper enjoyment of psychoanalysis is not in such a hurry. He enters the room of his friend from the bustle of the day, and even if the world outside should explode from all its mechanical energies, here there is still good old time. One is sympathetically asked how one has slept and what one has dreamt about. The sense of family, so wickedly neglected by life today, has its natural significance restored, and one discovers that what Aunt Augusta said when the maid dropped the plate is not ridiculous at all but, looked at in the proper way, more revealing than an expression of Goethe's. But more important than any individual detail, indeed most important of all, is that with such treatment the human being, even when softly and magnetically stroked, learns again to feel himself the measure of all things. Through centuries he has been told that he owes his behavior to a culture of much greater significance than he is. When in the last generation we finally largely got rid of culture, innovations and inventions took the upper hand, beside which the individual seemed to himself to be a nothing. But now psychoanalysis takes this stunted individual by the hand and proves to him that he need only have courage and gonads. May they never come to an end! This is my wish as a layman, but I think it agrees with that of the experts.

On that account I am made uneasy by a conjecture which is possibly only the result of my lay status but which might perhaps be correct. For as far as I know the previously mentioned Oedipus Complex stands today more than ever at the center of theoretical thought. Almost all phenomena are adduced to it, and I am afraid that after another generation or two there will no longer be an Oedipus! One must realize that it originates in the being of the small person who is supposed to find his pleasure in his mother's womb or lap* and be jealous of the father who displaces him there. But what if mothers no longer have a womb? One can already see where this is leading: the lap is not only that area of the body for which the word in its strictest sense was created, but signifies psychologically the whole incubating motherliness of woman, the breast, the warming fat, the pacifying and sheltering softness; it even signifies, and not wrongly, the skirt, whose broad folds form a mysterious nest. In this sense the basic experiences of psychoanalysis definitely derive from the clothes of the 1870's and 1880's and not from ski togs. And if you look at people in bathing suits, where is the womb or lap today? When I try to imagine the psychoanalytic longing to return to it in an embryonic state as I look at the running and swimming bodies of today's girls and women, much as I appreciate their unique beauty I don't see why the next generation should not just as happily want to return to the father's womb.

But then what?

Will we get an Orestes instead of an Oedipus? Or will psychoanalysis have to give up its blessed effects?

Translated by Burton Pike

*In German the same word means both "womb" and "lap".

The Blackbird

The two men I must mention in order to tell three short stories—
in the course of which it will become clear who the narrator
is—had been friends from childhood; let's call them Aone and
Atwo. Long term friendships such as theirs grow more and more
peculiar the older one gets. In the course of years one changes from
head to toe, from the smallest hair on your skin to your very heart,
but the relationship itself remains remarkably the same. It alters as
little as do the relations which every individual has with the various
persona that he successively calls "I". It doesn't matter whether
you feel like the thickheaded boy with blond hair who once was
photographed; no, basically you cannot even say that you like this
foolish little egoistic monster. Similarly, you are neither in accord,
nor contented, with your friends; indeed, many friends can't stand
each other. In a certain sense these are the deepest and best friendships. They contain the incomprehensible element with no adulter-
ation.

The upbringing shared by the two friends Aone and Atwo had
been nothing short of a religious one. They had, of course, both
been educated at a boarding school that commended itself on having
given appropriate emphasis to religious principles. The ambition of
the pupils, however, lay in never observing them. For example: the
institution's church was a large and beautiful one with a stone
steeple, and was reserved for the sole use of the school; no outsider
ever entered, and while a few students in the front pews alternately
knelt and stood as required by the holy rites, other groups could
always play cards in the rear by the confessional boxes, smoke
cigarettes on the stairs leading to the organ, or vanish up into the
steeple, under whose gabled roof a balcony was held aloft like a
plate with candles, and there, on this parapet, at a dizzying height,
acrobatic stunts were performed that could have cost the necks of
even less sin-laden boys.

One of these provocations of God consisted in doing a handstand
on this parapet. You slowly raised yourself up and then remained
there, eyes downward, standing on your hands and swaying back
and forth. Anyone who has performed this feat on solid ground
will know how much self-confidence, boldness, and luck are needed

to repeat it on a foot-wide ledge atop a church steeple. Many daring and agile lads would not attempt it, even though on flat land they could stroll about on their hands at will. For example, Aone didn't. Conversely, and this may well serve to introduce him as narrator, Atwo in his boyhood was the inventor of this test of aplomb. You rarely saw a body like his. He didn't have the physique which comes from sports, as do many, but rather seemed to be effortlessly woven from muscles by nature. Atop this body was a narrow, smallish head, with eyes like lightning coiled in velvet, and teeth which sooner made one think of the sleekness of a beast of prey than expect the meekness of a mystic.

In their college years both friends championed a materialistic theory of existence that regarded man as a physiological and economic machine, without soul or god. This he may very well be, though it didn't matter to them in the least; the lure of such a philosophy doesn't lie in its truth but in its demonic, pessimistic, terribly intellectual character. By this time their relationship to one another was already the comradeship of young men. Atwo was studying forestry and spoke of going far away as a forestry engineer, to Russia or to Asia, as soon as his studies were ended. Instead of such boyish dreams his friend had already hit upon a more grown-up fantasy and busied himself with the upward struggling working-class movement. When they met once again, shortly before the Great War, Atwo had his Russian exploits behind him, was employed in the office of a large corporation and seemed to have suffered considerable disappointments, even though he was doing tolerably well. In the meantime, his old school friend had gone from fighting in the class struggle to editing a newspaper which printed a great deal about social harmony and was owned by a big investor. From that time on they were inseparably bound by their mutual disdain for one another.

Once more, however, they lost touch and finally, when they were thrown together again for a short time, Atwo related the following, in the way that one dumps out a sackful of memories before a friend in order to continue on with the empty bag. Under these circumstances it matters little what Aone replied, and their conversation can be related almost as if it were a monologue. It would be more significant if one could describe exactly how Atwo looked, for his appearance had a decisive bearing on the meaning of his words.

But that's difficult. At best one might say that he called to mind a sharp, slender sinewy riding crop that, resting on its supple tip, leaned against a wall. In this half-erect, half-sunken posture he seemed quite at ease.

*   *   *

"Among the oddest places in the world are those Berlin courtyards," said Atwo, "where the backs of two, three, or four buildings point their behinds at each other. Cooks sit in rectangular openings in the middle of the walls and sing. You can tell by looking at the red-hued copper utensils on shelves how loudly they clatter. Far below, a man's voice bawls out abuse to one of the girls up above, or heavy wooden shoes clomp back and forth on the hard brick pavement. Slow. Hard. Restless. Meaningless. Endless. Is it so or not?

"The kitchens and bedrooms face the courtyards; they lie close to one another like love and digestion in the human body. Floor by floor the nuptial beds are stacked up above each other, for every bedroom in the building has the same location. The wall with the window, the wall between the bedroom and the bathroom, and the wall with the closet all fix the location of the bed to within half a meter. Likewise, floor by floor the dining rooms, the white-tiled bathrooms, and the balconies with their red lamp shades pile up, one on top of the other. Love, sleep, birth, digestion, unexpected reunions, careworn and sociable nights lie close above one another in these buildings like columns of stacked-up breadrolls in an automat. In middle-class apartment houses such as these your personal destiny has already been settled when you move in. You will admit that human freedom lies principally in when and where you do something, for what people do is almost always the same. It's a hell of a thing if in addition you make the layout of everything the same. Once I climbed on top of a wardrobe merely to exploit the vertical dimension, and I can say that the disagreeable conversation in which I was involved looked quite different from up there."

Atwo laughed at his recollection. Aone felt almost as if they were sitting on a balcony with a red lamp shade, which belonged to his own apartment, but he remained silent, for he knew all too well what he might have replied.

"Moreover I'll admit even today that there's something monstrous in this regularity," Atwo himself allowed. "At that time I thought that I saw something like a desert or an ocean in this specter of anthill living and desolation. Even though the thought of it turns my stomach, a Chicago slaughterhouse is, after all, something quite different than a flowerpot! But the remarkable thing was that while I had this apartment I used to think about my parents with unusual frequency. You'll recall that I had as good as lost all contact with them, but all of a sudden this sentence began running through my head: They have given you life. And this comical thought returned time and time again, like a persistent fly that can't be chased away. There's nothing particularly curious about this sanctimonious phrase, which gets drummed into everyone's head in childhood. But when I considered my apartment I said all the same, 'Look. Now you have bought your independence, for so and so many marks yearly rent!' Perhaps I even sometimes said, 'Now you have fashioned a life of your own.' And that's where things stood—in the middle between department store, death insurance, and pride. Yet it seemed to me exceptionally noteworthy, indeed even a mystery, that here something had been given to me whether I wanted it or not, and what's more, something which formed the basic legend of everything else. I believe this proposition concealed a treasure trove of irregularity and unfathomability that I had buried. And then came the story with the nightingale.

"It began on an evening like many others. I had stayed at home, and after my wife went to bed I sat down in the study; perhaps the only difference from similar evenings was that I didn't pick up a book or anything else, but even that had occurred before. After one a.m. the street begins to grow quieter. Conversations become fewer and fewer. It's lovely to follow with one's ear the advance of the night. By two, noise and laughter downstairs clearly indicate drunkenness and lateness. I became aware that I was waiting for something, though I had no inkling of what it might be. Toward three the sky began to get lighter—it was May. I felt my way through the dark apartment to the bedroom and noiselessly lay down. I no longer expected anything but sleep and, in the morning, a day like the one that had just ended. Soon I no longer knew if I was awake or asleep. A dark green light seeped through the drapes and between the blinds; thin white streaks of the dawn wound their way into the room. It could have been my last waking impression or a tranquil dream vision. Then I was awakened by something approaching.

Sounds came nearer. Once, twice I drowsily perceived them. Then they sat on top of the adjacent building, and from there leaped into the air like dolphins. Or I might have said like star flares, for the impression of spheres of light lingered. When they fell back down they burst softly against the windowpanes and sank slowly into the depths like great silver stars. I sensed the presence of magic. I lay awake on my bed, but differently than in the daytime; I felt like the figure on its coffin lid. It's very hard to describe, but when I reflect on it it was as if I had been turned inside out. I was no longer a solid, space-filling form, but something like a depression in space. The room was not hollow but was permeated by a substance that doesn't exist in the daytime, darkly transparent and darkly trans-palpable—I too was made of it. Time ran in fever-small, rapid pulse beats. Why shouldn't what has never happened before happen now? 'It's a nightingale that's singing out there,' I said to myself, half aloud.

"Well, perhaps there are indeed more nightingales in Berlin than I thought," continued Atwo. "I believed then there weren't any in these stone mountains, and that this one had flown to me from afar. 'To me!' I thought, and sat up with a smile. 'A heavenly bird! So they really exist!' In such a moment, you see, one is ready to believe in the supernatural in the most natural way, as though one had spent one's entire childhood in a magical world. Immediately I thought: 'I will follow the nightingale. Goodbye, my love. Good-bye, indeed, love, house, city . . . !' But before I had gotten up, before I had clearly decided whether I would climb up to the roofs or would follow it along the streets, the bird had become silent and had obviously flown farther off.

"Now it was singing on another roof for another sleeper," Atwo reflected. "You will suppose that this ends the story? It's only just the beginning, and I don't know what the ending will be!

"I was abandoned, and oppressed by a profound despondency. 'It wasn't a nightingale at all. It was a blackbird,' I said to myself, exactly as you would like to say. It's well known that they mimic other birds. I was fully awake now, and the stillness was irksome to me. I lit a candle and studied the woman who lay next to me. Her body looked a pale, brick-red color. The white border of the blanket lay across her skin like a strip of snow. Wide shadow-lines, whose origin couldn't quite be made out, although of course it had to be connected with the candle and the position of my arm, wound about her body. 'What does it matter,' I thought meanwhile, 'if it really was only a blackbird?' Oh, on the contrary, precisely the fact that it had been merely an ordinary blackbird that could so derange me—that is much more significant! You know that one only cries over a single disillusionment; after a second, a smile is already on the way. And the whole time I continued looking at my wife. All this was interconnected, though I don't know how. 'For years I have loved you, like nothing else in the world,' I thought, 'and now you lie there like a burnt-out husk of love. You have become totally strange to me, and now I have emerged at the other end of love.' Was that satiety? I don't remember having experienced satiety. I'll describe it to you like this: it's as if an emotion could tunnel through your heart as if through a mountain, on whose far side lay another world with the same valley, the same houses, and the same little bridges. But I simply didn't know what it was—I still don't know today. Perhaps I'm wrong to tell you this story in connection with two others that followed it. I can only tell you what I took it for when I experienced it: a signal had come to me from somewhere. That was my impression of it.

"I lay my head next to her unsuspecting, sleeping body. Her breast seemed to rise and fall excessively, and the walls of the room rose and fell about her like the high seas about a ship that is far from land. I probably would never have left, but if I were now to steal away, it seemed to me, I would remain the little boat abandoned in solitude and that a great and seaworthy ship had negligently sailed over me. I kissed the sleeper; she didn't feel it. I whispered something in her ear, and perhaps I did it so circumspectly that she didn't hear. Then I laughed at myself, and scoffed at the nightingale, but stealthily dressed. I believe I sobbed, but I really did leave. It was staggeringly easy, although I tried to tell myself that no respectable person would behave like this. As I recall, I was like a drunkard, who curses the street he's walking on to assure himself of his sobriety.

"Naturally, I've often thought of going back. At times I longed to return from across half the world, but I never did. She had become untouchable for me. I don't know whether or not you understand me, but one who is deeply aware of an injustice will no longer rectify it. And by the way, I don't want your absolution. I want to tell you my stories in order to find out whether or not they're true. For years I've been unable to speak my mind to anyone, and frankly, if I were to catch myself talking aloud about this I'd be uneasy.

"So make no mistake; my rationality concedes nothing to your enlightenment.

"Two years later I found myself in a tight spot. It was in South Tyrol, in a blind section of a battle-line that curved from the bloody trenches of Cima di Vezzena to Lake Caldonazzo. There the line ran deep in the valley like a sunny ripple, over two hills with lovely names, and climbed up again on the other side to lose itself in quiet mountains. It was in October. The sparsely-manned trenches were overhung with foliage. The lake burned soundlessly in blue. The hills lay there like great withered wreaths, 'like grave-wreaths,' I often thought, without fearing them. Hesitantly and divided, the valley flowed around them, but beyond the line we held it fled from such pleasant diversions and led like a trumpet-blast, brown, wide and heroic, into the hostile distance.

"In the middle of the night we occupied an advanced position. We were so exposed in the valley that the enemy could have hit us by throwing stones, but they were content with simple artillery fire. On mornings after such nights everyone wore a strange expression, which didn't disappear for several hours. Everyone's eyes were enlarged, and upon the army of shoulders the irregularly held heads looked like a trampled lawn. Nevertheless, on all those nights I often raised my head above the rim of the trench and cautiously, like a lover, looked back over my shoulder; then I'd see the Brenta Mountains, bright heavenly blue like stiffly pleated glass, standing in the night. On these nights the stars were especially large, and looked like they had been stamped out of gold paper, and shimmered greasily as if baked from dough, and the sky was blue even at night, and the moon's thin, maidenly crescent, all silver or all gold, floated enraptured in its midst. You must try to imagine how beautiful it was; in a secure existence nothing is that beautiful. Sometimes I couldn't bear it and, filled with joy and yearning, crept out into the night as far as the green-gold black trees. I raised myself up among them like a small, brown-green feather in the plumage of the quietly sitting, sharp-beaked bird Death, which is more bewitchingly black and iridescent than anything you've ever seen.

"By contrast, in the main sector during the daytime you could actually ride about. In such positions, where you have time for reflection, for terror, you first learn to know the danger. Each day it gathers its victims: a set weekly average, such and such percent. Even the division's general staff officers were reckoning as impersonally as an insurance company. Actually everyone does. One instinctively knows one's chances and feels secure, if not exactly in favorable circumstances. This is the remarkable peace one experiences when one is continually at the front lines. I have to say this beforehand so that you don't falsely imagine my situation. To be sure, it happens that you feel yourself suddenly compelled to search for a particular well-known face you have seen several days before— but it's no longer there. Such a face can be more shocking than is reasonable, and can hang in the air like the shimmer of a candle flame. So one has less fear of death than usual but is susceptible to all sorts of excitations. It's as if the fear of one's end, which weighs constantly upon one like a stone, had been rolled away, and now, in the indeterminate proximity of death, a strange inner freedom blossoms.

"Once during this time an enemy aircraft flew over our peaceful position. This didn't occur often because the mountain range, with its deep ravines opening narrowly between fortified peaks, had to be flown over at a high altitude. We were standing on one of the 'grave-wreaths,' and in a split second the sky was dotted with bursts of shrapnel from the batteries as if by a nimble powder-puff. It looked amusing, almost delightful. The sun shone through the airplane's tri-colored wings above our heads as if through church windows or colorful tissue paper, and the only thing the moment lacked was some music by Mozart. To be sure, the thought ran through my head that we were clustered together like a racetrack crowd and made an easy target. Someone even said, 'Better take cover!' But clearly there'd be no pleasure in scuttling down a hole in the ground like a field mouse. Transfixed, I heard a faint ringing sound approaching my upturned face. Of course, it could have been the other way round, so that I first heard the ringing sound and only then realized the approach of danger; but at the same moment I already knew: it is an aerial dart! These were pointed iron rods, no thicker than a carpenter's pencil, which airplanes used to drop at that time from high altitudes, and if one struck you in the head it would pierce your entire body and come out again through the soles of your feet; but they rarely hit anyone and were soon given up. So, then, this was my first one. Bombs and machine-gun fire sound quite different, and I knew at once what I was dealing with. I tensed, and the next second I had the strange sensation, at odds with all probability: 'It's going to hit me!'

"And do you know what it was like? Not like a terrifying presentiment but rather like a never expected piece of luck! At first I was puzzled that I should be the only one to hear the ringing. Then I thought the sound would disappear again. But it didn't. It was still far off, and as it drew nearer became perspectively louder. I carefully observed the other faces, but no one else had perceived it. And in that instant, when I realized that I alone heard this tenuous singing, something rose forth out of me toward it—a ray of life; every bit as endless as that of death which was coming from above. I'm not inventing this; I'm trying to describe it as simply as possible. I'm convinced that I have expressed myself with absolute sobriety. Of course, I know that to a certain degree it's like a dream where one imagines that one is speaking quite clearly while the words themselves are externally incoherent.

"This lasted for a long time during which I alone heard the approaching event. The sound was a thin, singing, simple high sound, like that which is produced when the rim of a glass is made to vibrate, but there was something unreal about it. 'You've never heard that before,' I said to myself. And this sound was directed at me. I was linked to this sound, and didn't doubt in the least that something decisive was about to happen to me. I didn't have a single thought of the kind one is supposed to have in the instant prior to death; everything I felt was directed toward the future. I must simply state that I was certain that in the next moment I would feel the presence of God in the presence of my body. That's no little thing for a person who hasn't believed in God since he was eight years old.

"Meanwhile the sound from above became more substantial; it swelled and grew menacing. I asked myself several times if I shouldn't give warning, but I didn't want to do that, even though I or one of the others might be struck. Perhaps this fancy—that high above the battlefield a voice was singing to me—was nothing but a damnable conceit. Perhaps God is nothing more than this: that we poor beggars, in the narrow confines of our existence, can vainly boast of having a rich relative in heaven. I don't know. But without a doubt the air had now begun to ring for the others as well. I noticed shadows of uneasiness flitting across their faces, but not a single one of them said a word either! I looked at these faces once again. Fellows to whom nothing could be further from their thoughts stood without knowing it like a group of disciples awaiting a message. And suddenly the singing had become an earthly sound, ten feet, a hundred feet above us, and then died away. He, it, was there. In the midst of us, but closest to me, something shattered into an unreal noiselessness, something was swallowed and silenced by the earth. My heartbeats were calm and regular. I couldn't have been frightened for even a fraction of a second. I wasn't unconscious for even the tiniest sliver of time, but the first thing I noticed was that everyone was looking at me. I was standing on the same spot as before, but my body had been wrenched savagely sideways and had executed a deep, semi-circular bow. I felt that I was coming to from a delirium and didn't know how long I'd been out. No one spoke to me. Finally someone said, 'Aerial dart,' and everyone wanted to look for it, but it was lodged a meter deep in the ground. At that moment I was inundated with a passionate feeling of gratitude and I believe my entire body blushed. If someone had said that God had entered my body I wouldn't have laughed, but neither would I have believed it. I wouldn't even have believed that I bore off a splinter from Him. Nevertheless, every time that I remember this I'd like to experience something of the sort once again, only more clearly.

*   *   *

"Actually, I did experience it again, but it was no more intelligible," Atwo began his last story. He seemed to have become uncertain, but precisely because of this one could perceive that he was ardently eager to hear himself tell it.

It concerned his mother, who had never possessed a large share of Atwo's love, though he maintained that hadn't been so. "Superficially we didn't get along," he said, "and, after all, that's only natural when an old woman lives in the same small town for decades and her son, according to her standards, had achieved nothing in the world. She made me as uneasy as the imperceptibly broadened reflection of myself in a mirror might, and I hurt her by not coming home for years at a time. Every month she would write me an anxious letter filled with questions; even though I usually didn't respond, there was some odd connection, and I remained close to her nevertheless, as was ultimately shown.

"Perhaps decades ago she had passionately impressed upon her mind the ineradicable image of a small boy, in which God only knows what hopes she may have placed, and since I was that long-since vanished boy her love clung to me as if every sun which till then had set still hovered somewhere between light and darkness. There you'd have this secret vanity again except it isn't vanity. For I can truly say I don't care for my own company, and the way so many people act—the way they complacently look at photographs of their younger selves, or enjoy remembering what they did at this or that time in their lives—this ego-savings-account system is totally incomprehensible to me. I'm neither particularly capricious, nor do I live just for the moment, but when something is over I'm over too; if I realize, in walking down a street, that I've often come this way before, or if I see the house I used to live in, I feel a sudden and intense dislike of myself, as though I had recalled a disgraceful deed. What has been flows away as one changes, and it seems to me that no matter how one changes one wouldn't do so at all if the person one relinquished were altogether irreproachable. But precisely because I usually feel this way it was amazing when I realized that all my life a person had clung to an image of me, in all probability one which never corresponded to me, but which was in a certain sense my charter, the mandate of my creation. Do you understand me when I say that in a figurative sense my mother was a lioness confined in the real existence of a very limited woman? She wasn't clever by our standards; she had neither self-restraint nor broad horizons; when I think back over my childhood one couldn't call her kind, either. She was irascible and at the mercy of her nerves, and you can imagine the sort of occurrences resulting from this combination of passion and narrow vision. But I maintain that there exists a stature or character which, when personified in our everyday experience, is as incomprehensible as when in fabled times gods assumed the shapes of serpents and fish.

"Soon after the aerial dart incident I was captured during combat in Russia. Later I took part in the great transformation there and wasn't in any particular hurry to return, for the new life long pleased me. I still admire it now, but I realized one day that I could no longer mouth several essential dogmas without yawning. This entailed danger to my life, so I fled to Germany, where individualism was in full, inflationary bloom. I engaged in all sorts of dubious enterprises, in part out of necessity and in part for the joy of once again being in an old country where one can do wrong without having to feel ashamed of oneself. Things didn't go very well for me; sometimes I was in an exceedingly bad way. Things weren't going too well for my parents either. Several times my mother wrote to me, 'We cannot help you, but if it would help to get the little you will one day inherit, it would be my wish to die.' She wrote that, even though I hadn't visited her in years, nor shown her any sign of affection whatever. I must confess that I thought it was a somewhat exaggerated manner of speaking to which I attributed no significance, although I never doubted the authenticity of the feeling, however sentimentally it might be expressed. But then something very odd occurred: my mother actually did fall ill, and it's possible she dragged my father along with her, as he was very devoted to her."

Atwo reflected. "She died of a disease that she must have had without anyone suspecting it. One could point to a variety of natural explanations for the coincidence, and I fear that you'll hold it against me if I don't do this, but once again the incidental circumstances were the most noteworthy. She had absolutely no wish to die. I know that she fought, and bitterly complained about, an early death. Her will to live, her resolutions and wishes were all opposed to the event. Nor can one say that a resolve at the root of her character opposed her superficial intentions; if that were so she would already have thought of suicide or voluntary indigence, which she hadn't done in the least. She was wholly a victim. But haven't you ever noticed that your body has another will beside your own? I believe that everything we experience as having apparent mastery over us: will, emotion, sensation, and ideas, does so only under orders of limited authority, and that during difficult illnesses and convalescences, in uncertain battles and at every critical turning point in one's destiny there is a kind of primal decision of one's whole body in which the ultimate power and truth reside. But be that as it may, what was certain was that I immediately had the impression of something entirely voluntary in my mother's illness. You may call it imagination, but the fact remains that from the moment I received news of her illness, although there seemed no cause for alarm, I was markedly and completely changed. A hardness that had surrounded me melted instantly away. I can say no more than this: the condition I found myself in from then on had a strong resemblance to my awakening on the night I left home, and to my awaiting the singing dart from on high. I wanted to journey to my mother at once, but she kept me away on all sorts of pretexts. First it was that she would be delighted to see me, but I should wait for her slight illness to pass so she could welcome me in full health; later she told me that my visit might prove too agitating for her at the moment. Finally, when I pressed, she said the decisive turn for the better was at hand, and I should be patient for just a while longer. It appears as if she were afraid that a reunion would raise doubts in her mind. Then everything resolved itself so hastily that I only just managed to arrive in time for the burial.

"I found that my father was also ill and, as I told you, soon I could do nothing but help him die. He had previously been a decent man, but during these weeks he was peculiarly obstinate and moody, as if he held a grudge against me and felt annoyed by my presence. After his burial I had to dispose of the household effects, and this lasted several weeks. I was in no hurry. The people of the small town visited me now and again, out of old habit, and told me where in the living room my father used to sit, and my mother, and they themselves. They scrutinized everything very carefully and offered to buy this or that piece. They're so basic, these provincial people, and once one said to me, after he had thoroughly investigated everything, that it was really terrible—an entire family stamped out within a few weeks! No one counted me. When I was alone I sat quietly and read children's books—I'd found a whole chest full of them in the attic. They were covered with dust and soot, partly dried out and partly moldy, and if you struck them they gave off clouds of soft blackness. The marbled endpapers had worn away, leaving groups of jagged islands behind. But when I forced my way into the pages I conquered their contents like a seafarer navigating between these dangers. Once I made a strange discovery: I noticed that the darkened spots at the top where you turn the pages and below in the margin were slightly different from those caused by moldering, then I found all kinds of unidentifiable marks, and finally wild, faded pencil-tracks on the title pages. All at once I was overcome by the realization that these signs of enthusiastic wear-and-tear, these hasty marks and pencil scratches were the traces of a child's fingers, my own fingers, preserved for thirty and more years in a chest under the roof, preserved and forgotten by the whole world. Now, I'll tell you, it may not be anything special for other people when they reflect upon themselves, but for me it was as though my world were turned upside down. I also rediscovered a room, which, thirty years ago and more, had been my nursery. Later it served as a linen closet and the like, but basically it was left as it had been when I used to sit at the sprucewood table under the kerosene lamp, the lamp whose chain was held by three dolphins. Now I sat there again many hours a day and read like a child, like a child whose feet don't reach the floor. For you see, we're used to our heads towering up into nothingness without support because we have something solid beneath our feet, but in childhood we're not quite secure at either end. Instead of the grasping claws of later life we still have delicate, flannellike hands, and we sit in front of a book as if we were sailing through space over precipices on a small leaf. I tell you, under that table my feet really no longer reached the floor.

"I had fixed up a bed in this room and slept there. Then the blackbird came again. Once, after midnight, I was awakened by a wonderful, magnificent song. I didn't wake up immediately, but listened to it for a long time in my sleep. It was the song of a nightingale, but the bird wasn't sitting in the garden bushes but on the roof of a nearby building. I began to sleep with my eyes open. 'There aren't any nightingales here,' I thought. 'It's a blackbird.'

You needn't think I've already told this story once today! When this thought occurred to me—there are no nightingales here, it's a blackbird—I awoke. It was four in the morning; the day entered my eyes. Sleep sank away as quickly as the traces of surf are absorbed in dry sand of the shore, and there in the open window, in light like a soft white woolen wrap, sat a blackbird. It was sitting there as surely as I am sitting here.

" 'I am your blackbird,' it said. 'Don't you recognize me?' I didn't really remember right away, but I felt extraordinarily happy when the bird spoke to me.

" 'I've already sat on this windowsill once before, don't you remember?' it continued, and now I replied:

" 'Yes, one day you sat there where you're sitting now, and I quickly shut the window.'

" 'I am your mother,' she said.

"Well, look, I may have dreamt that. But I didn't dream the bird. It sat there, then flew into the room, and I quickly shut the window. I went up into the attic and looked for a large wooden cage, which I remembered because the blackbird had already been there once before in my childhood, just as I mentioned. It had sat in the window and then flown into the room. I had used a cage, but it soon became tame and I didn't keep it locked up; it lived in my room unconfined and flew in and out. Then one day it didn't return, and now there it was again. I had no desire to try and determine whether or not it was the same blackbird. I found the cage, and along with it a new chest of books, and I can only say to you that I have never in my life been so good a person as I have since I've had the blackbird, though I probably can't describe to you what a good person is."

"Has she spoken often?" Aone asked slyly.

"No," responded Atwo, "she hasn't spoken. But I've had to provide her with birdseed and worms. It's a little awkward for me that she eats worms and I'm supposed to take her for my mother. But it's all right; it's just a question of getting used to it, and what don't you have to get used to in everyday life! Since then I've never let her go, and that's all I have to tell. That's the third story, and how it will end I don't know."

"But surely," Aone cautiously sought to confirm, "you implied that there's a single meaning in all of this?"

"Good heavens," countered Atwo. "Everything happened just as I said, and if I knew the meaning I wouldn't have had to relate all this to you. But it's like when you hear whispering or mere rustling, without being able to tell which it is!"

Translated by Thomas Frick and Wilhelm Wiegandt
(amended by Burton Pike)

Art and the Morality of the Crawl

Dear Ferdi, in spite of your nineteen years you still seem to be a beginner, since you ask me whether the crawl is an art or a science. I have already received the decisive explanation from fourteen-year-old boys that it is a science, but seventeen-year-olds are convinced they are exercising an art. Doubting is not in the spirit of our times. But I will answer your question as well as I can, and so cleverly that you will be able to take it up with the most celebrated hydrocephalics.

The paradox of the crawl is that $A < C$ and $B > D$, but nevertheless $A + B > C + D$. (In case you reacted negatively to learning mathematics, $<$ means less than and $>$ more than.) In words: In the crawl you swim worse with the legs alone or the arms alone, but much more quickly with arms and legs together.

How can that be? What physical or physiological processes produce this contradiction of motions? I may express to you my original hope of finding in the answer to this initial question the basis for our attempt to reach a decision about art or science. In the history of swimming one becomes aware at first glance of a rising scale of difficulty in which what became more and more difficult in the successive forms of swimming was not learning them but understanding what it was one had learned. In its basic typology the ordinary breaststroke is a quite understandable making a pathway for oneself through the water, not much different from the way one would move through any other mass. The leg motions in Spanish swimming, which followed the breaststroke, were similar to it, and one could also understand the extended circular sweep of the arms. (You know it? This motion of the arms was similar to the crawl's except that it extended farther forward, came down flatter on the water, and was drawn not only against the body but also past it.) But the cunning closing of the legs in both strokes, the scissors which one sometimes saw (closing of the legs while they casually cross), the rolling of many good "Spanish" swimmers, the stretching out horizontally or gently inclined hanging of the body, were in their effect hydrodynamic mysteries.

In the case of the crawl it is impossible to arrive at a satisfactory explanation with the simple mechanics of the inclined plane. Here one must apply streamlining, eddies, drops in pressure, glide resistances, and other nuisances of the theory of motion of a solid body in liquids which one knows from the construction of ships, turbines, and airplanes, in order to come finally to the obvious result that the body to be accounted for is not solid at all, but elastic and in variable motion. Still, in this manner it ought to be possible to get at least a rough picture of the physical relationships created by the upward and forward propulsion involved in the various techniques of swimming. That alone would suffice to point the training in this sport in certain directions, even ignoring the fact that such an investigation is not without a charm of its own.

Nor could one expect less from the observation from a biomechanical point of view, which compares the swimming of people with that of animals based on the possibilities offered by the way the body is constructed. In the water we are four-legged creatures. The instinctive attempts of a non-swimmer to hold himself above water have well-known similarities with the dog-paddle, even the ape-paddle as far as I can remember after seeing it a few times. Proceeding from that point, as a return to nature the crawl appears to be a kind of crafty non-swimming outfitted with all sorts of transposed motions learned from observing seals and more southerly master-swimmers. In there somewhere, aside from this direct line of development, is where the breaststroke really belongs as the first attempt to swim better than nature intended for one who has apparently taken his cue from various kinds of water animals, beetles, toads, and whatnot.

I think such an investigation can be quite absorbing, and since I want to please you because you take your sport so seriously, I have also made an effort to dig up the physiological and biological literature on swimming. I can not claim there isn't any, since I didn't have enough time to exhaust all the possibilities, but I can tell you that when I used the catalog and all the usual bibliographical aids in the largest technical library in Germany I could not turn up a sigle treatment of our subject.

So according to that the crawl does not seem to be a science after all.

That is quite bitter, because it pushes the crawl into the realm of art and personality. Truly, you did ask me right off what it means that the crawl is practised according to a *style,* just like art, and where one ends up with a phenomenon such as style. You yourself, of course, will have observed that all kinds of crawl have, as they must, certain peculiarities in common, such as the generally horizontal position of the body, the relaxed stretch of the legs, and the concomitant leaf-and-stalk and flyswatter-like motion of the feet.

On the other hand opinions differ about, for instance, the number and scansion of the beats of the foot in relation to the rhythm of the arms, about the path of the arms, about how straight the body should be, and above all how all these details should fit together. If, due to whatever circumstances, one must change one's teacher a few times, one inevitably runs the risk of drowning. That is how style manifests itself. You will see this about as clearly if you have occasion to observe famous swimmers: every one does everything his own way. If you observe these styles you will find all kinds of them, even within the same stroke, although of course body-build and accomplishment have a reciprocal influence on each other. Man and woman, who without question offer the water dissimilar conditions, do not swim in noticeably different styles. Even the contribution of the leg strokes, which seems to be the most mysterious, throws us after a long process of deduction into consternation, since it has been determined that a man missing a foot can be one of the best swimmers.

Therefore I would rather not answer your question about what style is and signifies in an area which makes as many taxing claims on the mind as sport; as a matter of fact I would not like to answer your question at all. Just this much: One always speaks of style not where a simple, unequivocal accomplishment is demanded, but where a certain arbitrary relationship prevails between task and solution. Style is a substitute for standardization, but by no means a capricious substitution. For always underlying a style there is a method, whether elaborated intentionally or not, which lets itself be perfected in its own way until it reaches a point where it can no longer go on in that particular manner. In this sense beauty has styles, and in a closely related way fashions, but the most important element is not that taste changes but that it remains the same, which is to say a something which is never clear about what it wants. We seem to possess the remarkable quality that if we once want something we can go on wanting it for so long until nothing remains to be wished for, but that on the whole we don't know what we *ought* to want. For the most part it is this way too in art, where styles sprout, become dense, and decay like trees. And so one can even speak of styles of morality, which betrays that morality is not as secure as it likes to think.

If you want to apply this to the crawl you will recognize that there too style is an art of balancing out ignorance, in this case ignorance about the rational conditions of swimming which, given its relatively simple purposiveness, will surely be ascertained in time. Then there will only be as much style as different kinds of physical talent call for different kinds of utilization; about as much style as in the case of a racing boat which always has its own individuality no matter how precise the formula it was built to. Swimming lays small claim to those higher mental processes involved in really competitive sports or in riding, where the relationship with a second living being comes into play. But as I write the expression *higher mental processes* a warning I have up to now repressed burns my tongue: in sport never seek the High, but always only the Low! Today these values have been confused, and in a manner which is so peculiar that a few words about it are in order.

We never hear anything but that sport educates the human being, by which is approximately understood that it bestows on its disciples all sorts of virtues, like frankness, sociability, honesty, presence of mind, clear and rapid thought. You know this of course: the great sportsman is not only a genius, but—as long as he doesn't take a percentage—a saint. But in truth any other occupation, if it were taken as seriously, would bestow the same virtues. The effect of sport which is morally different is at most an attitude of calm niceness and attention to oneself and others which one is also familiar with from the carefree first days of a summer vacation, as well as that secure relation to nature which expresses itself in the feeling that one could uproot trees. To look to sport for the development of higher moral and intellectual capacities comes from that *passé* psychology which believed that the animal is either a machine or, if it should see a sausage, that it wouldhave to construct a syllogism of the kind: this is a sausage, all sausages taste good, so I will now eat this sausage. However, the animal is neither a machine nor does it construct syllogisms, nor does the human being conclude and judge this way in stimulating situations. What does take place in rapid actions in the animal and the human being is a stratified interpenetration of fixed patterns of behavior proper to the species and the individual. Both respond almost mechanically to external stimuli; involved in this is an anticipatory attention which, in similar fashion, is already preparing a response for the next phase. There is, finally, a lasting, completely unconscious adaptation of performed reactions to the demands of the moment. Even a human being executes the most complicated actions *without awareness,* without *intellect,* from which one may perhaps also conclude that it is not the role of intellect to play a role in sports. It is a not unamusing contradiction that there are today detailed investigations by philosophers and biologists which are redefining anew the concept of human genius precisely by erecting it on the basis of a more profound examination of the nature of animals, while our sports writers are still busy insisting on the possession of moral plus theoretical understanding as a self-evident premise of the crawl and of sports.

Translated by Burton Pike

ACKNOWLEDGMENTS

Every reasonable effort has been made to locate the parties who hold rights to previously published translations reprinted here. We gratefully acknowledge permission to reprint the following:

Young Törless, translated by Eithne Wilkins and Ernest Kaiser. Copyright 1959 by Pantheon Books. Reprinted by permission of Pantheon Books.

Three Women ("Grigia," "The Lady from Portugal," "Tonka"), translated by Eithne Wilkins and Ernest Kaiser, excerpted from the book *Five Women* by Robert Musil. English translation copyright © 1965 by Martin Secker and Warburg, Ltd. Copyright © 1966 by Dell Publishing Co., Inc. Reprinted by permission of Delacourt Press/ Seymour Lawrence and Martin Secker and Warburg, Ltd.

"The Perfecting of a Love," translated by Eithne Wilkins and Ernest Kaiser, excerpted from the book *Five Women* by Robert Musil. English translation copyright © 1965 by Martin Secker and Warburg, Ltd. Copyright © 1966 by Dell Publishing Co., Inc. Reprinted by permission of Delacourt Press/Seymour Lawrence and Martin Secker and Warburg, Ltd.

"The Flypaper," "Can a Horse Laugh?" "Hare Catastrophe," "Monuments," "Oedipus Endangered," "The Blackbird," and "Art and the Morality of the Crawl" have been translated from *Gesammelte Werke in neun Bänden,* Vol. 7, by Robert Musil, edited by Adolf Frisé. Copyright © 1978 Rowohlt Verlag GmbH, Reinbek bei Hamburg. Translated by permission of Rowohlt Verlag.

"The Blackbird," translated by Thomas Frick and Wilhelm Wiegandt. © 1979, 1981 by Thomas Frick and Wilhelm Wiegandt. Simba Editions, Cambridge, Mass., 1981. Reprinted by permission.